Gender Equality and Work–Life Balance

Pressure to achieve work–life "balance" has recently become a significant part of the cultural fabric of working life in United States. A very few privileged employees tout their ability to find balance between their careers and the rest of their lives, but most employees face considerable organizational and economic constraints that hamper their ability to maintain a reasonable "balance" between paid work and other life aspects—and it is not only women who struggle. Increasingly, men also find it difficult to "do it all." Women have long noted the near impossibility of balancing multiple roles, but it is only recently that men have been encouraged to see themselves beyond their breadwinner selves.

Gender Equality and Work–Life Balance describes the work–life practices of men in the United States. The purpose is to increase gender equality at work for all employees. With a focus on leave policy inequalities, this book argues that men experience a phenomenon called the "glass handcuffs," which prevents them from leaving work to participate fully in their families, homes, and other life events. It highlights the cultural, institutional, organizational, and occupational conditions which make gender equality in work–life policy usage difficult. This social justice book ultimately draws conclusions about how to minimize inequalities at work.

Gender Equality and Work–Life Balance is unique as it laces together some theoretical concepts that have little previous association, including entrepreneurialism, leave policy, occupational identity, and the economic necessities of families. This book will therefore be of particular interest to researchers and academics alike in the disciplines of Communication, Gender Studies, Human Resource Management, Employment Relations, Sociology, and Cultural Studies.

Sarah Jane Blithe is Assistant Professor of Communication Studies at the University of Nevada, Reno, USA.

Routledge Research in Employment Relations

Series editors: Rick Delbridge and Edmund Heery
Cardiff Business School, UK

Aspects of the employment relationship are central to numerous courses at both undergraduate and postgraduate level.

Drawing from insights from industrial relations, human resource management and industrial sociology, this series provides an alternative source of research-based materials and texts, reviewing key developments in employment research.

Books published in this series are works of high academic merit, drawn from a wide range of academic studies in the social sciences.

For a full list of titles in this series, please visit www.routledge.com

Gender Equality and Work–Life Balance

Glass Handcuffs and Working Men in the U.S.

Sarah Jane Blithe

Routledge
Taylor & Francis Group

NEW YORK AND LONDON

First published 2015
by Routledge
711 Third Avenue, New York, NY 10017

and by Routledge
2 Park Square, Milton Park, Abingdon, Oxon OX14 4RN

First issued in paperback 2018

*Routledge is an imprint of the Taylor & Francis Group,
an informa business*

Library of Congress Cataloging-in-Publication Data

Blithe, Sarah.
  Gender equality and work-life balance : glass handcuffs and working men in the U.S. / by Sarah Blithe.
     pages cm. — (Routledge research in employment relations ; 35)
  Includes bibliographical references and index.
  1. Work and family—United States.   2. Work-life balance—
United States.   3. Parental leave—United States.   4. Fatherhood—
United States.   5. Discrimination in employment—United States.
I. Title.
  HD4904.25.B58 2015
  306.3'60973—dc23
  2015004562

ISBN 13: 978-1-138-60001-0 (pbk)
ISBN 13: 978-1-138-85677-6 (hbk)

Typeset in Sabon
by Apex CoVantage, LLC

For Kevin, the love of my life, who is my partner in all things, and our children, Brooklynn and Braxton, who fill my life with joy, laughter, and love.

Contents

PART III
Finding the Key: Why Understanding
the Glass Handcuffs Matters

Acknowledgments

Thank you to Niko, Kiya, and Kodiak, the very best furry writing buddies.

Thank you to my parents, Michael and Jane Coleman, for always supporting and encouraging my education—I love you and appreciate you.

With gratitude and love for all my family in Colorado, Arizona, and California, particularly my brothers, Mikey and Adam; my nieces; my goddaughters; and family-in-law, especially my sisters-in-law, Stephanie and Kelly, and my parents-in-law, Richard and Dianne Blithe, who consistently amaze me with their love, wisdom, and support.

This work would not have been possible without the incredible guidance from my graduate school advisor, Tim Kuhn.

I am indebted and grateful for my mentor, Karen Ashcraft, for her remarkably generous and always fun guidance in teaching, research, and life.

I am extremely grateful for the guidance of Catherine Ashcraft, who invited me into exciting research projects that assisted in the development of my research skills and led to the topic of this book.

My deepest thanks to the team at Routledge for supporting the development of this book and to Robert Swanson for the excellent indexing services.

I am so very thankful for the men who agreed to give their time to participate in the interviews for this study. Their words, ideas, successes, and struggles were quite inspiring to me, and I hope I have represented their feelings and experiences well.

I am also grateful to the colleagues, teachers, and researchers who read and assisted with various drafts of this project, provided incredible guidance in my writing, offered invaluable perspectives about research, and/or provided general encouragement and support for my research, including Janell Bauer, Jenny Beer, Stephanie Bor, Stephanie Brooks, Stephanie Coleman, Bob Craig, Stan Deetz, Elizabeth Eger, Lisa Flores, Susana Martinez Guillem, Jenna Hanchey, Katie Harris, Gwen Hullman, James Fortney, Michele Jackson, Matt Koschmann, Jennifer Lanterman, Katie Keeran, Jennifer Malkowski, Virginia McCarver, Jamie McDonald, Megan Morrissey, Kristina Ruiz-Mesa, Amy Pason, Jessica Robles, Christy-Dale Sims, Mary Stewart, Karen Tracy, Dani Watkins, and Amy Way. I am especially lucky to have the support of my amazing writing group colleagues and friends, Leslie Rill and

Anna Wolfe, and the astute editing assistance of Jenn Aglio, Kendra Hess, Bill Macauley, Angie White Davlyn, and Isabel Youngs.

Thank you to the Department of Communication at the University of Colorado Boulder for the generous dissertation fellowship.

Thank you to the National Center for Women & IT for the kind research fellowship.

Thank you to the College of Liberal Arts at the University of Nevada, Reno, for the Creative and Scholarly Activities Grant, which supported the final development of this book. Thanks to the department of Communication Studies at the University of Nevada, Reno for the ongoing research support.

Thank you to my dear friends for generally supporting me through this "hobby" of mine. I am so grateful for Ivana Bahula, Lauren and Chris Bickel, Renee Bohlen, Tina Cho, Shannon Cox, Amanda Evans, Angie and Stephen Halsey, Sophie and Cam Hartley, Anne and Bobby Kline, Scott and Valerie Krum, Kieonna Lane, Jana Larson, Natalie and Damon LaScala, Jen Moxon, Carrie O'Connor, Jassen Savoie, Elizabeth and Greg Schwieterman, Amber Snow, Tracy Stanisewski, and Candace Wickstrom. In loving memory of Erin Kilbane.

Nic, you are my soul mate. I am so very grateful for our conversations and your seemingly unending supply of support over the last 23 years. Thanks for always reminding me that research should matter and for being a totally awesome best friend.

1 Outlining the Glass Handcuffs Phenomenon

A recent cover of *Bloomberg BusinessWeek* featured a distressed man at his desk with a child trying to gain his attention. The words "LEAN OUT" splashed the cover. The article inside featured the "Deloitte Dads," a new group of fathers who assemble to provide support for each other as working dads. In an obvious take on Sheryl Sandberg's (2013) wildly popular *Lean In*, which urges women to achieve career success without worrying about balancing their work with family, the men in the Deloitte Dads support each other in strategies to become involved parents. The men discuss challenges in their roles as "providers" and are vocal about their desires to spend more time with their children. These men are not alone in their desire to live a more balanced life. Recently, pressure to achieve work–life "balance"[1] has become a frequent conversation and a significant part of the cultural fabric of working life in the United States—and it is not only women who struggle to figure it out. A 2013 study found that 50% of working fathers and 56% of working mothers felt it difficult to manage work and family (Parker & Wang, 2013).

Very few privileged employees tout their ability to find balance between their careers and the rest of their lives, but most employees face considerable organizational and economic constraints that hamper their ability to maintain a reasonable balance between paid work and other life aspects. The "life" part of work–life encompasses familial concerns, but it also includes a number of other life priorities, such as education, civic and community service, military service, religious commitments, physical activity, health, other kinds of care work, volunteer work, and personal hobbies. In the face of the near impossibility of actually achieving balance, some national and organizational policies address the need for employee balance and can support some workers in balancing their work and nonwork time.

Many organizations, however, have been slow to create new and meaningful policies to support the work–life requirements for their employees and national policies do not cover all workers, leaving many employees— men and women—struggling to manage their work and other life pursuits. Golden (2000) explained that "individuals are living more complex internal as well as external lives, which are potentially richer but also considerably more challenging" (p. 20). Thus, while life might be richer with a diversity of commitments and experiences, it is also more difficult to manage. Most work–life policies are reserved for white- and gold-collar jobs (knowledge-work jobs that incorporate technology, entrepreneurialism, capitalism, and consumer culture) and are not accessible for most employees (Kirby & Krone, 2002; Nadesan, 2002). It is ironic that "a greater premium is placed on intimacy between parents and children at the very point that people have less real time to devote to these relationships" (Golden, 2000, p. 12). College men exiting top programs expect to be highly involved fathers and expect their partners to have careers (Kimmel, 2013, as cited in Kolhatkar, 2013). According to Kolhatkar (2013), "men spend three times as much time with their children as their grandfathers did" (p. 4). Despite these changes in men's family expectations and responsibilities, there have been few significant changes in work policies and cultures to accommodate the difference.

To further exacerbate the work–life crunch, current salaries do not wield as much buying power compared with previous generations, and thus many modern couples dually seek work outside of the home in order to "recreate the same standard of living they enjoyed as children" (Golden, 2001, p. 247). (See Wieland, Bauer, and Deetz's [2009] work on corporate colonization through careerism and a consumption-based quality of life for further discussion of this issue.) However, these men often experience acute work–life pressure when they get into the workforce and realize that existing organizational policy does not wholly support or even reflect these fundamental attitude shifts about care work.

In organizations that do have work–life policies available, cultural practice rarely allows the full implementation of such policies. The use of work–life policies is highly dependent on gender, race, and class (National Partnership for Women & Families, 2013). Furthermore, employees who access work–life policies are subject to stereotypes that they are less committed, too expensive, and not as promotable as other employees (Kirby & Krone, 2002; Kolhatkar, 2013; U.S. Department of Labor, 2012). Currently, using work–life policies, especially taking a leave of absence from work, hurts career progress and prevents wage growth (Glass, 2004), although the extent of the problem is unclear. Glass (2004) found that working from home just 5 hours a week results in an average 27% reduction in wages for working women, even though the research also shows that "using work-family policies reduces the job stress and fatigue, turnover, and labor force interruptions that reduce productivity per hour among mothers" (p. 371).

In the United States, researchers report much conflicting data about leaves of absence. Part of this problem is that only 40% of U.S. workers can legally take leaves of absence. In addition, Kamerman and Moss (2011) explained that

> leave policy, more than many other social policies, is at the intersection of the economic (since it bears on labour force participation and

labour market regulation), the social (since it bears on children, families and gender equality), and the demographic (since it bears on fertility). This generates a complex situation of different potential objectives and potential conflicts between objectives, even within the same broad field. (p. 9)

This pattern sustains systems of organizational inequality and leaves workers unable to achieve balance without repercussion, even as work–life policy usage helps individuals become better employees.

The purpose of this book is to work toward gender justice and equality by exploring organizational work–life policies and practices. This book argues that achieving equity in U.S. organizations rests not only on individuals' equal access to equity policies but also on individuals' equal use of and participation in equity policies and programs. Foundational to this project are the economic and moral assumptions that gender equity at home and work is desirable. In many ways, equality in paid work is the prevailing morally responsible answer to centuries of institutional inequality and discrimination. Equally important is the potential for equality at home, which is a morally driven pursuit that both alleviates uneven pressures of care work and invites equal participation in enjoyable home-based pursuits. Women disproportionately take up the majority of care work in the United States for a wide range of family members, including young children, adult children, grandparents, grandchildren, parents, parents-in-law, domestic partners, spouses, and siblings (National Alliance for Caregiving, 2009; Ness, 2014).

There are economic reasons that necessitate equity as well, such as the economic imparity of retaining qualified women in many fields (Ashcraft, Kuhn, & Cooren, 2009; Ashcraft & Blithe, 2009), narrowing the wage and wealth gaps, or protecting productive male workers from stress-related health implications that take them out of the workforce (Glass, 2004). Research suggests that diverse organizations and work teams perform better than more homogeneous teams, and diverse organizations and teams are more competitive, more innovative, and more successful at reaching their customers or other target audiences when both men and women work together (Azoulay, Ding, & Stuart, 2007; Ding, Murray, & Stuart, 2006; Murray & Graham, 2007).

These kinds of economic impacts bear some weight in how arguments for and against gender equity in work–life policies unfold. This book focuses particularly on policies and practices around workers' leaves of absence, which, in the United States, are highly subject to gender inequality in both policy language and practice (Albiston, 2010; National Partnership for Women & Families, 2013; U.S. Department of Labor, 2012). Drawing on data from interviews with men from a variety of occupations, this book takes a unique approach to work–life policy research by focusing on the lived work–life and leave experiences of men.

WHY MEN?

Focusing on men in a gender justice project about work–life issues may seem counterintuitive, as most research presents work–life as a concern of women (see Ashcraft & Mumby, 2004; Buzzanell & Turner, 2003; and Tracy & Rivera, 2009, for notable exceptions). However, such a focus is necessary— particularly in this historical moment. To begin, men are gendered beings who struggle with work–life balance. Women have long noted the near impossibility of balancing it all and continually struggle with organizational work–life policies, but it is only recently that men have been encouraged to see themselves beyond their breadwinner roles. In the face of increasing pressure to maintain their economic status while also participating in care work and self-improvement, the work–life tensions for men have reached a threshold (Aumann, Galinsky, & Matos, 2011; Harrington, Van Deusen, & Humberd, 2011; National Partnership for Women & Families, 2012). Employed men in the United States have reported increasing interest in being involved in the lives of their children but worry about sacrificing their economic stability and security (National Partnership for Women & Families, 2012). The lack of viable policies to assist men in balancing family and work creates stress for many employed men and makes it difficult for them to participate actively in the home (see Appendix A for notes about using Standpoint Theory to study issues from the standpoint of a particular identity).

The second reason that a focus on men is important is because of the myriad benefits that result from men's participation at home. Multiple studies report that children with engaged fathers are healthier (Galtry, 2002; Tanaka, 2005) and more successful (Croft, 2014; National Partnership for Women & Families, 2012). Furthermore, men themselves see health benefits when they are not as stressed in their management of dual roles, and coupled men who contribute to care work report having happier relationships with their partners and children.

Finally, because men do not use work–life policies in the same ways as women, taking time away from work remains a stigmatized practice that results in significant material consequences. Put simply, if men do not use work–life policies for families, women will never be able to use the policies without financial penalties. Particularly because men continually inhabit gatekeeping and mentoring roles that shape organizational culture, policy, and practice (Tracy & Rivera, 2009), they *must* demonstrate that using work–life policies is an acceptable practice for *all* employees. Achieving gender equity would include an improvement in the lives of both women *and* men (National Partnership for Women & Families, 2013; Tracy & Rivera, 2009).

THE GLASS HANDCUFFS

As pressure increases for men to participate in child rearing, personal health, and work–life balance, the discursive and material inability of men to take time off from work is problematic. Fewer than 2% of new fathers take a parental leave of absence from work in the United States, and only 16% of men take leave of absence at all, most often for personal health crises (U.S. Department of Labor, 2012). However, there is consistent and increasing pressure for men to take a more active role in the family and to personally take control of their own mental and physical well-being through work–life balance.

The "glass handcuffs" metaphor addresses this paradox and explains the invisible mechanisms that keep men continually working while simultaneously keeping them away from family and other nonwork pursuits. Men consistently wear one side of the invisible constraint while the other side locks onto their paid-work places or positions. They remain locked in the public sphere and have difficulty breaking away to participate in the private sphere. Although men around the world experience this extreme attachment to work, men in the United States are particularly vulnerable and have the least support to engage in their lives outside of work. Only 14% of men in the United States have any kind of access to paternity leave with even a small amount of pay, while at least 66 other countries provide fathers paid leave for a new child (National Partnership for Women & Families, 2012).

Four main logics chain men to their work: (a) the assumption that men cannot take leave, (b) the presumption that men should not take leave, (c) the assumption that men do not need to take leave, and (d) men's lack of desire to take time completely away from work. The glass handcuffs serve as a metaphor that can capture each of these logics, which individuals can feel but not see in the relationship among men, families, and work, and can explain why men do not usually take leaves of absence.

The first evident logic men used to describe their inability to leave work was the belief that *men cannot take a leave of absence* because they cannot afford to take time off without pay or because they were afraid they would lose their jobs. This suggests a serious material constraint precluding men from taking leaves of absence. Because of sex segregation in occupations and job roles, men are still the breadwinners in many families. In some families, men continue their roles as sole breadwinners and 76% of married men out earn their wives in heterosexual dual-income families. Thus, taking a leave of absence carries financial constraints for many men. Particularly in the case of parental leave, men reported that they *had* to work to support their wives who were staying home or on leave themselves.

Other men admitted that they would not take leaves of absence, even if they could afford it, because they were afraid of losing their jobs, which would be financially disastrous. The frequency of layoffs was one reason men with jobs were fearful to leave. Many men in this study personally experienced a layoff and feared it would happen again, believing that their managers would discover that they were replaceable in their absence. Many men said that their organizational or occupational cultures did not support leave-taking practices for men and that men who took leaves of absence were vulnerable to layoffs or other repositioning in the company. The financial concerns and job security fears are what keep these men at work. The glass handcuffs metaphor captures this tendency because it suggests that men cannot take leave, even as personal economic fears and realities are not noticeably visible from the outside.

The glass handcuffs metaphor also captures the second logic men used to explain why they do not leave work: the assumption that *men should not take leaves of absence*. The data in this study revealed that most men felt responsible for their own career success. Many men lamented that they wanted more time for their families and their hobbies but felt compelled to sacrifice these pursuits, at least to some extent, in order to succeed at work. These men wanted more time for their nonwork lives but felt they were unable to have it. This created an inequality with women in the accessibility of work–life policies. Individually protecting one's career also led to unhealthy behavior reported by the men in this study. Repeated stories about extreme dedication and work hours exemplified the tendency to work through anything (e.g., children's birth, personal health scares, and sleep). Male employees positioned this potentially dangerous tendency to work though anything as a necessary step to advance quickly in their careers.

Taking leaves of absence went directly against organizational demands for time commitments and, as such, seemed to suggest a lack of dedication except in (and even in) the most extreme cases of injury or personal health issues. The stigma attached to workers (particularly men) taking leaves of absence persuaded many men in this study to believe that doing so would be detrimental to their careers and that they must avoid such practices in order to succeed at work. Taking vacation time, working virtually, and quitting are some ways in which the men in this study described avoiding "damaging" leaves of absence. This stigma against leave-taking is so great that many men actually quit their jobs when they wanted to take significant time off. Taking time between jobs was an acceptable way that many men took time away from work. It seems surprising that many men believe that taking a leave of absence is detrimental to their careers, yet quitting can help achieve work–life balance without hindering career progress. However, the stigma attached to leave and the pervasive assumption that men should not take leave made the men in this study believe that quitting was a better alternative to achieve time off.

The third logic used to validate men's constant participation in paid work is the framing that *men do not need leave*. Many men cited virtual work as a phenomenon that has made leaves of absence unnecessary. Because they could work from anywhere, many men worked virtually during times when they might otherwise have taken a leave of absence. Men described working virtually during their own health problems or when they had children. Virtual work allowed men to take more time away from a physical workplace without getting too far behind on their work. As such, the workers who talked about virtual work praised the practice and their organizations for allowing them to have an increased work–life balance. However, the desire to keep up with work and the reluctance to leave work are concurrently evidence of the glass handcuffs, an invisible desire to continue engaging in work and the perception that leaving for any reason is unnecessary.

Some men in this study also felt that they did not need leaves of absence because they participated in traditional, gendered roles in their families. In this subset, leave equals family and family equals women's responsibility. These particular men have partners to handle situations that require leave. For example, some men in this study described how their wives took care of ailing parents or children's needs, and, as a result, their own presence was not necessary.

Finally, the last logic men drew on to describe why they did not take leaves of absence was that they *did not want to take a leave of absence* because they loved their jobs so much. The glass handcuffs metaphor is useful here because it illuminates how some men bond to their occupations by love and passion. The many men who described their tendencies and inabilities to let go of work had an invisible pull to their occupations. It was difficult for them to describe, but they explained their feelings of an innate drive and connection to work. These men did not want to stop working and pushed back against the notion that work and life are separate spheres. Instead, for these men, work is life and life is work. The glass handcuffs can explain the seamless bond here, in that men do not take leaves of absence when they do not want to leave work because they are passionate about their jobs. In this frame, the glass handcuffs are not unwelcome, but still keep men continually working.

The use of glass metaphors to explain problems in working environments is prevalent because glass captures the essence of something people cannot always see but can feel. In other words, one can quite literally feel a collision with a glass door, even if the door was invisible beforehand. Glass metaphors are particularly helpful in capturing notions of power in organizations and help specifically to understand how subtle biases toward certain bodies in organizations (e.g., white women and workers of color) face intangible discrimination at work. Ashcraft (2013) explained that

> the utility of glass metaphors lies in their capacity to name and evoke systemic patterns that are otherwise elusive. They provide tangible abbreviations or proxies that redirect us from individual explanations (e.g. willful prejudice) to institutional accounts, surfacing hidden dynamics at work that call for further explanation. (p. 12)

Glass metaphors serve as a discursive resource that helps people talk about the goings-on of organizational life that are otherwise difficult to describe, and these metaphors can help us to understand and analyze the hidden dynamics that can harm some employees at work.

The *glass ceiling* is likely the best-known glass metaphor and describes an invisible barrier that white women and workers of color hit when climbing the ranks of an organization. The glass ceiling captures the numerical inequality of women at the top of organizations and inequality in compensation at all levels of organizations (Ashcraft & Blithe, 2009; Powell, 1999). The glass-ceiling metaphor has become so pervasive in describing organizational life that the Federal Glass Ceiling Commission (1995) emerged to study progress, opportunities, and constraints relative to the glass ceiling.

As such, the glass ceiling has largely become a catchall for most racial and gender inequality in organizations, which suggests that inequality occurs in a variety of ways. However, it is necessary to be more precise in the way we talk about inequalities as they occur for white women, women of color, men of color, and white men (Cotter, Hermsen, Ovadia, & Vannemen, 2001; Maume, 1999). Some scholars have started to understand more invisible constraints, and have posited other glass metaphors to describe nuances in inequitable organizational practice. The glass escalator refers to the intense pressure men working in female-dominated occupations or specialties face to move into more traditionally masculine professions. For example, Christine L. Williams (1992) found that while people praised a male public librarian for his excellence in storytelling, they also critiqued him for not advancing. Williams also tracked male nurses and teachers who were pushed or fast-tracked into administration by both men in managerial positions and their female peers.

In essence, the glass handcuffs metaphor captures the unseen apparatus, composed of discourses, practices, material constraints, and gendered assumptions that condition men to work nonstop and cautions them against spending too much time on nonwork pursuits. Unlike the *golden handcuffs*, which are explicit moves employers take to retain employees through noncompete agreements and financial incentives such as stock options (see, e.g., Kafker, 1993; Sengupta, Whitfield, & McNabb, 2007), the glass handcuffs explain the *invisible* constraints that keeps workers, particularly male workers, at work.

Making the glass handcuffs visible is necessary to begin to address structural inequality in leave-taking practice. If men cannot and will not leave work, there can never be equal participation for men at home or for women at work. While glass metaphors aid in seeing gender and racial inequalities at work, glass, of course, *can be broken*. Thus, the glass handcuffs metaphor suggests these invisible barriers between men and women at work and home can be shattered though the processes of imagining work and workers in new ways. It is in this spirit that I make visible the glass handcuffs phenomenon, its causes, implications, and opportunities to break the constraints.

CURRENT ORGANIZATIONAL SCENE FROM WHICH THE GLASS HANDCUFFS EMERGE

It is unsurprising that work–life policies do not work well for men, because policy writers never designed policies with the typical male worker in mind.

As the U.S. workforce has changed over the past 20 years, organizations and governments created new, "Band-Aid" policies to meet the needs of the diverse workforce. Historically, specific kinds of workers in specific kinds of bodies determined how jobs developed. In the United States, the majority of jobs developed around the needs and abilities of young or middle-aged, able-bodied men with stay-at-home wives (Acker, 1990; Albiston, 2010). (Although low-income and working-class women worked in a variety of jobs throughout history, many positions *developed* for working- and middle-class men.) This "ideal-type" worker was unencumbered by outside obligations—his single obligation was to earn a living. He was flexible, dedicated, and loyal to his company. This worker was always available and completely committed to work, and he had no real need or expectation to purposely take time away from work. In response, organizations developed workplace cultures and policies around this particular type of ideal worker that did not include policies to support time away from work.

In today's society, workers rarely homogenously fit this "ideal type" because of broad changes to the U.S. workforce (Acker, 1990). As such, in order to better understand organizations and their policies, it is imperative to consider changes in U.S. employment demographics. The major factors related to primary changes in today's workforce discussed here include increases in women workers, dual-income families, single parents, workers with disabilities, aging workers, and chronic presenteeism. The subsequent sections briefly describe these changes, and how and why the changes impact leaves of absence and other work–life policies—all of which are important to understand in order to see how U.S. work–life policies are woefully inadequate to support U.S. workers.

Additional Women

A dramatic increase of women into the paid workforce created shockwaves in the demographics of U.S. workers. Six out of 10 U.S. American women currently take up paid-work positions, and these women comprise about half of the entire U.S. workforce (Center for American Progress, 2012). In 1975, nearly half of families with children had a stay-at-home mother and employed father (Center for American Progress, 2012). However, in 2012, only 20% of all families with children subscribed to this traditional family model (Vespa, Lewis, & Kreider, 2013). Increases in the educational levels of women have contributed to both the numbers of women in the workplace and to a rise in access to higher paying jobs. For example, women between the ages of 25 and 34 currently earn more college degrees than do men of the same age group (Moe & Shandy, 2010). For women, this education leads to more competitive, better paying jobs and women's numerically equal participation in the U.S. American workforce.

As the presence of women in the U.S. workforce increased, so did the need for workers' leaves of absence. Because women employed outside of the home still carry the majority of the responsibility for child care and the home (Klein, Izquierdo, & Bradbury, 2013; Moe & Shandy, 2010), most women cannot adequately satisfy their employers' historical expectation to be available around the clock. Care work, including child care, elder care, pet care, and home care, requires working women to spend a significant amount of time away from work. The demands of care work are not always predetermined and frequently require unplanned breaks away from work. Hochschild (1989) described the tendency for employed women to retain the household responsibility as the "second shift," referring to the household work that primarily women shoulder in addition to their paid employment (see also Halpern & Cheung, 2008). Recent data (see, e.g., Alberts & Trethewey, 2007; Bond, Thompson, Galinsky, & Prottas, 2002; Klein et al., 2013; Moe & Shandy, 2010; Parker & Wang, 2013) revealed that employed women spend more time on child care and house work than men, with some research documenting that employed women spend approximately 41 hours per week more than employed men do on household tasks (approximately 62 hours per week for employed women, as compared to only 21 hours per week for their employed cohabiting men).[2] This heavy work burden can leave many women exhausted, depressed, and physically ill.

Despite the inequitable division of labor at home, leaders in organizations most often underestimate how great the imbalance is and how it disproportionately challenges female employees (Tracy & Rivera, 2009). Because managers and executives are most often partnered men, their personal experience is quite different from most female employees. In U.S. organizations, the few women who have achieved executive status most often do not have children and, as such, have a different understanding of work–life balance than working mothers (Hewlett, 2005). Although these women most certainly face gender-based discrimination at work, their assumptions about the imbalance of gender roles and family may not reflect that majority of employees' experiences. When the work–life experience of organizational leaders is significantly different from a group of employees, inequality persists in the ways policies and practices unfold. Women, for example, use work–life policies more often to manage their care-work responsibilities, whereas men use them more often to tend to their personal health. Thus, using work–life policies for care work carries more of a stigma, as people in the upper echelons of organizations usually only use these policies for personal health. This paradox suggests that work–life policies have little chance of achieving actual equality in organizations (Tracy & Rivera, 2009).

Dual-Income Families, Single-Parent Families, and Female Breadwinners

Today's workforce is also changing due to new family patterns. New family patterns including dual-income families, single-parent families, and female-breadwinner families exist in the context of increases in women in the workplace, a rising divorce rate, a rising number of never-married parents, and male unemployment. These family situations heighten the potential need for workers' need to take leaves of absence because there is not a stay-at-home partner to deal with care-work issues. These newer family types require different organizational accommodations around workers' periodic time away from work.

At present, dual-income families comprise approximately 60% of U.S. American families, and dual-earner families with children are the most common family structure today (Parker & Wang, 2013). In 15% of these dual earner families, the mother is the breadwinner (Parker & Wang, 2013). This significant proportion of household income is vitally important for the maintenance of the family and is not the "pocket change" or vacation funds of middle- and upper class women's wages in the past. Rather, in coupled families where both adults work, the dual employment is usually an economic necessity (Hattery, 2001). For example, Oliver and Shapiro (2006) found that more than one third of married couples require dual earnings in order to generate between $25,000 and $50,000 (a living wage). This need for a second worker increases in non-white families. For example, two thirds of all African American families require dual incomes to make a living wage (Oliver & Shapiro, 2006).

Dual-income families are a relatively new phenomenon in the United States. In 1970, only one third of married couples classified themselves as dual-income families. However, by 2000, nearly 60% of married couples earned dual wages. These dual-earning couples often jointly work 80 hours per week, though many couples report working significantly more. In fact, in 2000, nearly 15% of couples jointly worked 100 hours or more per week (Moe & Shandy, 2010). When employed parents have obligations to paid employment and the responsibility of children and home, leaves of absence become more necessary. For example, when there is no stay-at-home partner to deal with sick children or parents, one or both workers must likely adjust work schedules (see, e.g., Golden, 2001).

In recent years, hype about female breadwinners outnumbering male breadwinners hit a frenzied level as men saw record unemployment in the early part of the Great Recession (California Budget Project, 2010; Parker & Wang, 2013; Wang, Parker & Taylor, 2013). Female breadwinners include women in dual-income families who out earn their partners, never-married single-mother families, and divorced single-mother households (Behson, 2013). The characterization of female breadwinners as replacing male breadwinners is inaccurate. The surge of women earning more than their partners has receded as men have reclaimed their higher earning jobs in the wake of the recession (California Budget Project, 2010; American Association of University Women, 2015). However, single mothers and dual-income mothers with children still have requirements for care work that are different from most gatekeepers in organizations, which requires policy consideration.

In much the same way as dual-income families, single-parent families have increased needs for time away from work. Single parents must work but may have fewer safety nets to help them cover care obligations when something goes wrong. Single-parent families are increasingly present in U.S. American society, in large part as the result of a growing divorce rate and the rise of never-married parents. The majority of single parent families are single-mother families, which puts greater exigency on women to use work–life policies (Albiston, 2010; Bolzendahl & Olafsdottir, 2008). In 2013, about 30% of families with children were single-parent families, and primarily single women led these families (Parker & Wang, 2013). The increase in single-parent families has left many working mothers as the only source of financial support for their families, and this makes single mothers' work critical for economic survival (Ciabatarri, 2007; Nelson, 2005). While single-parent workers may feel a need to exercise their rights to leaves of absence more acutely than do other workers (e.g., workers from dual-income families), using these policies can have serious, negative implications for their career progressions.

Workers with Disabilities

In addition to familial structure changes, at present U.S. workers also are more likely to have a disability than in years past. This is important because many disabilities require accommodations in the workplace, particularly with regard to time away from work. The number of people with disabilities entering the U.S. workforce has increased in recent years, in part due to legal reforms promoting education for children with disabilities and improved medical care. For example, medical advancements (e.g., new treatments) and medical technology (e.g., lighter and more portable wheel chairs) improve the length and quality of life for people with serious illnesses or injuries, so individuals with these conditions regularly enter the workforce and remain in the workforce longer. Additionally, because the probability of having a disability increases with age, and because individuals in the baby-boomer generation have remained in the workforce, the U.S. workforce has recently aged significantly, and as a result, employees with disabilities represent a significant and growing population in the workforce. In 2013, 12% of the U.S. population had a disability, and a majority of these individuals were employed (Albiston, 2010).

Despite the addition of workers with disabilities, most organizational policies do not reflect the potentially unique needs of these employees to take time away from work—often unexpectedly. For example, people with social anxiety disorder, lupus, or bipolar disorder often require unexpected time away from work in order to manage their own health. Employers unfamiliar with the nuances of these medical situations regularly punish and dismiss people with disabilities, finding their need for accommodation "unreasonable" (Albiston, 2010). The typical routine and patterned structure of most work often conflicts with the surprising and unexpected health-related reasons that disabled employees need to temporarily leave work. If leave were more accessible for employees with disabilities, managing work and health could be an easier endeavor. However, the stigma and material consequences for employees who temporarily leave work for "unapproved" reasons have put employees with disabilities at risk for dismissal.

Aging Workers

The U.S. American workforce is also aging, and the needs of an aging population are important considerations for leaves of absence policies. The average life expectancy in the United States is rising (currently 80.8 for women and 78.3 for men; U.S. Census Bureau, 2012). At present, 21% of the U.S. population is 55 or older (U.S. Census Bureau, 2014), and it is expected that by 2030, 20% of the population will be 65 or older (Smith, 2004). Like workers with disabilities, older workers need time away from work for health-related reasons more often than other workers.

As the number of older adults in the U.S. population increases, so does the need for elder care. Smith (2004) defined elder care as the "informal care of the elderly by family and friends" (p. 353). Elder care functions as a personal safety net for everyone, and by 2020, 40% of workers may need to provide elder care (Smith, 2004; Tracy, 2008). However, women are the primary providers of elder care, and this type of work is subject to gendered norms about who can and should conduct such care. For example, U.S. women can expect to spend 18 years caring for elderly relatives (Smith, 2004). Doress-Worters (1994) described "caregiver stress" or "caregiver burden" and examined the effects of elder care on caregivers and found that women may experience role strain as a result of taking on these roles in the context of several others (p. 597). To add to this stress, many workers find themselves in a *caregiving sandwich*—a situation in which they must provide care for both their young children and for their aging parents (Doress-Worters, 1994). Indeed, Smith (2004) claimed that elder care induces more stress than child care for workers because there are more unanticipated caregiving situations. For these reasons, Smith (2004) argued that elder care is perhaps one of the most important aspects of work–life and, as such, is highly affected by organizational availability of leaves of absence.

In addition to aforementioned demographic shifts in the U.S. workforce, a new cultural assumption of "chronic presenteeism" pervades, which describes the tendency of U.S. workers to be physically present at work, regardless of other life events, such as illness (Sheridan, 2004, p. 210). Organizations perpetually attempt to measure workers' performance, an effort that becomes more difficult when flexible programs and technology enable different patterns for performing work. Continually, *face time*, which describes the hours employees work at an actual office, is a measure of workers' performance. This has continued despite advances in technology that make working outside the office possible. Researchers have linked face time to a number of problems, such as organizational pressure for employees to come to work during illness, grief, and other times during which they might stay home. In extreme cases, face-time requirements (either real or imagined) can create a culture of organizational commitment that pressures employees to work 24-hour shifts. Sheridan (2004) found that men, in particular, see no choice but to engage in an unrelenting work schedule in which they can only show their worth by performing their work when others are watching. Although some studies have revealed that work performance actually declines as the work hours increase (Heiler, 1998; Simpson, 1998), face time continues to dominate performance assumptions. Such assumptions, however, disproportionately impact women and workers with disabilities as their increased responsibilities outside of work have the potential to significantly affect their ability to put in the same hours as men (Sheridan, 2004).

The effort to "unlock" the glass handcuffs requires a close look at the contexts from which the phenomenon emerges, the causes of the glass handcuffs, implications, and suggested courses of action to remedy this particular version of work–life inequality. In Chapters 2, 3, and 4, I set the stage by presenting some information about the contexts for the glass handcuffs phenomenon. I explore in Chapter 2 organizational inequality, including subtler forms of gender-based discrimination that prevent women and other marginalized groups, including people of color, from reaching the upper echelons of organizations. These discrete biases against women, and especially against women of color, mothers, pregnant women, and women in childbearing years, function as invisible barriers to women's career advancement (Moe & Shandy, 2010; Smith, 2004).

In Chapter 3 I situate leaves of absence policies by examining the international development of policies to help employees manage work and nonwork. I reveal a history from the first maternity leave rights in Germany in 1883 to now, explicating the development of leave policies internationally before moving into a discussion about leave policies in the United States. I conclude the chapter by identifying particular arguments and points of inequality in the Family Medical Leave Act of 1993 (FMLA).

The fourth chapter includes data from the interviews about men's perceptions about work–life balance, about leaves of absence, and about what these concepts mean to men. It explains how many men conceive of work–life as work–family and outlines the ways in which some men feel excluded from the work–family concept. In this chapter, I also present data about how most of the men in this study view themselves as personally balanced but also consider themselves outliers when compared to the majority of unbalanced men. I end the chapter with a discussion about instances in which the men believed leaves of absence are appropriate, such as to avoid burnout.

After covering the historical context for the glass handcuffs, the book moves to identify and explain some causes for the glass handcuffs. I present in Chapter 5 textual analysis data from books by and about prominent industry leaders. By drawing out the discourses from respected men about how to act at work and how to think about work–life balance, this chapter presents some data about how macro discourses serve to secure the glass handcuffs.

In Chapter 6, I discuss the propensity of men to draw on discourses of occupational uniqueness and their personal-occupational identities to explain their inability to leave work. By framing their occupations as different from other occupations, men can explain away the need for or ability to take time away from work. This feeling of occupational uniqueness does influence not only how men perceive their industries but also how they perceive themselves as branded with an occupational identity that precludes their ability to take a leave of absence. Occupational identity influences how men understand and act in relation to leave policies, because this is part of the everyday practice of workers. It is here that occupational identity quite obviously influences the leave-taking practices of individual workers by occupation. This chapter analyzes how the notion of occupational uniqueness and occupational identity work as causes of the glass handcuffs phenomenon.

I explore entrepreneurialism as a constraint to work–life policies, particularly leaves of absence, in Chapter 7. The discourse of entrepreneurialism reflects an ideology that workers are personally responsible for their own success. At work, this leads to assumptions that good workers are autonomous, engaged in self-surveillance and self-improvement, and can and will do whatever it takes to succeed and achieve. These "do-it-yourself "or "pull-yourself-up-by-your-bootstraps" mentalities are particular Western constructions that situate the accomplishment of work and career as the responsibility of the worker. This "entrepreneurial ideal" is always present yet impossible to achieve. Entrepreneurial discourses function in racist, gendered, and classed ways. Discussions of work–life balance tangle within this discursive frame.

Gender is perhaps the most encompassing cause of the glass handcuffs. In Chapter 8, I present a historical overview of relevant gender constructs and interview data that illustrate how men drew on gendered rationales to explain the impossibility or limited availability of leaves of absence. After discussing the gendered rationales related to leaves of absence, I discuss the economic constraints that prevent men from taking leaves. When their wages are required to support the family, either as sole breadwinners or as significant contributors to the family income, leaves of absence are not possible for many men. This chapter outlines the real and perceived economic consequences that inhibit men from taking leaves of absence.

In Chapter 9, I present ways men reframe leaves of absence as unnecessary. The men in this study drew on four primary arguments to explain this view: (a) Virtual work enables them to work from home if necessary, (b) vacation time or flextime can maintain work–life balance, (c) quitting their jobs at crucial life moments allows men to gain time, (d) a work–life distinction is irrelevant. These framings and practices circumvent formal leaves of absence. In this chapter, I provide evidence and examples of each of these arguments and analyze how they collectively harm all employees in organizations. Positioning leaves of absence as unnecessary is problematic, particularly for employees who may need to take more time away from work.

After fleshing out the causes of the glass handcuffs, in Chapter 10, I provide arguments about why understanding the glass handcuffs matters and present a number of serious implications that can arise. For example, the wage and wealth gaps and the *maternal wall* continue to disadvantage all women in the workforce. When men do not take time away from work for family, it sets precedents that taking time off for work is unacceptable or not desirable. Until men are free to leave, women will continue to face penalties at work for leaving. Other impacts discussed in this chapter include the health, behavioral, and economic effects of increased day care use and health implications for men who are overworked. This chapter also presents some actionable conclusions from the previous analysis of the glass handcuffs, including (a) reforming the FMLA (b) instating a sick-day policy, (c) revaluing care work, (d) studying the effects of other work–life policies and technologies, (e) broadening the "life" in work–life conversations, (f) focusing on the importance of occupational identity, (g) insisting on managerial support and executive modeling of work–life practices, (h) getting men involved in the equity movement, and (i) shifting gendered expectations at home. As this list suggests, much more work is required to throw organizational inequality off balance.

NOTES

1. The term *balance* is a point of contention in work–life research. To speak of work–life "balance" implies that balance is indeed possible or desirable and that anyone who is not sufficiently "balanced" is doing something wrong (Kirby, Golden, Medved, Jorgenson, & Buzzanell, 2003). I use the term *balance* throughout the book but do not continually identify the problematic nature of the word in the text. Let it suffice that the very concept of achieving work–life balance (and its related terms, such as "unbalanced") are political and problematic, even as the concepts enjoy wide mass-market appeal.
2. Same-sex couples see more equity in this division of labor.

REFERENCES

Acker, J. (1990). Hierarchies, jobs, bodies: A theory of gendered organizations. *Gender and Society*, 4(2), 139–158. doi:10.1177/089124390004002002
Alberts, J., & Trethewey, A. (2007). Love, honor and thank. *Greater Good*, 4(1), 20–22.

Albiston, C. (2010). *Institutional inequality and the mobilization of the family and medical leave act: Rights on leave.* Cambridge, England: Cambridge University Press.

American Association of University Women. (2015). The simple truth about the gender pay gap. Retrieved from: http://www.aauw.org/files/2015/02/The-Simple-Truth_Spring-2015.pdf

Ashcraft, C., & Blithe, S. (2009). *Women in IT: The facts* (NCWIT 2009). Boulder, CO: National Center for Women & Information Technology.

Ashcraft, K. L. (2013). The glass slipper: "Incorporating" occupational identity in management studies. *Academy of Management Review, 38*(1), 6–31. doi:10.5465/amr.10.0219

Ashcraft, K. L., Kuhn, T., & Cooren, F. (2009). Constitutional amendments: "Materializing" organizational communication. *The Academy of Management Annals, 3*(1), 1–64. doi:10.1080/19416520903047186

Ashcraft, K. L., & Mumby, D. K. (2004). *Reworking gender: A feminist communicology of organization.* Thousand Oaks, CA: Sage.

Aumann, K., Galinsky, E., & Matos, K. (2011). The new male mystique. Retrieved from http://familiesandwork.org/site/research/reports/ newmalemystique.pdf

Azoulay, P., Ding, W., & Stuart, T. (2007). The determinants of faculty patenting behavior: Demographics or opportunities? *Journal of Economic Behavior & Organization, 63*(4), 599–623.

Behson, S. (2013, June 3). The Pew Research Report, breadwinner moms, misleading headlines and the challenges of dual-income households. [Blog comment]. Retrieved from http://fathersworkandfamily.com/2013/06/03/the-pew-research-report-bread winner-moms-misleading-headlines-and-the-challenges-of-dual-income-househol ds/?blogsub=confirming#blog_subscription-2

Bolzendahl, C., & Olafsdottir, S. (2008). Gender group interest or gender ideology? Understanding U.S. support for family policy within the liberal welfare regime. *Sociological Perspectives, 51*(2), 281–304. doi:10.1525/sop.2008.51.2.281

Bond, J. T., Thompson, C., Galinsky, E., & Prottas, D. (2002). Highlights of the National Study of the Changing Workforce executive summary. Retrieved from www.familiesandwork.org

Buzzanell, P. M., & Turner, L. H. (2003). Emotion work revealed by job loss discourse: Backgrounding-foregrounding of feelings, construction of normalcy, and (re)instituting of traditional masculinities. *Journal of Applied Communication Research, 31*(1), 27–57. doi:10.1080/00909880305375

California Budget Project. (2010, May). How the other half fared: The impact of the Great Recession on women. *Policy Points,* pp. 1–9.

Center for American Progress. (2012). White House summit on working families. Retrieved from http://workingfamiliessummit.org/wp-content/uploads/2014/06/ Ed-Board-Memo.pdf

Ciabatarri, T. (2007). Single mothers, social capital, and work-family conflict. *Journal of Family Issues, 28*(1), 34–60. doi:10.1177/0192513X06292809

Cotter, D., Hermsen, J., Ovadia, S., & Vannemen, R. (2001). The glass ceiling effect. *Social Forces, 80*(2), 655–682. doi:10.1353/sof.2001.0091

Croft, A. (2014, May 28). Dads who do chores bolster daughters' aspirations. Retrieved from http://news.ubc.ca/2014/05/28/dads-who-do-chores-bolster-daughters-aspira tions/

Ding, W., Murray, F., & Stuart, T. (2006). An empirical study of gender differences in patenting in the academic life sciences. *Science, 313,* 665–667.

Doress-Worters, P. (1994). Adding elder care to women's multiple roles: A critical review of the caregiver stress and multiple roles literatures. *Sex Roles, 31*(9–10), 597–616. doi:10.1007/BF01544282

Federal Glass Ceiling Commission. (1995). *Good for business: Making full use of the nation's human capital.* Washington, DC: U.S. Department of Labor Publications.

Galtry, J. (2002). Child health: An underplayed variable in parental leave policy debates? *Community, Work & Family, 5*(3), 257–278. doi:10.1080/1366880022 000041775

Glass, J. (2004). Blessing or curse? Work–family policies and mother's wage growth over time. *Work and Occupations, 31*(3), 367–394. doi:10.1177/0730888404266364

Golden, A. G. (2000). What we talk about when we talk about work and family: A discourse analysis of parental accounts. *The Electronic Journal of Communication, 10*(3–4), n.p. Retrieved from http://www.cios.org/EJCPUBLIC/010/3/010315.html

Golden, A. G. (2001). Modernity and the communicative management of multiple roles: The case of the worker–parent. *The Journal of Family Communication, 1*(4), 233–264. doi:10.1207/S15327698JFC0104_02

Halpern, D. F., & Cheung, F. M. (2008). *Women at the top: Powerful leaders tell us how to combine work and family*. Malden, MA: Blackwell.

Harrington, B., Van Deusen, F., & Humberd, B. (2011). *The new dad: Caring, committed and conflicted*. Retrieved from http://www.bc.edu/content/dam/files/centers/cwf/pdf/FH-Study-Web-2.pdf

Hattery, A. (2001). *Women, work, and family: Balancing and weaving*. Thousand Oaks, CA: Sage.

Heiler, K. (1998). The "petty pilfering of minutes" or what has happened to the length of the working day in Australia? *International Journal of Manpower, 19*(4), 266–280. doi:10.1108/01437729810220383

Hewlett, S. (2005). Addressing the time crunch of high earners. In J. Heymann & C. Beem (Eds.), *Unfinished work: Building equality and democracy in an era of working families* (pp. 156–179). New York, NY: The New Press.

Hochschild, A. R. (1989). *The second shift*. New York, NY: Penguin Books.

Kafker, S. (1993). Golden handcuffs: Enforceability of non-competition clauses in professional partnership agreements of accountants, physicians, and attorneys. *American Business Law Journal, 31*(1), 31–58. doi:10.1111/j.1744–1714.1993.tb00674.x

Kamerman, S., & Moss, P. (Eds.). (2011). *The politics of parental leave policies: Children, parenting, gender and the labour market*. Bristol, England: The Policy Press.

Kirby, E., Golden, A., Medved, C., Jorgenson, J., & Buzzanell, P. (2003). An organizational communication challenge to the discourse of work and family research: From problematics to empowerment. *Communication Yearbook, 27,* 1–43.

Kirby, E., & Krone, K. (2002). The policy exists but you can't really use it: Communication and the structuration of work-family policies. *Journal of Applied Communication Research, 30*(1), 50–77. doi:10.1080/00909880216577

Klein, W., Izquierdo, C., & Bradbury, T. (2013, March 1). The difference between a happy marriage and miserable one: Chores. *The Atlantic.* Retrieved from http://www.theatlantic.com/sexes/archive/2013/03/the-difference-between-a-happy-marriage and-miserable-one-chores/273615/

Kolhatkar, S. (2013, May 30). Alpha dads: Men get serious about work-life balance. *Bloomberg Businessweek.* Retrieved from http://www.businessweek.com/articles/2013-05-30/alpha-dads-men-get-serious-about-work-life-balance

Maume, D. (1999). Glass ceilings and glass escalators: Occupational segregation and race and sex differences in managerial promotions. *Work and Occupations, 26*(4), 483–509. doi:10.1177/0730888499026004005

Moe, K., & Shandy, D. (2010). *Glass ceilings & 100-hour couples: What the opt-out phenomenon can teach us about work and family*. Athens: The University of Georgia Press.

Murray, F., & Graham, L. (2007). Buying science and selling science: Gender differences in the market for commercial science. *Industrial and Corporate Change, 16*(4), 657–689. doi:10.1093/icc/dtm021

Nadesan, M. H. (2002). Engineering the entrepreneurial infant: Brain science, infant development toys, and governmentality. *Cultural Studies, 16*(3), 401–432. doi:10.1080/09502380210128315

National Alliance for Caregiving. (2009, November). *Caregiving in the U.S.* Retrieved from http://www.caregiving.org/data/Caregiving_in_the_US_2009_full_report.pdf

National Partnership for Women & Families. (2012). *Dads expect better: Top states for new dads.* Retrieved from http://www.nationalpartnership.org/research-library/work-family/paid-leave/dads-expect-better-report.pdf

National Partnership for Women & Families. (2013). A look at the U.S. Department of Labor's 2012 Family and Medical Leave Act employee and worksite surveys [Fact sheet]. Retrieved from http://www.nationalpartnership.org/research-library/work-family/fmla/dol-fmla-survey-key-findings-2012.pdf

Nelson, M. K. (2005). *The social economy of single motherhood: Raising children in rural America.* New York, NY: Routledge.

Ness, D. (2014). Showing thanks for family caregivers this month. Retrieved from http://www.nationalpartnership.org/blog/showing-thanks-for-family-caregivers-this-month.html

Oliver, M. L., & Shapiro, T. M. (2006). *Black wealth/white wealth: A new perspective on racial inequality.* New York, NY: Routledge.

Parker, K., & Wang, W. (2013). *Modern parenthood: Roles of moms and dads converge as they balance work and family.* Retrieved from http://www.pewsocialtrends.org/files/2013/03/FINAL_modern_parenthood_03-2013.pdf

Powell, G. N. (1999). Reflections on the glass ceiling: Recent trends and future prospects. In G. N. Powell (Ed.), *Handbook of gender and work* (pp. 325–346). Thousand Oaks, CA: Sage.

Sandberg, S. (2013). *Lean in.* New York, NY: Random House.

Sengupta, S., Whitfield, K., & McNabb, B. (2007). Employee share ownership and performance: Golden path or golden handcuffs? *The International Journal of Human Resource Management, 18*(8), 1507–1538. doi:10.1080/09585190701502620

Sheridan, A. (2004). Chronic presenteeism: The multiple dimensions to men's absence from part-time work. *Gender, Work & Organization, 11*(2), 207–225. doi:10.1111/j.1468–0432.2004.00229.x

Simpson, R. (1998). Presenteeism, power and organizational change: Long hours as a career barrier and the impact in the working lives of women managers. *British Journal of Management, 9*(Suppl. 1), 37–50. doi:10.1111/1467–8551.9.s1.5

Smith, P. R. (2004). Elder care, gender, and work: The work-family issue of the 21st century. *Berkeley Journal of Employment and Labor Law, 25*, 351–398.

Tanaka, S. (2005). Parental leave and child health across OECD countries. *The Economic Journal, 115*(501), F7–F28. doi:10.1111/j.0013–0133.2005.00970.x

Tracy, S. J. (2008). Dialectic, contradiction, or double bind? Analyzing and theorizing employee reactions to organization tension. *Journal of Applied Communication Research, 32*(2), 119–146. doi:10.1080/00909880420002210025

Tracy, S. J., & Rivera, K. D. (2009). Endorsing equity and applauding stay-at-home moms: How male voices on work-life reveal adverse sexism and flickers of transformation. *Management Communication Quarterly, 24*, 3–43. doi:10.1177/0893318909352248

U.S. Census Bureau. (2012). Table 104. Expectation of Life at Birth, 1970 to 2008, and Projections, 2010 to 2020. *Statistical Abstract of the United States: 2012.* Retrieved from http://www.census.gov/compendia/statab/2012/tables/12s0104.pdf

U.S. Census Bureau. (2014). Infoplease demographic statistics. Retrieved from http://www.infoplease.com/us/census/data/demographic.html

U.S. Department of Labor. (2012). *Family and medical leave in 2012: Technical report.* Retrieved from http://www.dol.gov/asp/evaluation/fmla/FMLA-2012-Technical-Report.pdf

Vespa, J., Lewis, J., & Kreider, R. (2013). Table 10. Children's Economic Situation by Family Structure: CPS 20121—Con. (Numbers in thousands). In *America's families and living arrangements: 2012* (pp. 25–26). Washington, DC: U.S. Census. Retrieved from http://www.census.gov/prod/2013pubs/p20-570.pdf

Wang, W., Parker, K., & Taylor, P. (2013). Breadwinner moms: Mothers are the sole or primary provider in four-in-ten households with children; public conflicted about the growing trend. Retrieved from PEW Research Center website: http://www.pewsocialtrends.org/2013/05/29/breadwinner-moms/

Wieland, S. M. B., Bauer, J. C., & Deetz S. (2009). Excessive careerism and destructive life stresses: The role of entrepreneurialism in colonizing identities. In P. Lutgen-Sandvik & B. Sypher (Eds.) *The destructive side of organizational communication: Processes, consequences and constructive ways of organizing* (pp. 99–120). London and New York: Routledge.

Williams, C.L. (1992). The glass escalator: Hidden advantages for men in the "female" professions. *Social problems, 39*(3), 253–267.

Part I

Contexts for the
Glass Handcuffs Phenomenon

2 Organizational Contexts for the Glass Handcuffs Phenomenon

In order to understand how the glass handcuffs phenomenon occurs, it is necessary to comprehend the existing contexts that frame the current working environment in the United States. In this chapter, I begin with some theoretical work about how communication constructs organizations, which makes transparent the permeable nature of organizational cultures and policies—relevant for thinking about how inequalities in organizations might be undone. Next, I present some of the most pressing areas of structural inequality for issues of work–life, including biased organizational logics, occupational segregation, the wage and wealth gaps, the maternal wall, and unconscious bias. Finally, I discuss organizational inequity as it relates to leaves of absence policies.

THE COMMUNICATIVE CONSTITUTION OF ORGANIZATIONS

Traditional conceptions of organizational communication considered communication as message transmission (Axley, 1984) and organizations as things. The idea that the shape of the organization shapes the kind of communication that occurs at work and that the organization exists separately from communication pervaded much early organizational communication scholarship and still dominates in much business and management research. This model drives many undergraduate organizational communication classes that teach "effective communication" and seek to coordinate message transmission and build skills. In this view, communication accomplishes goals within the boundary of the organization, and merely expresses organizational realities that preexist (Ashcraft, Kuhn, & Cooren, 2009). While this view of communication is an important part of organizational and business communication, scholars have transcended this limiting model and broadened the concept of organization. Rather than viewing an organization as a "container" (R. Smith, 1993), these scholars began to understand an organization as something that is created through communication. From this perspective, aspects of an organization, such as culture or policies, are not independent "things" but rather fluid constructions that make up the organization (Ashcraft et al., 2009).

The *linguistic turn* in the late 1960s centered language as a necessary component of social realities (Rorty, 1967). From this premise stemmed a growing trend to consider communication for its ability to produce social realities (McPhee & Zaug, 2000; Searle, 1995; Taylor & Van Every, 2000) in addition to the traditional view that communication expresses social realities (K. Ashcraft et al., 2009). Recently termed the Communicative Constitution of Organizations (CCO) (Putnam & Nicotera, 2008), this perspective views organizational structures as the manifestations of constant negotiation (Taylor & Van Every, 2000). From a CCO perspective, communication is the process that determines the possible versions of social realities for people at work. As such, it is more accurate to describe "organization" as a verb rather than a noun (Putnam & Nicotera, 2008; Weick, 1979) and organizations are physical manifestations of human interactions (Koschmann, 2012).

The CCO view of communication creates possibilities for new ways of viewing organizational structures, forms of power, inequalities, and policy discrepancies. CCO scholars do not suggest that organizations are wholly discursive (Putnam & Nicotera, 2009) but, rather, the highly discursive nature of organizations suggests that seemingly rigid structures are malleable (see K. Ashcraft et al., 2009, for an analysis of the material component of CCO work). Policies and inequalities at work are thus the result of human interaction and are not immutable "things" (Koschmann, 2012). This view opens up the possibility to challenge, contest, and dismantle organizational systems (Deetz, 1992), to question how central organizational concepts, the validity of organizational structures, and power relationships came to be part of organizational life (K. Ashcraft et al., 2009; Koschmann, 2012).

The shift to a CCO view of organizational communication has been a major ontological shift and an integral step in understanding how organizations fit within larger society (Cheney, 2000). Explaining how organizations are produced through the *process* of communication helps to explain, understand, and make visible more dimensions of organizational life (McPhee & Zaug, 2000; Putnam & McPhee, 2008; Putnam & Nicotera, 2009). Explicating the processual role of communication in constituting organization, K. Ashcraft et al. (2009) defined communication as the

> ongoing, dynamic, interactive process of manipulating symbols toward the creation, maintenance, destruction, and/or transformation of meanings, which are axial—not peripheral—to organizational existence and organizing phenomena . . . taking communication (as defined here) seriously means treating discursive struggle as a generative process. A communicative explanation is thus any account that hones our understanding of how communication constitutes organizational reality, clarifies how communication works as an organizing mechanism, or illuminates communication (rather than, for instance, physical location) as the site of organization. (pp. 22–23)

Indeed, the conception of communication as a *generative process* is highly useful for studying organizations because process theory reveals explanations for rather than descriptions of organizational life (Van de Ven & Poole, 2005). Put simply, communication is the explanation for how organizations and our experiences of organizations come to exist.

Considering this historical development of organizational communication is important because it provides a framework for identifying important turns in the theoretical consideration of organizational life and illuminates the potential and possibilities that arise from shifting ontological thought from "things" to "processes." This is an important consideration for this project because it makes visible the constructed (and therefore potentially contested) nature of organizational facets such as policies, practices, and organizational culture. CCO reveals how "facts" and seemingly cemented organizational ideologies are actually liquid. Through this lens, power, domination, and inequalities in organizations are reversible, while occupational stories become contestable narratives. It is through communication that the politics of all organizational facets develop, and also how norms, roles, and expectations frame the actions of individuals (K. Ashcraft et al., 2009). Unfortunately, the historical development of these organizational facets has been far from equitable.

STRUCTURAL INEQUALITY

In 2010, *The Economist* hailed organizational equality for women at work, complete with Rosie the Riveter on its cover and the text "We did it!" Claiming that organizations had finally reached equal numerical participation by men and women in the U.S. workforce, the article represents a growing colloquial argument that gender equality at work has been achieved. In some ways, the article celebrates actual progress at work. Men and women are competitive in terms of pay for similar jobs with similar hours during the first two years of their careers. Childless men and women remain fairly wage comparable over the term of their careers. This wage competitiveness is surprising, considering that, on a wide scale, women earn less than men do and are far less likely to hold leadership positions at work. In addition, women's educational achievement has increased substantially: women earn more college degrees than their male counterparts and 60% of undergraduate students are women. Women attend the same kinds of higher education institutions and have a higher grade point average than men (3.3 vs. 3.18), which will presumably set them up for success at work after graduation (Bureau of Labor Statistics, 2011; Corbett & Hill, 2012; Institute for Women's Policy Research, 2010; Moe & Shandy, 2010).

However, equal *numerical participation* in work is not the same as *achieving equality*. Myriad gender oppressions continue to persist in U.S. workplaces, which prevent the attainment of true equality. In this section,

I draw out some of the most prevalent areas of gender inequality in the U.S. workforce, which include (a) biased organizational logics, (b) occupational segregation, (c) the wage and wealth gaps, (d) the maternal wall, and (e) unconscious bias. While there are certainly many other ways employees experience discrimination at work, these are some of the most influential areas pertaining to work–life issues.

Biased Organizational Logics

Organizational logics are important to understand because they underscore hidden scripts that disadvantage some employees. Organizations, and U.S. organizations in particular, tend to organize in ways that preserve an unequal social order (see, e.g., Baines, 2010; Grimes, 2002; Tienari, Quack, & Theobald, 2002). Large-scale, seemingly impenetrable systems of inequality characterize most U.S. organizations. *Inequality regimes* (Acker, 2006) and *institutional inequality* (Albiston, 2010) explain the ways that organizations and other institutions developed historically such that people in power determined which ways of acting in organizations (how to organize work, how pay, benefits, respect, and pleasure at work are determined, how individuals attain promotions, etc.) were appropriate. These concepts explain how "commonsense" ways of acting were produced to posit some identities and ways of being as more desirable to others (Acker, 2006; Albiston, 2010). Inequality regimes and institutional inequality describe how work came to be work: set in a particular political context, developed and maintained by people in power, and perpetually reproduced by individuals enacting expectations at work every day. The *historical construction* of inequalities, however, is important to emphasize because constructions can be deconstructed. Recognizing institutional inequality offers a means for social change by facilitating the reinterpretation of taken-for-granted meanings.

The well-known division of social order into masculine and feminine is a core piece of inequality in organizations. This order assumes two persistent logics across contexts: first, that males are different from females and, second, that masculine norms are prioritized in a well-defined hierarchy (Hirdman, 1990). This gender system is identifiable in most societies around the world and throughout history and has a profound impact on the construction of identities. Male bodies are ascribed masculine characteristics while female bodies are ascribed feminine characteristics, and bodies and characteristics that are labeled "feminine" are regarded as less than whatever is deemed as masculine (Butler, 1999; Lindgren & Packendorff, 2006). This gender system has been both evident and problematic in organizations, particularly as more and more women with their ascribed femininities have entered the workforce. Indeed, Lindgren and Packendorff (2006), drawing on Ferguson (1984), claimed, "bureaucratic organizations and industrial mass production can be seen as contributing to a gender order that manifested itself in the whole life of modern human beings" (p. 842). Thus, it is not surprising that organizations, which are patterned after social order, highly prioritize masculinity over femininity; however, it is troubling that this pattern is continually reinforced in practice.

One particular problem in the structural organization of work is that it emerged around a white middle-class universal/ideal worker (Acker, 1990; Albiston, 2010). This universal/ideal worker is disembodied and asexual (Acker, 1990), available to work full time, does not have domestic responsibilities, and is able-bodied and healthy (Albiston, 2010). Furthermore, the most effective universal/ideal workers are able to set their personal lives and emotions aside (Judiesch & Lyness, 1999), likely because this universal/ideal worker has no relationships or responsibilities outside of the workplace and has no outside attachments or obligations (Fenstermaker & West, 2002). While the universal worker ideal unfairly disadvantages white women, women of color, single parents, people with disabilities and serious medical conditions, mothers, dual-income couples, people working in less affluent jobs, and men who cannot or will not conform to the ideal (C. Connell, 2010; R. W. Connell & Wood, 2005), it is a significant part of U.S. organizational life and sets the tone for modern U.S. workplaces.

Occupational Segregation

When looking closely at the "equal participation" of women in the U.S. workforce, a clear pattern of occupational segregation occurs. There are large gender discrepancies in college majors and in occupations. Thus, while women make up a majority of health care (88%) and education (81%) majors, they account for only 19% of computer and information science majors, and 18% of engineering and engineering technology majors (Corbett & Hill, 2012). The percentages are lower for actual graduation rates, as women frequently change majors out of science, technology, engineering, and mathematics (STEM) fields before they finish their education. A similar pattern happens in occupations. While there are more women elementary school teachers, women make up only 17% of Congress, 17% of corporate board members, and only 3% of *Fortune* 500 companies CEOs (Kunin, 2012). These statistics are even more shocking when broken down by race. Women of color have almost no representation as CEOs and very little as board members for major companies (McCarver & Blithe, 2014).

Vertical occupational segregation describes the tendency for women to represent such a small percent of the upper echelons of organizations, which occurs in *every* occupation, including female dominated industries (Charles & Grusky, 2004; McCall, 2001). For example, as mentioned previously, women are a numerical majority in teaching; however, most principals are men. In medicine, nurses are mostly women, but doctors, who earn more money and reside higher on the occupational hierarchically, are mostly men. Vertical occupational segregation is evident even within the occupational category of "doctor," where comparisons show that more surgeons are men, but pediatricians tend to have an equitable gender distribution. Surgeons also earn more money and reputations as the some of the most skilled doctors. In essence, this describes the clustering of white men in leadership and power positions, while women do not advance as far in that particular occupation. To reiterate, vertical occupational segregation occurs in all occupations, in varying degrees, even in female dominated occupations.

Horizontal occupational segregation, also called "pink-collar ghettos" (Stallard, Ehrenreich, & Sklar, 1983) or "occupational ghettos (Charles & Grusky 2004), explains the division of work by gender. Women perpetually make up the dominant numerical demographic in low wage occupations such as education, health services, transportation and utilities, and local government, and are highly concentrated in administrative support jobs (Bureau of Labor Statistics, 2011). Horizontal occupational segregation patterns have remained relatively stable over time. When considering occupational segregation, it is clear that claiming work equality based on numerical participation in the workforce in general is misleading. Deep inequalities exist by occupation, both within and across occupational spaces.

The Wage and Wealth Gaps

The "wage gap" explains the numerical difference in the wages of women compared to men, when controlled for a number of factors including grade point average (GPA), occupation, job specialty, number of hours worked, degrees, educational institution, industry, organizational level, and job position responsibility (McCarver & Blithe, 2014). When all of these factors are equal, women still make less than men do. Occupational segregation is a big part of the wage gap, and accounts for about one third of wage discrepancies (Bureau of Labor Statistics, 2011; Corbett & Hill, 2012), yet much of the gap is explained only by gender (and race) inequality. Currently, the wage gap is an average of 82% across all occupations (The WAGE Project, 2013). Nevertheless, the wage gap fluctuates by occupation and geographic location. For example, in Louisiana the wage gap is 68.7% and in California it is 89.9% for full-time workers across occupations. However, there is a 68% discrepancy in construction, and only an 89% difference for K–12 teachers (McCarver & Blithe, 2014). There are no occupations that do not have a wage gap, and in every case it is women who earn less money (Bureau of Labor Statistics, 2011; Corbett & Hill, 2012; The WAGE Project, 2013). The wage gap widens for women of color—African American women earn about 68% of all men's earnings, and Latinas earn approximately 57% of all men's earnings. The gap also widens with age: 84% earned for women aged 25 to 34, but only 60% earned compared to all men for women aged 55 to 64 (The WAGE Project, 2013). Over time, the wage gap has severe implications for women. Throughout their lives, college educated women will earn a half-million dollars less than their equally qualified male counterparts (Carnevale, Rose, & Cheah, 2011).

The wage gap is a significant problem that contributes, in part, to the even more troubling gender *wealth gap*. The wealth gap captures the total economic resources available compared to overall debt between women and men. It is a more comprehensive indicator of overall economic viability and stability. Like the wage gap, the wealth gap demonstrates that women earn less overall when compared to men. In addition, the wealth gap also captures gender inequalities in stock options, paid vacation, health insurance, and favorable tax codes, all of which favor men. Since 1998, the gender wealth gap has increased, despite a narrowing of the wage gap (Chang, 2012). Women own about 36% of overall wealth, and never-married women account for only 6% of this figure. The wealth gap increases when broken down by race and parental status—women of color and all mothers face substantially lower overall total wealth figures. Despite mainstream claims to the contrary, the wage gap and wealth gap illuminate structural inequalities deeply rooted in U.S. organizational life that impact the ways in which men and women relate to paid work.

The Maternal Wall

The *maternal wall* describes an invisible and often unconscious bias preventing the upward mobility of working mothers. These discrete biases against women, and especially against women of color, mothers, pregnant women, and women in childbearing years, function as invisible barriers to women's career advancement (I. Smith, 2009). Discriminatory biases perpetuate the stereotype that women lack the commitment of childless employees, and are damaging to any woman who is assumed to potentially have or want a family (Moe & Shandy, 2010). Albiston (2010) explained that

> mothers earn less than men, whether or not those men have children; mothers also earn less than women who do not have children. These wage penalties remain even after controlling for factors that might differentiate mothers and nonmothers, such as human capital investments, part-time employment, the mother-friendly characteristics of jobs held by mothers, and other important differences in the characteristics, skills, and behaviors of mothers and nonmothers. (p. 66)

In part, the maternal wall bias explains why the wage gap begins to increase around the age most women have children.

Discrimination claims based on the *maternal wall* are on the rise. For example, Calvert (2009) explained that family responsibilities discrimination (FRD), also called caregiver discrimination, occurs when employees face discrimination based on their family caregiving responsibilities. Claims of FRD comprise a substantial portion of work–life lawsuits filed. FRD manifests itself in many ways, including when organizations refuse to hire pregnant women, resist promoting mothers of young children, punish male employees for taking time off to care for their children, and give unwarranted negative evaluations to employees who take leave to care for aging parents. FRD is typically caused by unexamined biases about how "employees with family caregiving responsibilities will or should act" (Calvert, 2009, p. 3). FRD represents one example of how organizational assumptions about how employees might or should act contribute to employers' unconscious discriminatory practices.

Unconscious Bias

Many gender inequalities in the workforce are discreet, often unintentional, forms of discrimination. Unconscious biases draw on preexisting beliefs, values, norms, and organizational practices, and influence the actions of all workers. Put simply, people often believe that what they have experienced in life is the "right" way, which makes change and imaging new systems, policies, and practices difficult. However, left unchecked, unconscious biases systematically disadvantage white women and workers of color, primarily because they have not been a part of the historical script of organizational life (C. Ashcraft & Blithe, 2009). This kind of discrimination typically goes unchallenged in everyday practice and can be hard to prove, yet it can severely impede the career advancement of all women. Two examples of unconscious biases that are particularly relevant for this project include microinequities and stereotyping.

Microinequities are unstated and subtle messages that accumulate over time to debase and discourage women in the workplace. These might include the use (or nonuse) of titles, order in group e-mails, gestures, tone of voice, looks, and other aspects of work–life that are difficult to capture and explain, but that make women feel devalued at work. In a classic example, if male executives repeatedly engaged in informal networking or socializing at strip clubs or on golf courses, female employees who did not enjoy those activities might miss out of work conversations that occurred. In a more recent example, studies have shown that letters of recommendation for women use the applicant's first names and are shorter than are letters of recommendation for men that use "Mr." instead of first-name familiarity (Trix & Psenka, 2003). It is nearly impossible to prove or even explain this type of discrimination at work, but microinequities greatly contribute to the kind of jobs women take, and how far they advance in their careers (C. Ashcraft & Blithe, 2009). In a similar way, gender stereotypes influence how people perceive women at work. For example, women are frequently cast as "work mothers," "ice queens," and "overemotional." Men displaying nurturing tendencies, little emotion, or too much emotion at work are not typically subject to the same kinds of stereotypes. These biases play a role in promotion, salary, role placement and hiring decisions, and contribute to gender inequality at work.

Organizational Equity and Leaves of Absence

Some scholars have started attending to leave policy and practice as a particularly relevant point in organizational equity (see, e.g., K. Ashcraft, 1999; Buzzanell, 2003; Kirby & Krone, 2002; Martin, 1990) For example, Kim (1998) explained that

> family leave policy introduces gender equality issues underscoring the fact that work–family conflict is not only a woman's issue but also a man's issue . . . If, however, traditional role bias and stereotypes are pervasive in organizations, the goals of family leave benefits for employees might be distorted during the policy implementation process. (p. 80)

Although the United States has made some progress in designing laws about leave policies, there are still far too many implementation problems to observe much progress. Many employees do not actually use leave policies because they have internalized cultural and organizational messages that workers who use leave policies are uncommitted and will not advance (Glass, 2004; Schultz, 2007).

Most employees can relate stories of colleagues or acquaintances who have suffered as a result of taking a leave of absence. As such, studying the cultural discourses about leave-taking is important if leave policies are to be implemented. As Albiston (2010) explained,

> understanding what FMLA rights will mean requires examining how workers come to comprehend and claim their rights, especially when they encounter conflict over taking leave. In addition, workers do not mobilize their rights in a cultural vacuum. FMLA rights remain embedded within existing power relations, institutions, and culture, including deeply entrenched beliefs and practices associated with work, gender, and disability. (p. ix)

Untangling how these factors work together to suppress equity progress is a central goal of this project.

Like all organizational policies, leave of absence policies typically rely on biased organizational logics that systematically discriminate by gender, race, class, and ability by assuming an ideal type worker will use the policy. However, because fewer than 10% of U.S. families consist of a stay-at-home mother and a working father (Grill, 1996; Moe & Shandy, 2010), few employees actually embody this ideal. Regardless, work schedules revolve around assumptions that workers' availability is constant, which results in an organizational value on face time. Workers who engage in less face time (such as some workers with disabilities or some parent workers) frequently collect penalties at work (Golden, 2000). Face time is still a premium in most workplaces, which poses a problem to the pursuit of flexible work and threatens workers' chances of actual work–nonwork balance. As such, the constructed importance of face time is one of the larger obstacles for workers who want to take a leave of absence, especially if there is a heavy emphasis on visibility as a mark of commitment in the organization. Valuing face time is a crucial example of the way the organizations adopted the dominant worker standpoint without critique.

Furthermore, it is imperative to reiterate that inequality regimes (and their inscriptions on leave practice and usage) go well beyond gender. Race, class, sexuality, and ability, for example, are all also organized into institutional and hierarchical orders of inequality. Thus, interrogating the way leave policies are raced is just as important as analyzing the hegemonic masculinity that organizes the lives of women and men at work. Race is typically ignored in organizational analyses, an oversight that actually reproduces and sustains implicit whiteness (K. Ashcraft & Allen, 2003). When white scholars and policy makers choose to ignore whiteness, race inequalities in policy use are exacerbated (Grimes, 2002). However, despite the knowledge that organizations and social institutions and practices are raced, very few analyses focus on how FMLA and other leave policies might be raced.

Armenia and Gerstel (2006) argued that treating women and men as homogenous groups does not capture the family variations necessary to understand leave practice. Rather, household composition and income, health status, and wage gaps are all raced variables that contribute to one's ability and/or willingness to take a leave of absence. African Americans and Latina/os—populations that may have greater health problems and/or different demands from relatives—may require leave more than may white workers. However, these populations are also less likely to access leave because they frequently (and statistically) have less access to leave (Armenia & Gerstel, 2006). Armenia and Gerstel only examined family leave and found that, while white men were significantly less likely to take family leaves than were women, men of color showed no significant difference in their propensity to take leave than white women or women of color. The authors also found that the presence of a spouse or partner significantly increased employees' chances of taking a leave across all races and concluded that unpaid leaves reproduce occupational segregation and wage disparities across genders and races and do little to promote equity. The findings in this study suggest that analyzing leave policies should move well beyond a focus on women, because the use and understandings of work–life policies and leaves differ by social identity.

Understanding how people use leave policy across class is also important. Low-income workers infrequently take leave even for emergencies for fear of losing their jobs (Whittiker, 1991). Critics of the FMLA have pointed to its classed design, particularly in regards to the 50-person threshold, the length of tenure with an organization, and the hours worked that qualify employees for FMLA coverage, which excludes many workers (e.g., seasonal laborers, migrant workers, domestic workers, child care workers, home health care providers, and most jobs held by low-wage workers of color, particularly women of color). Furthermore, these statutes also exclude people who are unemployed and people with medical conditions who cannot work full time (Albiston, 2010).

In addition to the structural inequalities that lead to race and class discrimination, U.S. organizations (and thus leave policies) are inherently ableist. Historically, disability and work have been constructed as mutually exclusive categories and, as such, the FMLA unfairly discriminates against people with disabilities who are frequently segregated into less secure and nonstandard jobs (Albiston, 2010). People with disabilities and women have historically been classified as nonworkers; thus, they have been excluded from the way work is structured and face difficulty when they attempt to exercise their rights to take a leave from work in institutions that require uninterrupted work. Similarly, courts have generally found that long leaves of absence, unpaid leaves of indefinite duration, and excessive or erratic absences are not reasonable accommodations for people with disabilities in the workplace (Albiston, 2010).

For the previously mentioned reasons, leave policy in the United States clearly reveals a bias toward particular kinds of workers, to the detriment of most others. As Bornstein (2000) explained,

> exclusions from the Act reflect a moral code, pronouncing which individuals and families are entitled to the coverage and security of a national policy, and which are not. While certain individuals and families are rewarded, protected, and benefited by the coverage of the Act, others are disadvantaged, punished, disregarded, and ignored. (p. 81)

As long as U.S. organizations continue to structure work around the universal worker ideal, leave policies will inevitably be rife with inequality. Many policies that aim to remedy inequality can only operate at a surface level because the structural foundation from which the policies developed is unequal (Buzzanell, 1995). The social order and deeply rooted assumptions about gender and ability remain too powerful and immune to change from policies that do not address the structural, institutional nature of inequality. Surface equality policies do not significantly propel organizations toward equity; rather, organizations still have considerable work to do in order to move beyond inequality regimes. Significant organizational overhaul and deep policy analysis that considers social identity are required in order for leave policies to create more equity at work and home.

REFERENCES

Acker, J. (1990). Hierarchies, jobs, bodies: A theory of gendered organizations. *Gender & Society, 4*(2), 139–158. doi:10.1177/089124390004002002

Acker, J. (2006). Inequality regimes: Gender, class, and race in organizations. *Gender & Society, 20*(4), 441–464. doi:10.1177/0891243206289499

Acker, J. (2009). Du plafond de verre aux régimes d'inégalité [From glass ceiling to inequality regimes]. *Sociologie du travail, 51*, 199–217. doi:10.1016/j. soctra.2009.03.004

Albiston, C. (2010). *Institutional inequality and the mobilization of the family and medical leave act: Rights on leave.* Cambridge, England: Cambridge University Press.

Armenia, A., & Gerstel, N. (2006). Family leaves, the FMLA and gender neutrality: The intersection of race and gender. *Social Science Research, 35*(4), 871–891. doi:10.1016/j.ssresearch.2004.12.002

Ashcraft, C., & Blithe, S. (2009). *Women in IT: The facts* (NCWIT 2009). Boulder, CO: National Center for Women & Information Technology.

Ashcraft, K.L. (1999). Managing maternity leave: A qualitative analysis of temporary executive succession. *Administrative Science Quarterly, 44*(2), 240–280. doi:10.2307/2666996

Ashcraft, K.L., & Allen, B. (2003). The racial foundation of organizational communication. *Communication Theory, 13*(1), 5–38. doi:10.1111/j.1468–2885.2003. tb00280.x

Ashcraft, K.L., Kuhn, T., & Cooren, F. (2009). Constitutional amendments: "Materializing" organizational communication. *The Academy of Management Annals, 3*(1), 1–64. doi:10.1080/19416520903047186

Axley, S. (1984). Managerial and organizational communication in terms of the conduit metaphor. *Academy of Management Review, 9*(3), 428–437.

Baines, D. (2010). Gender mainstreaming in a development project: Intersectionality in a post-colonial un-doing? *Gender, Work and Organization, 17*(2), 119–149. doi:10.1111/j.1468–0432.2009.00454.x

Bornstein, L. (2000). Inclusions and exclusions in work–family policy: The public values and moral code embedded in the Family and Medical Leave Act. *Columbia Journal of Gender and Law, 10*(1), 77–85.

Bureau of Labor Statistics. (2011). *Women at work.* Washington, DC: Author.

Butler, J. (1999). *Gender trouble: Feminism and the subversion of identity.* London, England: Routledge.

Buzzanell, P.M. (1995). Reframing the glass ceiling as a socially constructed process: Implications for understanding and change. *Communication Monographs, 62*(4), 327–354. doi:10.1080/03637759509376366

Buzzanell, P.M. (2003). A feminist standpoint analysis of maternity and maternity leave for women with disabilities. *Women and Language, 26*(2), 53–65.

Calvert, C. (2009). *Work life law: Testimony before the joint economic committee hearing on balancing work and family in the recession.* San Francisco, CA: The Center for WorkLife Law.

Carnevale, A., Rose, S., & Cheah, B. (2011). *The college payoff: Education, occupations, lifetime earnings.* Washington, DC: Georgetown University Center on Education and the Workforce.

Chang, M.L. (2012). *Shortchanged: Why women have less wealth and what can be done about it,* New York, NY: Oxford University Press.

Charles, M., & Grusky, D. (2004) *Occupational ghettos: The worldwide segregation of women and men.* Stanford, CA: Stanford University Press.

Cheney, G. (2000). Thinking differently about organizational communication: Why, how, and where? *Management Communication Quarterly, 14*(1), 132–141.

Connell, C. (2010). Doing, undoing, or redoing gender? Learning from the workplace experiences of transpeople. *Gender & Society, 24*(1), 31–55. doi:10.1177/089 1243209356429

Connell, R.W., & Wood, J. (2005). Globalization and business masculinities. *Men and Masculinities, 7*(4), 347–364. doi:10.1177/1097184X03260969

Corbett, C., & Hill, C. (2012). *Graduating to a pay gap: The warnings of women and men one year after graduation.* Washington, DC: American Association of University Women.

Deetz, S. A. (1992). *Democracy in an age of corporate colonization: Developments in communication and the politics of everyday life.* Albany: State University of New York.

Fenstermaker, S., & West, C. (Eds.). (2002). *Doing gender, doing difference: Inequality, power, and institutional change.* New York, NY: Routledge.

Ferguson, K. (1984). *The feminist case against bureaucracy.* Philadelphia, PA: Temple University Press.

Glass, J. (2004). Blessing or curse? Work–family policies and mother's wage growth over time. *Work and Occupations, 31*(3), 367–394. doi:10.1177/073088840 4266364

Golden, A. G. (2000). What we talk about when we talk about work and family: A discourse analysis of parental accounts. *The Electronic Journal of Communication, 10*(3–4), n.p. Retrieved from http://www.cios.org/EJCPUBLIC/010/3/010315.html

Grill, A. (1996). The myth of unpaid family leave: Can the United States implement a paid leave policy based on the Swedish model? *Comparative Labor Law Journal, 17,* 373–397.

Grimes, S. (2002). Challenging the status quo? Whiteness in the diversity management literature. *Management Communication Quarterly, 15*(3), 381–409. doi:10.1177/0893318902153003

Hirdman, Y. (1990). Genussystemet [The gender system]. In *Statens Offentliga Utredningar* [Swedish government official reports], *Demokrati och makt I Sverige,* (pp. 73–114). Stockholm: SOU.

Institute for Women's Policy Research. (2010). *Are women now half the labor force? The truth about women and equal participation in the labor force.* Washington, DC: Author.

Judiesch, M., & Lyness, K. (1999). Left behind? The impact of leaves of absence on managers' career success. *The Academy of Management Journal, 42*(6), 641–651. doi:10.2307/256985

Kim, S. (1998). Toward understanding family leave policy in public organizations: Family leave use and conceptual framework for the family leave implementation process. *Public Productivity & Management Review, 22*(1), 71–87.

Kirby, E., & Krone, K. (2002). The policy exists but you can't really use it: Communication and the structuration of work-family policies. *Journal of Applied Communication Research, 30*(1), 50–77. doi:10.1080/00909880216577

Koschmann, M. (Producer). (2012, May 8). *What is organizational communication?* Video retrieved from http://www.youtube.com/watch?v=e5oXygLGMuY

Kunin, M. (2012). *The new feminist agenda: Defining the next revolution for women, work, and family.* White River Junction, VT: Chelsea Green Publishing.

Lindgren, M., & Packendorff, J. (2006). What's new in new forms of organizing? On the construction of gender in project-based work. *Journal of Management Studies, 43*(4), 841–866. doi:10.1111/j.1467–6486.2006.00613.x

Martin, J. (1990). Deconstructing organizational taboos: The suppression of gender conflict in organizations. *Organization Science, 1*(4), 339–357. doi:10.1287/orsc.1.4.339

McCall, L. (2001). *Complex inequality: Gender, class, and race in the new economy.* New York, NY: Routledge.

McCarver, V., & Blithe, S. J. (2014, May). *This is not where we thought we would be: Still striving for the good life through feminism.* Paper presented at the annual meeting of the International Communication Association, Seattle, WA.

McPhee, R. D., & Zaug, P. (2000). The communicative constitution of organizations: A framework for explanation. *The Electronic Journal of Communication*, 10(1–2). http://www.cios.org/www/ejc/v10n1200.Htm

Moe, K., & Shandy, D. (2010). *Glass ceilings & 100-hour couples: What the opt-out phenomenon can teach us about work and family*. Athens: The University of Georgia.

Putnam, L., & McPhee, R. (2008, November). *Theory building: Comparing approaches to "communication constitutes organizations."* Paper presented at the 94th National Communication Association Conference, San Diego, CA.

Putnam, L. L., & Nicotera, A. M. (Eds.). (2008). *Building theories of organization: The constitutive role of communication*. Oxford, England: Routledge.

Putnam, L. L., & Nicotera, A. M. (2009). Communicative constitution of organization is a question: Critical issues for addressing it. *Management Communication Quarterly*. doi: 10.1177/08933189093511581

Rorty, R. (Ed.). (1967). *The linguistic turn: Recent essays in philosophical method*. Chicago, IL: University of Chicago Press.

Schultz, N. (2007, November). *The challenge of negotiating family leave in higher education for women faculty: An issue of policy, practice, and access*. Paper presented at the meeting of the National Communication Association, Chicago, IL.

Searle, J. R. (1995). *The construction of social reality*. New York, NY: The Free Press.

Smith, I. A. (2009). Failure to progress: What having a baby taught me about Aristotle, advanced degrees, developmental delays, and other natural disasters. In E. Evans & C. Grant (Eds.), *Mama PhD: Women write about motherhood and academic life* (pp. 93–102). New Brunswick, NJ: Rutgers University Press.

Smith, R. C. (1993). *Images of organizational communication: Root-metaphors of the organization-communication relation*. Paper presented at the International Communication Association Conference.

Stallard, K., Ehrenreich, B., & Sklar, H. (1983). *Poverty in the American dream: Women & children first*. Cambridge, MA: South End Press.

Taylor, J. R., & Van Every, E. J. (2000). *The emergent organization. Communication as site and surface*. Mahwah, NJ: Erlbaum.

Tienari, J., Quack, S., & Theobald, H. (2002). Organizational reforms, "ideal workers" and gender orders: A cross-societal comparison. *Organization Studies*, 23(2), 249–279. doi:10.1177/0170840602232004

Trix, F., & Psenka, C. (2003). *Exploring the color of glass: Letters of recommendation for female and male medical faculty. Discourse & Society*, 14(2), 191–220.

Van de Ven, A. H., & Poole, M. S. (2005). Alternative approaches for studying organizational change. *Organization Studies*, 26(9), 1377–1404.

The WAGE Project, Inc. (2013). Who is affected by the wage gap? Retrieved from WAGE Women Are Getting Even website: http://www.wageproject.org/files/who.php

Weick, K. E. (1979). *The social psychology of organizations* (2nd ed.). Reading, MA: Addison-Wesley.

Whittiker, D. (1991). Should we have a national leave policy: A survey of leave policies, problems, and solutions. *Howard Law Journal, 411*, 414–415.

3   Situating Leave of Absence Policies

If you or any American has to choose between being a good parent and being successful in your careers, you have paid a terrible price, and so has your country.

—President Bill Clinton, May 23, 1999

The glass handcuffs emerged from a complicated history of organizational leave development. The concept of leaves of absence began in the late 1800s. However, how, where, and why policies developed is highly contextual and differs drastically across time and geographic regions. To understand the importance of leave policy access and to see the inequity in current U.S. policies and practice, it is necessary to know the history of leave development, and the international scene for current leave of absence policies. In this chapter, I first define leave. Next, I explicate the development of leave policies internationally and move into a discussion about leave policies in the United States. I conclude by identifying particular arguments and points of inequality in the Family Medical Leave Act of 1993 (FMLA). I examine and explain each critique such that embedded policy inequalities are illuminated, and set the context for how the glass handcuffs emerge.

DEFINING LEAVES OF ABSENCE

Leaves of absence are prolonged periods that employees take away from work. In the United States, employees typically take leaves of absence at the arrival of a new child, for active military duty, and for personal health crises, although sometimes employees also use leaves for other caregiving situations such as adoption or a child's health crisis, bereavement, and other special circumstances. The concept of a leave of absence assumes that employees sometimes need extended time away, but that they want or need to retain their jobs. Leaves are different from other types of time away from work, such as vacation, sick, or personal time, although people frequently conflate leaves of absence with these types of time off. All time away from work programs share some historical development.

Currently, organizations in the United States present leaves of absence as a benefit given by organizations, legally available for about 40% of U.S. employees. Covered employees may not realize their benefits because organizational culture prevents leave policy usage. That there is inequality in U.S. leave policy is indisputable, but whether employees should have or need leaves of absence at all and how to organize policies are highly contested points. As is discussed in detail in this chapter, proponents of leave policy often consider leaves of absence a right rather than a benefit. They point to multiple positive outcomes from extended time away from work, including many health benefits for fathers, mothers, children, and all over-worked employees, increased equality for employed women and people with disabilities at work, financial benefits for families who might avoid expensive early child care and additional medical expenses associated with this arrangement, and greater equality between men and women at home. Arguments for leave are beginning to broaden even more in scope to include single, childless, and other employees that have needs not previously defined in policy, such as elder care and stress management. Like other work–life and diversity policies, supporters for leaves of absence see moral value in equal access to work policies, and explicate economic rationales for promoting equality at work.

INTERNATIONAL LEAVE HISTORY

Employers and employees have long been concerned about how to manage time away from work. While sick time and vacation time cropped up first, parental leaves have a shorter history. The first maternity leave rights occurred in Germany in 1883, and by the beginning of World War I, 21 countries had established such policies, with leaves spanning from 4 to 12 weeks and approximately half of these policies offering paid leave for women following childbirth. Subsequently, the International Labour Office hosted the first Maternity Protection Convention in 1919, specifying that pregnant women could not work for the first 6 weeks after "confinement," that they could take six weeks of leave before confinement with a note from a doctor, and would maintain all benefits for themselves and their children during the leave. Furthermore, the convention ensured nursing mothers the right to 30 minutes of time to stop working two times a day for breastfeeding. Shortly after the convention, most industrialized countries implemented some sort of maternity leave policy (Kamerman & Moss, 2011).

In 1967, Hungary developed child care leave, intended for women after their maternity leave expired. While lawmakers specifically designed the policy for women, the concept of child care leave opened the door for new fathers to take a leave of absence. As a result of the development of child care leave, parental leaves, intended specifically for both parents after maternity, started gaining traction in national policies around the world. These leaves allowed fathers, in addition to mothers, to spend more time at home and more time on child care around the period of their children's births (Kamerman & Moss, 2011).

Today, every country that is part of the Organization for Economic Co-operation and Development (OECD) provides paid maternity and parental leaves except for the United States (Kamerman & Moss, 2011). In the United States, the FMLA, which makes some provisions for workers taking leave, is non-comprehensive and completely unpaid. Other countries differ in policy implementation, primarily in terms of how workers are paid (e.g., by individuals, by the government, by employers, or through a combination of these sources), lengths of workers' leave (typically ranging from 3 months to 5 years), who can use leave time (e.g., mothers, fathers, or both), how leave time can be used (e.g., including part-time options), and whether leave is considered a family entitlement or an individual entitlement (Kamerman & Moss, 2011). For example, some countries, such as Norway, Iceland, and Sweden, have implemented leave specifically for fathers collectively called *fathers' quotas*. Brandth and Kvande (2002) found that leave specifically mandated increased men's actual use of parental leave by as much as 75%. These nations designed fathers' quotas to encourage fathers to have more contact with and care for their children and to help achieve gender equity by strengthening the ties of fathers to homes and mothers to workplaces.

LEAVE IN THE UNITED STATES

Leave policies in the United States are highly controversial, both in their history and in current status. In 1993, President Bill Clinton signed the FMLA as his first piece of legislation after a contentious Congressional battle and two vetoes from former president George H. W. Bush. The FMLA was the first national policy in the United States that aimed to balance work and family conflict. It is similar to other labor laws (e.g., child labor laws, health and safety laws, Social Security, and the minimum wage), which establish minimum standards for employment. Positioning leave as a minimum work standard assumes that employees have the right to leave work for medical or familial concerns and that these concerns are legitimate (Albiston, 2010).

The FMLA guarantees up to twelve weeks of unpaid, job-protected leave on the employee's request for any of the following reasons: (a) caring for a new child, including birth, adoption, or foster care (within 1 year), (b) caring for a seriously ill family member (e.g., a spouse, child, or parent); (c) managing or recovering from a serious medical condition that prevents the employee from performing his or her job; (d) caring for a family member injured in military service (up to 26 weeks in a single year); (e) personal deployment or addressing difficult situations that arise from a family member's military service (e.g., the employee's son, daughter, parent, spouse or next of kin who is on covered active duty; U.S. Department of Labor, 2012).

Federal law does not mandate that organizations allot their employees personal leave, sick leave, or bereavement leave; rather, these types of leave are options that employers can offer at will. These additional leave policies often interact with FMLA policies (i.e., when employees first use all of their sick or vacation time as part of their parental leave).

The federal goals of the policy include increasing family stability and integrity, helping employees balance their work demands and family needs, supporting family structure change, improving productivity and the quality of work environment in organizations, and creating workforce diversity and equal employment opportunity. Finding women disproportionally responsible for family caretaking on top of their increasing integration into the paid work force, Congress initially designed the Act to relieve stress on employed women. However, they wrote it in gender-neutral terminology (Bornstein, 2000). This neutrality likely happened during the contentious squabbling that occurred during the passage of the act, and potentially serves as a means to expand all workers' rights, regardless of gender.

The FMLA guarantees leave for covered employees and covered employers may not interfere with rights or protections afforded by the Act or deny leave for qualifying employees. Federal laws also protect employees from retaliation by their employers for exercising their FMLA rights. The FMLA requires that on employees' return to work; organizations must restore employees to their previous or equivalent job with, at minimum, the same pay and benefits. The act also protects employee benefits while employees are on leave. To qualify for the FMLA, employees must have worked for their employer for at least twelve months and at least 1,250 hours within the past year leading up to the leave, and the company must have a minimum of 50 employees within a 75-mile radius (U.S. Department of Labor, 2012). One exception to this coverage is employees in the highest paid 10% of an organization, whose absence might cause serious economic turmoil to a company (U.S. Department of Labor, 2012).

As written, the federal FMLA considers "family" to be immediate family only, including parents, spouses, and children. Individuals are parents when they are in "loco parentis" and have day-to-day responsibilities of care or provide financial support for a child. Courts can confer or deny loco parentis status on a case-by-case basis, determined by the age of the child, the degree of financial support, and the degree to which the child is dependent on the employee. Employers regularly require employees utilizing FMLA benefits to document their relationship to the child before approving FMLA rights. Loco parentis begins to widen the FMLA's definition of family, but it is open to employer interpretation. Amendments for service members, however, specifically include next of kin and adult children. Some states have expanded the language of family to include domestic partners and domestic partner's children, civil union partners, parents-in-law, grandparents, grandparents-in-law, grandchildren, stepparents, siblings related to the worker by blood, legal custody, and persons with whom the employees lives.

Some states have also modified the FMLA to lower the required number of employees for organizational coverage. Vermont, for example, requires companies with as few as 10 employees to provide parental leave. Other states have expanded the FMLA to include time off work for other responsibilities, such as organ or bone marrow donation (e.g., Connecticut), addressing domestic violence, stalking, or sexual assault (e.g., Colorado, Florida, Hawaii, and Illinois), and for parents to attend their children's educational activities or medical visits (e.g., California, Washington, D.C.; U.S. Department of Labor, 2012).

Despite initial fear and serious opposition from U.S. employers, most businesses implemented the FMLA with little trouble. Organizations supporting FMLA policies report lower absenteeism and higher employee morale and loyalty, and have experienced little disruption to the workplace. Ninety percent of covered organizations asserted that administering FMLA policies was easy (National Partnership for Women & Families, 2013a; U.S. Department of Labor, 2012). Moreover, there are little to no costs associated with implementing the Act. For example, many organizations report that the act is costless to implement and that it has reduced costs associated with employee turnover. A recent Department of Labor report that studied effects of FMLA usage on the 20th anniversary of the act concluded that FMLA compliance actually had either a positive or no noticeable effect on employee productivity, morale, absenteeism, and business profitability (National Partnership for Women & Families, 2013a; U.S. Department of Labor, 2012). Furthermore, the report confirmed that misuse of the FMLA is quite rare. Only 2.5% of FMLA covered workplaces cited misuse, and experts confirmed only 1.6% of reported cases constituted misuse (National Partnership for Women & Families, 2013a; U.S. Department of Labor, 2012).

Thirteen percent of *employees* used the FMLA in 2012 (U.S. Department of Labor, 2012). Of leave takers, 57% left to tend to a personal illness; 22% left to care for a new child; 19% percent took leave to care for a spouse, child, or parent with a serious medical condition; and 2% took leave for military deployment or caregiving (U.S. Department of Labor, 2012). This breakdown represents combined reasons why leave takers took time off; however, employees' reasons for taking leave differed drastically by gender. Women made up 56% of leave takers and primarily used the FMLA to care for family, whereas men were more likely to use the FMLA to take care of their own personal health issues. Leave-taking practices vary by other demographic features such as age,[1] family income, and ethnicity. For example, families least likely to have FMLA rights include low-income families, families with low levels of education, and Latinos (Ness, 2014). Additionally, low-income, part-time, young, never married workers, and Latinos are least likely to meet FMLA requirements, even if they work for an organization covered by the FMLA (Ness, 2014). Most leave takers took relatively short leaves. Almost half of leaves lasted 10 days or fewer, and only one fifth of leaves lasted more than 60 days (U.S. Department of Labor, 2012).

Overall, the FMLA has had a positive impact on workers and organizations (National Partnership for Women & Families, 2013a). Employees who took leave believed their leaves were important and necessary to manage complex lives (U.S. Department of Labor, 2001). Without the FMLA, the aforementioned leave takers might have lost their jobs, sacrificed their health, or neglected children or other family members. Thus, advocates see the FMLA as an important victory in gender equality, and believe the culture of the United States is slowly changing as a result of the Act (National Partnership for Women & Families, 2013b). However, some of the same advocates of FMLA-level serious critiques of the act and continually push for further reform.

PROBLEMS WITH THE FMLA

Although the FMLA passed, myriad diverse groups continually critique the Act, including for example, feminists, many of whom critique the FMLA because they claim it does not do enough for U.S. workers. The act is still a source of contention in the United States. In general, FMLA is critiqued because (a) it is unpaid, which exacerbates inequalities; (b) it does not reconcile state and federal conflicts; (c) there is a tension between government and private management of leave; (d) it does not attempt to address cultural attitudes in the United States; (e) there is evidence of harmful workplace consequences for people who take leave; (f) it does not take infant, child, or maternal health into account; (g) it does not cover enough people; (h) it does not do enough; and (i) it is the worst leave policy of all economically stable countries in the world. I briefly unpack each critique in the following subsections.

Unpaid Leave Exacerbates Discrimination Across Gender, Race, Class, and Ability Lines

The first critique of the FMLA is that leave employees may take is not paid. Despite the fact that the United States is the only OECD country (of 38 total OECD countries) that does not support its citizens with paid leave, there have been few serious attempts to provide such a benefit (OECD, 2011). The issue of unpaid leave in the United States is perhaps the biggest problem identified with the FMLA, in that it obstructs equitable use of the policy across gender, class, race, occupation, and familial status. Millions of U.S. workers cannot afford to take unpaid leave (Wu, 2011). Moreover, lost pay is the most frequently reported reason that employees do not exercise their rights to take leaves. Nearly half of workers who needed leave but did not take it cited lost wages as a barrier to taking leave (National Partnership for Women & Families, 2013a). Women composed 64% of workers who needed leave but did not take it, and Latino workers, non-white workers, unmarried workers, and employees earning less than $35,000 per year were most likely to forgo a leave of absence, even though they needed one (National Partnership for Women & Families, 2013a).

FMLA privileges people who can financially support themselves for 12 weeks without pay. This most often includes upper middle-class women who have a partner to financially support them. Because leave is usually unpaid, taking leave is much more difficult for low-income families or families with only one income. More than half of lower earning and middle-income workers did not receive any kind of pay while on leave (National Partnership for Women & Families, 2013a). These workers reported limiting their spending, using savings, put off paying bills, cutting leaves short, borrowing money and using public assistance to subsidize their family expenditures while on leave (National Partnership for Women & Families, 2013a). Additionally, in coupled families with higher-earning men, it is likely that men, specifically, cannot afford to take unpaid leave. In the United States, gender, class, occupation, familial structure, and race intertwine such that many cannot financially afford to take unpaid time away from work. In this way, leave-taking is a seriously classed, raced, and heteronormative practice.

Paid leave is likely the only way that all parents in the United States would have the ability to care for their newly born children. Because of the decline in real wages over the past few decades, coupled with a reduction in the purchasing power of the U.S. dollar, most U.S. families must have two paychecks to maintain the same standard of living as was possible with a single income in the 1950s. This has made unpaid leave impractical or even impossible for the majority of U.S. citizens (Albiston, 2010; Grill, 1996; National Partnership for Women & Families, 2013b). Advocates suggest a national paid family and medical leave insurance program, modeled after some successful state paid leave programs (e.g., a few states have paid-leave programs, including Connecticut, New Jersey, California, and Washington; National Partnership for Women & Families, 2012) as the only way leave policies will work for most U.S. Americans.

Some scholars have suggested that an increase in *men* taking leave would help reduce stereotypical gendered work roles; however, most men need paid leave (Bornstein, 2000; National Partnership for Women & Families, 2012). Because the provider/breadwinner role puts the economic burden of unpaid leave most heavily on men, men are less likely than women to be able to take leaves of absence. Thus, in order for men to truly be able to take on more responsibility at home and in care work, leave policies must advance so that paid leave is more readily available to men and women (National Partnership for Women & Families, 2012).

State/Federal Conflicts

The second critique against the FMLA is that it does not reconcile state and federal conflicts. These conflicts arise in both the implementation and study of employees' leave-taking practice because state and company policies often conflict with the guidelines of the FMLA. Throughout history, the United States has centered family as the cornerstone of U.S. American civilization. However, the founders gave responsibility for the maintenance and stability of families to the states, not the federal government. Federal interventions into individual cases most likely focused on individuals rather than families (Wisensale, 1997). In his inaugural speech, Ronald Reagan (1981) voiced this ideology:

> Government is not the solution to our problems; government is the problem. It is my intention to curb the size and influence of the federal establishment and to demand recognition of the distinction between the powers granted to the federal government and those reserved to the states or to the people.

Indeed, the United States still struggles with how much federal regulation is necessary in family concerns, and states frequently intervene to set up different standards for families depending on where those family members live. As such, despite the fact that most U.S. citizens support family-friendly policies, the difficulty and structure of U.S. political decision-making may make transferring opinion into policy impossible (Huber & Stephens, 2001).

Government versus Private Social Policies

A third enduring challenge with changing or improving FMLA leave policies is the ongoing tension between government and private control and/or responsibility of social policies. Particularly in the United States, privatization has a stronghold and citizens oscillate back and forth regarding how much governmental intervention they will tolerate. Critics on both sides debate whether the government should or should not provide "pro-family" policies (e.g., paid family leave). Supporters of governmental intervention assert that the government must play a role in supporting leave policies, particularly in light of the changing workforce. Yet, U.S. citizens are hesitant to give too much power to the government. Opposition to the FMLA focused on market-driven leave options that would provide alternatives in leave practices. However, this market proved to be uneven and bereft of useful options. For example, while fiercely opposing the FMLA, President H. W. George Bush argued that innovative private benefit plans would grow to accommodate workers and that the FMLA would stifle the development of such initiatives (Whittaker, 1991). This opposition to governmental intervention (Bolzendahl & Olafsdottir, 2008) is a truism for U.S. citizens on the political or economic right. However, alternate studies have shown that U.S. Americans are not opposed to government intervention. For example, U.S. Americans could actually be ideologically opposed to high government intervention but also increasingly unable to manage the pressure they face as nontraditional workers raising families.

The United States is quite unique in its decision to use employment to deliver social welfare benefits (Bornstein, 2000). Some other countries (e.g., Great Britain, Australia, and New Zealand) also emphasize private solutions to social issues, rather than promoting governmental public programs. However, when compared to these nations, the United States lags well behind in institutionalizing social welfare policy and family policy in particular (Bolzendahl & Olafsdottir, 2008). The current system of distributing social benefits through workplaces allows for the intertwining of private benefits and social policy. For example, when commercial organizations manage benefits and family stability, those employers become the administrators of public wellness. This corporate power enables employers to privilege or exclude values based on economic views. Social policy becomes an economic issue, and the emphasis of these policies shifts to focus on business costs rather than on social needs (Bornstein, 2000).

The FMLA is, thus, inherently a clash between market driven policy and family values, which results in a complicated, disjointed, contradictory, and limited program that fails to alleviate work–family conflicts. The failure of the FMLA to remedy these discrepancies can result in confusion about *how* and *if* employees can exercise FMLA rights, wage penalties, and litigation, and can lower career satisfaction and employment prospects, especially for women (Buzzanell, 2003). Complications from the public/private debate about policy responsibility suggest a need to move discussions about leave policies from the corporate arena into a civic space that incorporates the needs of both organizations and families (Meisenbach, Remke, Buzzanell, & Liu, 2008). Then discursively moving leave policies out of such colonization[2] might be useful for citizens in need of leave.

Cultural Attitudes and Discourses about Families and Leaves of Absence

A fourth critique of FMLA is that it does not attempt to address cultural attitudes in the United States. A number of negative attitudes about family exist within, and even pervade, the United States (Grill, 1996; Moe & Shandy, 2010; Wisensale, 1997).[3] Government policies reflect cultural attitudes. As Wisensale (1997) related, "the Reagan administration consistently opposed federally funded child care and family leave. Why, this administration argued, should the American taxpayers pick up the tab for babysitting the kids of the middle class" (p. 79)? The repeated discourses about individualism influence cultural attitudes about families and leaves of absence. When children become "choices" to be managed, then leaves of absence also become choices that workers could avoid if they selected a particular life path.

At the organizational level, there are frequently extensive pressures (e.g., supervisory, peer, and self-induced pressures) that encourage employees not to make use of available work-life policies. Employees sometimes consider work–family policies as a form of preferential treatment (Williams & Westfall, 2006) that privileges parents and discriminates against childless employees, causing resentment towards employees who use the policies. Kirby and Krone (2002) studied employees' usage of organizations' leave policy and found that coworkers were frequently resentful of other employees' use of work–family policies. None of the study participants evidenced collective attitudes about balancing work and family or even expressed appreciation that work–family benefits were available to their coworkers. Furthermore, participants seemed oblivious to the tradeoffs made by working parents (e.g., not recognizing that part-time workers earned less).

The now-disbanded Childfree Network organized women and men workers without children and spoke out about "workplace inequities," including covering at work for absent people with kids, tax breaks for families with kids, and insurers paying for fertility procedures. Thus, even if policies exist in organizations, organizational culture (including management and executive leadership) must also support the use of the policies. A recent academic article (Dow, 2008) suggested tips for colleague-friendly parenting in the academy, including "try not to bring infants/young children to the office" and "recognize that colleagues are not required to accommodate parenting philosophies; that is, what parents are convinced is good for their children may be bad for their collegial relationships" (pp. 161, 163). The potential to harm working parents with these kinds of ideologies increases the frustration of nonparent workers is clear. Work–life issues still remain contentious and complicated in the United States. These attitudes are, however, much different from those in other contexts.

The culture puzzle becomes even more complicated when viewed through the lens of *organizational* cultures. Leave and other work–life policies have little value when placed in organizational contexts that do not support those policies (Albiston, 2010; Kirby & Krone, 2002; Moe & Shandy, 2010). If an organizational culture is not wholly supportive of work–life policy use, workers will face difficulties in accessing the policies. Kirby and Krone (2002) explained, "although organizational policies are a form of structure, they are produced and reproduced through processes of interpretation and interaction" (p. 51). Most organizational cultures in the United States assume that committed workers come to work even if they are sick, or when they have family conflicts. Employees often viewed workers who took leaves of absence (either because they were unwilling or because they were unable to work while sick) as shirking their work or as generally less valuable employees (Albiston, 2010). Stories about retaliation against employees taking leave keep potential leave takers from exercising their rights.[4]

Actual Workplace Consequences of Taking Leave

There are several actual workplace consequences for employees who choose to take a leave of absence. Leave takers receive fewer rewards and are perceived as less productive, less committed, and less effective (Allen & Russell, 1999; Judiesch & Lyness, 1999; Williams & Westfall, 2006). Leave-takers also face a depreciation of their human capital when they are away from work (Judiesch & Lyness, 1999; Williams & Westfall, 2006). Employees who take more than one leave of absence are only 25% as likely to receive a promotion as an employee who takes only one leave (Judiesch & Lyness, 1999). Managers who take a single leave of absence received significantly fewer promotions, smaller salary increases and lower performance ratings (Judiesch & Lyness, 1999; Williams & Westfall, 2006). These consequences are particularly salient for male leave takers. Men taking parental leave are particularly vulnerable and are significantly less likely to receive rewards (Allen & Russell, 1999).

Many employees fear entering onto the *mommy track*, which describes a slowing or a halting of career growth. Women with children have the slowest wage growth and account for most of the gender gap in wages (Glass, 2004). In fact, mothers earn only about half as much as men with equal qualifications and regularly see a slowing in their career progress. In more extreme cases, employed mothers hit the *maternal wall* (Williams & Segal, 2003), losing their jobs, experiencing wage reduction, demotion, or other kinds of discrimination related to their status as mothers or because of the perception that they may become pregnant (Gely & Chandler, 2004; Williams & Westfall, 2006).

Infant, Child, and Maternal Health

A sixth critique of the FMLA is that it does not take infant, child, or maternal health into account, although these are important factors that should be part of leave policy discussions (Berger, Hill, & Waldfogel, 2005; Galtry, 2002; Kamerman, 2007; Kamerman & Moss, 2011). The language of children's rights in not yet a serious consideration in leave policy discussions and children are usually in the margins of the FMLA and other leave policy research.

Multiple studies have confirmed that there are correlations between longer leaves of absence and health (Berger, Hill & Waldfogel, 2005; Galtry, 2002; Tanaka, 2005). Breastfeeding, in particular, is an important factor of infant health because it decreases the likelihood of a number of infant diseases (e.g., sudden infant death syndrome, or SIDS), is associated with infants' increased cognitive development, and, additionally, has a number of health benefits for mothers. Moreover, the American Academy of Pediatrics and the World Health Organization both stress the importance of

6 months of exclusive breastfeeding for infants. However, the return to work is a major factor in the termination of breastfeeding for employed women, and most current leave policies only cover 12 weeks of employees' time away from work. As a result, in the United States, mothers breastfeed their infants at significantly shorter durations than do mothers in other parts of the world (Berger, Hill, & Waldfogel, 2005; Galtry, 2002).

The FMLA Does Not Cover Enough People

Only about 59% of U.S. employees are eligible for FMLA (National Partnership for Women & Families, 2013a). The 41% of workers not covered work in businesses with fewer than 50 employees, work part-time (fewer than 1,250 total hours in 1 year, which is about 24 hours a week), or have not been employed for 12 months at their organization (U.S. Department of Labor, 2012). Analysts estimate that reducing the employer-size threshold to 25 workers would give FMLA protections to an additional 8.5 million workers, and leave advocates argue that the minimum hours and organizational tenure required for FMLA should be lowered to extend protections to even more workers (National Partnership for Women & Families, 2013a).

For employees who can access FMLA protections, many workers still face coverage difficulties based on their familial situation. Currently, the act does not cover employees who must care for domestic partners, same-sex spouses, adult children, siblings, grandchildren, grandparents, parents-in-law, and other family members (National Partnership for Women & Families, 2013b). However, more than one-third of caregivers care for these family members (National Alliance for Caregiving, 2009). Broadening the definition of "family" is an important step in making the FMLA available to more employees who need job protection.

The FMLA Does Not Do Enough

Advocates for leave reform argue that the FMLA does not do enough for employees. In particular, it does not cover bereavement, children's activities or school meetings, or time to recover from domestic violence, sexual assault or stalking (National Partnership for Women & Families, 2012, 2013b). These situations affect millions of workers every day in the United States, yet only privileged employees can take time away from work to attend to these important life events. In addition, the FMLA does not allow employees to take short-term sick time. About 43 million workers cannot earn any paid sick time in their current positions, and federal protection would enable these employees to take a sick day without jeopardizing their jobs (National Partnership for Women & Families, 2013b; Ness, 2014).

When FMLA finally became law, its supporters knew that the act was quite limited in scope. Because its passage was so contentious, legislators whittled the protections down in order to help the act pass. This "something-is-better-than-nothing" approach meant that having some employees covered would be better than having no employees covered. Most supporters at the time believed that getting some legislation passed would set precedence so that further legislation could follow in the form of more expansive protections (Selmi, 2004). However, as discussed, expanded coverage did not follow, and the FMLA still does not do much to help U.S. workers manage work–life conflicts.

The FMLA Is the Worst Leave Policy of All Economically Stable Countries

In terms of organizational leave offerings, the United States ranks the lowest of all OECD countries (high-income, "developed" countries). By comparison, Swedish parents can take up to 13 months off work while the government pays up to 80% of their wages. Parents can take up to 90 additional days of leave at a reduced payment, either all at once or in smaller chunks of time, until their children are 8 years old. Additionally, fathers receive two *Pappa* months, which is time only given to fathers. As another example, Norway allows workers 9 weeks of maternity leave, a 10-week "daddy quota," which is time given specifically for fathers, and an additional 27 weeks of parental leave at 100% compensation or 37 weeks at 80% compensation. Norwegian parents can use their leave (46 to 56 weeks) part-time until their children are 3 years old. Iceland offers parents 3-month maternity leaves and daddy quotas as well as an additional 3 months of parental leave that either parent can take until their children are 18 months old. Finland offers parents 4 months' maternity leave and a 1-month daddy quota with an additional 6 months of parental leave at 70% compensation. If both parents work part-time, the leave may last up to 44 weeks. Denmark offers 18 weeks of maternity leave and 32 weeks of parental leave at 90% compensation, which parents can extend by reducing other benefits.

Although these Nordic countries are extreme examples, other parts of the world are working to introduce leave policies that better support everyone. New Zealand, for example, has continually worked to improve its leave policies and now offers taxpayer-funded paid leave for eligible parents. As another example, in Germany, one parent per family can stay at home to care for children, regardless of whether this parent worked previously. Germany also offers a mother-protection period of 8 weeks where women do not work, followed by 3 years of job protection for one parent to stay home and care for the children, which all parents are entitled to, including part-time workers. This job protection time is paid, tax free, by the government and employers, as a child-rearing benefit and as a percent of previous salary (Ondrich, Spiess, Yang, & Wagner, 2003).

CONCLUSION

In this chapter, I have presented the complicated history and the current status of leave policy from which the glass handcuffs emerge. While the concept of taking extended time away from work is not new, the development of leave policies in the United States has made it very difficult for many women and most men to step out of their jobs for a time, even when serious health or caregiving needs arise. It is particularly troublesome that U.S. employees are not equally covered, and that inequalities in policy coverage and access are striking along gender, race, sexuality, class, and ability lines. From here, it is easier to see how and why leave inequality operates in the United States, and makes the glass handcuffs phenomenon possible and probable for men. In the next chapters I draw out the main causes for the glass handcuffs, which all grow from the fertile ground of inequality in U.S. employment policies.

NOTES

1. In 1998, Kim found women were most likely to take leave between the ages of 18 to 35, whereas men were most likely to take leave between the ages of 35 to 49.
2. Deetz's (1992) work on corporate colonization reveals the intense control of the corporation's infringement onto the lives of citizens.
3. For example, drawing on economist Nancy Folbre, Moe and Shandy (2010) argued that

   > Americans view children as pets. In this current society, having children is sharply identified as a personal choice and parents are deemed responsible for all the care of them. This completely ignores that fact that children will become the next contributing members of our society. This is an extraordinary value for society which receives no compensation. (p. 5)

   Grill (1996) expressed a similar argument in a comparison of U.S. attitudes and Swedish attitudes, noting that Swedish employers are willing to sacrifice for the good of society and encourage employees to take leave. She claimed that

   > the Swedish sense of collective responsibility for child rearing is relatively unknown in American society. Americans are very tax-averse and would decrease social expenditures rather than increase taxes in order to balance the government's budget." (Grill, 1996, p. 388)

4. In her study of meaning making around problematic or denied leave requests, Albiston (2010) described a new father who believed it was unthinkable to take more than one or two weeks of leave. This father claimed that his organization just was not open to men taking FMLA leave because men did not have the necessary biological recovery that might warrant a longer leave. In fact, *every* man in Albiston's study claimed to have experienced hostility and skepticism from employers and coworkers. Many of these men agreed that *as men*, they should prioritize work in their lives. Moreover, another of

Albiston's respondents took leave to care for his terminally ill wife. This respondent seemed fairly understanding when he received a disciplinary letter about his leave use, and when his employer, coworkers, and even his wife questioned his decision to take leave.

REFERENCES

Albiston, C. (2010). *Institutional inequality and the mobilization of the family and medical leave act: Rights on leave.* Cambridge, England: Cambridge University Press.

Allen, T. D., & Russell, J. A. (1999). Parental leave of absence: Some not so family-friendly implications. *Journal of Applied Social Psychology, 29*(1), 166–191. doi:10.1111/j.1559–1816.1999.tb01380.x

Berger, L., Hill, J., & Waldfogel, J. (2005). Maternity leave, early maternal employment and child health and development in the US. *The Economic Journal, 115*(501), F29–F47.

Bolzendahl, C., & Olafsdottir, S. (2008). Gender group interest or gender ideology? Understanding U.S. support for family policy within the liberal welfare regime. *Sociological Perspectives, 51*(2), 281–304. doi:10.1525/sop.2008.51.2.281

Bornstein, L. (2000). Inclusions and exclusions in work–family policy: The public values and moral code embedded in the Family and Medical Leave Act. *Columbia Journal of Gender and Law, 10*(1), 77–85.

Brandth, B., & Kvande, E. (2002). Flexible work and flexible fathers. *Work, Employment & Society, 15*(2), 251–267. doi:10.1177/09500170122118940

Buzzanell, P. M. (2003). A feminist standpoint analysis of maternity and maternity leave for women with disabilities. *Women and Language, 26*(2), 53–65.

Dow, B. (2008). Does it take a department to raise a child? *Women's Studies in Communication, 31*(2), 158–165. doi:10.1080/07491409.2008.10162528

Galtry, J. (2002). Child health: An underplayed variable in parental leave policy debates? *Community, Work & Family, 5*(3), 257–278. doi:10.1080/13668800 22000041775

Gely, R., & Chandler, T. D. (2004). Maternity leave under the FMLA: An analysis of the litigation experience. *Washington University Journal of Law & Policy, 15*, 143–168.

Glass, J. (2004). Blessing or curse? Work–family policies and mother's wage growth over time. *Work and Occupations, 31*(3), 367–394. doi:10.1177/0730888404266364

Grill, A. (1996). The myth of unpaid family leave: Can the United States implement a paid leave policy based on the Swedish model? *Comparative Labor Law Journal, 17*, 373–397.

Huber, E., & Stephens, J. (2001). *Development and crisis of the welfare state: Parties and policies in global markets.* Chicago, IL: University of Chicago Press Books.

Judiesch, M., & Lyness, K. (1999). Left behind? The impact of leaves of absence on managers' career success. *The Academy of Management Journal, 42*(6), 641–651.

Kamerman, S. (2007). Maternity, paternity, and parental leave policies: The potential impacts on children and their families. In R. E. Tremblay, R. G. Barr, R. D. e. V. Peters (Eds.), *Encyclopedia on Early Childhood Development* (Rev. ed., pp. 1–4). Montreal, Quebec, Canada: Centre of Excellence for Early Childhood Development. Retrieved from http://www.child-encyclopedia.com/sites/default/files/textes-experts/en/593/maternity-paternity-and-parental-leave-policies-the-potential-impacts-on-children-and-their-families.pdf

Kamerman, S., & Moss, P. (Eds.). (2011). *The politics of parental leave policies: Children, parenting, gender and the labour market.* Bristol, England: The Policy Press.

Kirby, E., & Krone, K. (2002). The policy exists but you can't really use it: Communication and the structuration of work-family policies. *Journal of Applied Communication Research, 30*(1), 50–77. doi:10.1080/00909880216577

Meisenbach, R., Remke, R., Buzzanell, P., & Liu, M. (2008). "They allowed": Pentadic mapping of women's maternity leave discourse as organizational rhetoric. *Communication Monographs, 75*(1), 1–24. doi:10.1080/03637750801952727

Moe, K., & Shandy, D. (2010). *Glass ceilings & 100-hour couples: What the opt-out phenomenon can teach us about work and family.* Athens: The University of Georgia Press.

National Alliance for Caregiving. (2009, November). *Caregiving in the U.S. 2009.* National Retrieved from http://www.caregiving.org/data/Caregiving_in_the_US_2009_ full_report.pdf

National Partnership for Women & Families. (2012). *Dads expect better: Top states for new dads.* Retrieved from http://www.nationalpartnership.org/research-library/work-family/paid-leave/dads-expect-better-report.pdf

National Partnership for Women & Families. (2013a). *A look at the U.S. Department of Labor's 2012 Family and Medical Leave Act employee and worksite surveys.* Retrieved from http://www.nationalpartnership.org/research-library/work-family/fmla/dol-fmla-survey-key-findings-2012.pdf

National Partnership for Women & Families. (2013b). Written statement of Judith L. Lichtman submitted to the U.S. House Committee on Education and the Workforce, Subcommittee on Workforce Protections, Hearing on H.R. 1406, the Working Families Flexibility Act. Retrieved from http://edworkforce.house.gov/uploadedfiles/lichtman_testimony.pdf

Ness, D. (2014). Showing thanks for family caregivers this month. Retrieved from http://www.nationalpartnership.org/blog/showing-thanks-for-family-caregivers-this-month.html

Organisation for Economic Coordination and Development. (2011). Executive summary. In *The future of families to 2030* (pp. 9–13). Paris, France: OECD Publishing. doi:10.1787/9789264168367-2-en

Ondrich, J., Spiess, C., Yang, Q., & Wagner, G. (2003). The liberalization of maternity leave policy and the return to work after childbirth in Germany. *Review of Economics of the Household, 1*(1), 77–110.

Reagan, R. (1981). Inaugural address January 20, 1981. Washington, DC: United States Government Printing Office.

Selmi, M. (2004). Is something better than nothing? Critical reflections on ten years of the FMLA. *Washington University Journal of Law & Policy, 15*, 65–91.

Tanaka, S. (2005). Parental leave and child health across OECD countries. *The Economic Journal, 115*(501), F7–F28. doi:10.1111/j.0013–0133.2005.00970.x

U.S. Department of Labor. (2001). *Balancing the needs of families and employers: Family and medical leave surveys, 2000 update.* Retrieved from http://www.dol.gov/whd/fmla/cover-statement.pdf

U.S. Department of Labor. (2012). *Family and Medical Leave in 2012: Technical report.* Retrieved from http://www.dol.gov/asp/evaluation/fmla/FMLA-2012-Technical-Report.pdf

Whittiker, D. (1991). Should we have a national leave policy: A survey of leave policies, problems, and solutions. *Howard Law Journal, 411*, 414–415.

Williams, J.C., & Segal, N. (2003). Beyond the maternal wall: Relief for family caregivers who are discriminated against on the job. *Harvard Women's Law Journal, 26*, 77–162.

Williams, J. C., & Westfall, E. S. (2006). Deconstructing the maternal wall: Strategies for vindicating the civil rights of careers in the workplace. *Duke Journal of Gender Law & Policy, 13*, 31–53.

Wisensale, S. (1997). The White House and Congress on child care and family leave policy: From Carter to Clinton. *Policy Studies Journal, 25*(1), 75–86. doi:10.1111/j.1541–0072.1997.tb00007.

Wu, P. (2011, February 5). On the FMLA anniversary, let's focus on the unmet needs of working Families [Blog comment]. Retrieved from http://www.nationalpartnership.org/blog/general/on-the-fmla-anniversary.html

4 Perceptions and Meanings of Work–Life Balance and Leaves of Absence for Men

At the dawn of 2015, as individuals flipped the calendar and began to consider how to change their lives for the better, work–life balance[1] emerged as a top New Year's Resolution (Cabral-Levesque, 2015; Newman, 2014; Robinson, 2015). Pressure to achieve an ideal balanced state is a relatively new phenomenon for men. For decades, research, popular media, and individuals have sorted through what balance means and looks like for women. Men, however, were invited into the conversation about balance long after. As such, most of the conversation about balance is set in context by women's experience of balance. One unexpected finding from this study was the very different ways in which men talked about work–life balance and work–life policies.

Despite all of the issues with current leave policies in the United States, most men interviewed for this study believed they were quite "balanced" without using leave. However, the ways that they spoke about balance frequently differed from colloquial and academic discussions of work–life. In this chapter, I draw out some excerpts from the interviews about what the men had to say about work–life balance and leaves of absence as a means of framing the broader discussion about the glass handcuffs. I also present data from the interviews that reveal the ways the men who feel balanced believe they are different, or outliers from the larger *un*balanced population. I conclude the chapter with a discussion of when the men found leaves of absences acceptable, particularly to manage burnout.

MEN AND WORK–LIFE "BALANCE"

Quite a few of the men in this study claimed that they thought about work–life balance frequently. For some of them, considering work–life balance was a new development, and many experienced pressure to get the balance "right." Although they did feel balanced, for the men thinking about work–life, it was frequently a stressful endeavor. For example, Stanley, a graduate student explained:

> I don't think a lot of people realize how difficult it is to be a student and to teach and try and have some semblance of a healthy social life and do

groceries and laundry on your own. And so balancing all of those things and try and find time of all those things is really kind of scary at times.

Arie, another graduate student, shared similar feelings:

I'm involved in a lot of different projects for a lot of different people, both in teaching and research and you know, in my classes. So it's difficult for me to manage all of those responsibilities in the limited amount of time that I have and still find time to spend with my growing family. So that's the stress. That's the problem that I'm facing.

Arie, who was expecting to become a father at the time of the interview, later described his work–life management a "confusing mix of where I'm trying to figure out as I go through this transition how I can best allocate my time. And it's kind of a new thing." His changing family circumstances provided a reason to consider what work–life "balance" might mean in his life.

Ace, an information technology support specialist, described work–life balance as

the ability to have a life outside of work. You know, the days of working 80 hours a week, you know, are still there, but a lot of companies will accommodate and say, "Okay, yeah. We love you to work all this, but you can work from home," or if you have to go to your son's concert, then you can go and do that. Like you can break out during the middle of the day or leave early, and you can just kind of make it up at some point. I know a lot of companies do that as well, but that's kind of the way it's balancing. So then you're not missing out on life in general, whether you have kids or not.

For Ace, less face time in the office and the ability to flex his hours around commitments for his children and his health equated to greater balance. Many men found that "permission" to leave work—particularly if it helped them to attend activities—would make them feel more balanced.

Rocket, a marketing director, shared Ace's view about flexibility. He thought work–life balance didn't make much sense in traditional understandings of the concept. Instead, he thought about developing a healthy relationship to work through flexibility. He explained:

I usually characterize it as work/life flexibility now because balance, I never quite understood what that was, and I feel like my true work–life balance, it would be like I'd only work two days a week and I'd have five days a week off, you know, so it was hard for me to kind of pen it into a 40-hour week or whatever kind of box.

So that's when I started thinking about work–life flexibility, and what's important to me about that, especially at an executive level where I operate now is that with family, with kids and everything else, there's times when I really want to have that flexibility to leave work, say, at noon to catch my daughter's play at school or something like that, knowing that I'll have to make up that time whenever—in the evening, on the weekend or something like that. So having that flexibility allows me to do that, and otherwise wouldn't be able to kind of fit it within a balance.

Work–life *flexibility* characterized Rocket's relationship with work better than "balance," and he explained that having organizational permission to check in and out of his workday helped him feel better about his relationships with kids and his own "sanity."

Chip, a real estate advisor, saw work–life as an emerging conversation for men:

I think the company right now in the current understanding of what disconnecting from work, there just seems to be a huge movement to actually kind of shift that conversation . . . Without the ability to pause work, you're just like, "I just want to go zonk out and watch TV" when you get home because you're so exhausted . . . You're pushing so hard throughout the day that you're not taking the time to kind of recharge a little bit and give yourself those moments to kind of just reconnect with the mind and body, or even just the two halves of the brain. I think that really just allowing your brain to resync up is a pretty important thing.

Chip, like Rocket and Ace, believed that the ability to leave work for even short periods during the day helped him feel balanced.

As the examples here demonstrate, many men in this study thought about work–life balance—sometimes frequently and strategically. The next few chapters will show how the men's personal relationships with work–life and leave policies manifest in a few ways. However, part of understanding why the glass handcuffs phenomenon is important rests with knowing that many men *think* about balance and leave. Most men had strong opinions about both work–life balance and leave of absence policies specifically. However, throughout the interviews, men's answers to the interview prompts were peppered with phrases such as "Does this make sense?" or "I don't know," or "I'm sure it is just me." When so many men make such disclaimers in concert, their hesitation to talk about balance despite their thought-out opinions on it suggest that although they are interested in the topic, it also is one of which they are not usually included.

COMPARTMENTALIZING WORK–LIFE

Many men in this study took a somewhat classic view of work–life balance. They conceptualized the two as completely separate and talked about achieving balance through strict compartmentalization. As Vincent explained, "No matter what you do, no one's ever going to be happy with their work–life allocations. It is different for everybody. But if you can keep work at work, then your home life can be relaxing." Although Vincent also spoke about bringing work home and working on vacations, he made an effort to keep work away from his home life. Another interviewee explicitly described compartmentalization:

> I think I do a pretty decent job of keeping my work at work. I try to compartmentalize in a lot of ways. That my work stays in a certain location and between certain hours I strongly avoid bringing my work home in the evenings or over the weekend. I want to come home and not think about it. Um to me I think that's a good and important balance. Um, seems like once you open the door to taking your work home and checking your work email in the evenings and over the weekend you've made yourself available uh, twenty four seven, it becomes very difficult to separate yourself. Um, which I think is a, what I consider to be a balance, being able to separate and say, "I'm not at work, I'm not going to think about work, and I'm not going to do work."

This interviewee believed complete separation assisted him in stopping work from leaking into his home life. In a similar way, Pat shared his view of balance:

> It means that you know when you're off the clock that you can enjoy your own life, and you know when you're in your office, and you're getting paid for it, then, then you know, you put in the work that they are paying you for, but you have to have that equal balance in both and I think, you know in this position that I have now, I'm an hourly employee. Which again is one of the only positions that's hourly, and it, it's really interesting because um, I'm able to just, you know, when I clock out at five I just, I make it a point that I don't answer any emails when I, over the weekend, although I have access to it. We all have access to, to things like that, you know, now with communication devices we have and it seems like everyone loads up their phone so that they can check their work email, but it's, I make it a, I make it a point to not do that when I'm, when I'm not here. And if I hear my, you know, if I happen to see an email in my, in my inbox on my phone, I just don't answer it until I get back to work.

Separating work and home life served as a means to protect Pat's personal time from the possible encroachment of work. Collin, an insurance manager, explained his separation of work and life this way:

> So balance to me means having the ability to turn work on and off. Like for me, I turn work on at 7:00 in the morning and I turn it

off at 3:00 in the afternoon. And at 3:15 when I get home I turn family on.

Turning work or family on and off was a strategy this interviewee used to facilitate balance in his life.

Even men who had quite fused work–life situations (such as a work-from-home situation) tried to compartmentalize work and life by hours of the day or had a specific home office where they kept business hours. Compartmentalization was one of the more concrete strategies the men spoke about. Chip explained his highly developed plan to compartmentalize work and nonwork tasks. He shared the following:

> I actually try to analyze once a month and say what are my goals? What is my time dedication to those goals for work, but at the same time I think I try to reserve about 20 to 30 percent of my total available free day time to also personal either development or growth, and that could also be fitness or mindfulness, actually being able to meditate or do yoga or something along those lines really actually can create a huge spike in productivity if I do it halfway through the day. So I try to kind of life hack my days . . . You know, it's becoming pretty apparent that multitasking for most people or pretty much everybody is not beneficial. It doesn't work as well as we can make it work so I really try to compartmentalize my day into hour-and-a-half increments and blocks.

Throughout his interview, Chip emphatically believed that strategically compartmentalizing work and nonwork tasks increased his health, happiness, and productivity.

WORK–LIFE = WORK–FAMILY

When asked to describe what "balance" meant to them personally, interviewees talked about some parts of their lives outside of work that were important enough to them to warrant consideration for balance. Almost all the men interviewed talked about spending time with their families as the primary nonwork pursuit involved in balance. For instance, Christopher explained:

> It is my wife and my daughter. When I'm not working, they essentially consume my life. Like, I really don't have too many hobbies, and of course, my family just started, so I'm sure that's gonna change soon. But, when I'm not at work, I'm on my way home with them, and when I'm on travel, when I'm going back to the hotel for the night, my first thought is of them and I can't wait to Skype, take a video, and make sure they can see me.

Christopher's emphasis on his family eclipsed other ways that he might have described balance. For him, family was all encompassing. In a similar example, Jarvis explained:

> I got to make it to my kids' baseball games. I got to, you know, help them with their homework, and take vacations with them and, I think [that] it really all revolves around doing things with my family.

In yet another example, Jesse explained how the importance of balancing family led him to work virtually, so that he could simultaneously take care of his son while his wife worked. He shared the following:

> Family means everything, it means everything to me. I've just been the type of person where, you know, I know work is work, [and that] you've gotta do it, but if it kind of interfered to [the point] where I couldn't be myself, or be around my family, or whatever, I'd just do something else. I would just do something else. It's just too important to me . . . And so, me, I'm home, I get to see him ride his bike and play t-ball and do everything else and stuff. It's real important to me.

For Jesse, virtual work enabled him to engage with his family in a more meaningful way. Juan, another work-from-home small-business owner explained how work–life balance equated to work–family:

> Work–life balance to me means I still stay connected to my wife in a meaningful way so that, come the end of the work week, she's not basically throwing two kids at me and saying, you know, I'm out of here. It means, knowing what size your kids wear at all times. It means knowing what their favorite food is.

Juan believed that his engagement in the day-to-day activities of his children and a positive relationship with his spouse equated to work–life balance.

When describing his perception about work–life balance, one interviewee explained:

> I make sure that I spend time with my kids. I make sure that I spend time with my wife. And I make sure that I do some of the little things in life that oftentimes people overlook, like call my mom or send my mom a card.

As these examples illustrate, many of the interviewees, and particularly fathers, discussed the importance of spending time with their families, broadly defined as children, parents, spouses, and partners.

NONFAMILY "LIFE" FACTORS

Although many men cited family as very important, some interviewees resisted the imposition of a family assumption in work–life policies. One interviewee said,

> Those policies really are more for people who have kids, and it isn't really fair. Me and my friends work way more—many, many more hours—than some of them. But it's not like I can tell my manager that I should get to leave early because I need to work out or want to play [a video game]. It's kind of a weird and annoying thing.

This interviewee elaborated that his pursuits were equally important to him personally but that he felt that his nonwork pursuits were not validated in the same ways that other employees' nonwork pursuits were.

Quentin also spoke about the perception that nonwork is frequently conflated with family:

> I've seen things on projects before where its seven at night and everyone is still working. The project's going on and someone says, "I really have to go and put my kids to bed, so I'm going to have to pick this up later." People don't seem to have a big deal about that, but I've also seen the same thing where a single guy says, "Hey, I've got to go let my dogs out, they've been in the house all day without anyone," and people scoff at that. So I can definitely see how there is a little bit of discrimination there between life outside. Most people do interpret that to just be family outside. But that's definitely not 100% of the case.

A number of men echoed this sentiment. In fact, many interviewees mentioned activities such as going to the gym or participating in other recreational activities more often than, and actually before, they mentioned balance in terms of their families. For example, one father shared the following:

> I think taking care of yourself is a good, you know, is a good work life balance. You know, making sure that your exercising and getting rest and of course if you're up late, you know, at home working on, on things then if, if, you know your stressed out then you're not getting your sleep and your rest and you know going to the gym or taking a yoga class and, and just, you know, taking care of yourself.

Many of the men cited working out or other physical activity as vitally important for their conception of work–life balance. One participant explained balance as "getting out and going for a trail run on Mondays or Wednesdays if I want to." In this way, he could attain balance in a couple of hours. After family, working out seemed to be the next most important aspect of nonwork time for most of the men interviewed. However, other aspects of nonwork life popped up. For example, one man explained that general socializing was important to him:

> For me, my friends are my family as well, so making sure that you still [maintain] your social connection outside of the office too. And also that means inside the office, you know, that means if it's Friday and it's five o'clock, maybe having a drink or something after work with some of your colleagues and getting to know them outside the office is always kind of helpful as well.

For this interviewee, even if he was socializing with people from work, he valued the time spent not discussing work-related issues. In a similar example, one graduate student explained what work–life meant to him personally:

> I mean so family is a big part of it. I think social life is a really big part of it as well, you know being able to have time to hang out with people that aren't from work or affiliated with school is really important.

Many men mentioned socializing as an important nonwork commitment. In general, single men, men without children, and the younger men interviewed mentioned the value of nonwork social time as important for their conception of balance.

Quite a few interviewees named travel as important for work–life balance. One coach interviewed explained: "Balance means travel! Definitely travel. Actually, mostly travel. (laughter) I would have to put travel at the top of that list." While this interviewee was quite passionate about traveling, other men interviewed mentioned travel with friends and family as important to achieving work–life balance.

A few other activities emerged as important nonwork commitments. Church, volunteering, education, and hunting figured into some of the men's conception of a healthy work–life balance. For example, one accountant shared,

> I've had [an employee] work for me . . . who likes to spend her summers volunteering at a camp. And we would give her unpaid time off for a period of two months each summer to go and do her volunteering. And then she would come back in the fall. We believe volunteering is an important part of being well rounded and being balanced as a person.

This man believed employee time off for volunteer activity was supported in his workplace but believed the nonprofit status of his organization might play a role in the valuation of volunteer work.

One interviewee claimed that he would take more time off during hunting season: "Hunting season is the only thing that makes me want to stay away from work more than a week at a time." Three men in the study mentioned hunting as important and as an activity that typically required about a week of time away from work. Some men described hunts that would take them away from work for 2 weeks, and in some cases they made annual trips.

A final theme that emerged from the interviews was the importance of education. One interviewee explained that work and family commitments made up the majority of his life but that his commitment to education also figured in:

> And then there's another sphere that's involved there as well, where I have intentionally committed myself to furthering my education. And that doesn't necessarily mean through formal programs or anything like that but it could just be from reading books, textbooks, insurance designations, stuff like that where I'm dedicating probably ten to 20 hours a month to that pursuit to further my knowledge so I can increase both my depth and breadth of knowledge within not necessarily my business for my company, but in my industry as well.

A few other men mentioned formal or informal education as important to their overall conception of balance, which they believed facilitated personal growth and career growth.

PERCEPTIONS OF LEAVE OF ABSENCE POLICIES

When asked about leaves of absence, some men conflated any time away from work with a leave of absence, while others were quite clear of their different kinds of time off. They presented some mixed data about whether or not leaves of absence are possible through the use of personal or vacation time, but the caps on the use of this time gave these employees the perception that they should not use the time in large blocks. For example, Doug explained:

> You get your ten, fourteen, or 20 vacation days, and you can choose to use them however you want. Some places I've worked at, if you don't use [these vacation days] by the end of the year, you lose [them].

The requirement to relinquish accumulated vacation time at the end of the year meant that employees could not accumulate more time to use in large blocks. Employees are responsible for deciding how to use their vacation days. This responsibility directly ties to how employees think about taking leaves of absence.

As another example, Jarvis experienced an extreme case of organizational vacation time maintenance and explained:

> My company doesn't accrue vacation time. I think [that] they are trying to limit or eliminate balance sheet liabilities . . . There were people who had maybe a year's worth of vacation or two years' worth of vacation or something accrued, where it would be sitting on the balance sheet and they would owe that person, and that person would retire and get two extra years of salary. You know what I mean, that the company would have to pay at the time that that person retired.
>
> So, my company just got rid of it. I mean, they just said, 'We're not going to accrue it, [so] work it out with your supervisor.' If you got to take time off and you're not going to, you know, more senior people are not going to get more than less senior people, and if you take more than what your supervisor thinks is enough, then you can be fired, but if you don't then you can just take it. So, there are no accruals at all [anymore]. There is an implication that you might take two weeks a year, but I'm not sure about more. I guess I could try it and see if they fired me.

In Jarvis's case, his organization eliminated vacation time so that longer blocks of time, if even possible, were not probable for employees. When Jarvis said, "I guess I could try it and see if they fired me," he was joking and quickly followed up with an assurance that he would not personally take such a gamble with his career. Yet his frustration and sense of disempowerment was clear.

One of the graduate students interviewed explained that he did not believe leaves of absence were possible for student employees. He explained: "The way that it's set up, I don't think that [leaves] would be an option. Certainly not as anything that's paid." Gerard, a nightclub security worker, observed that leaves of absence were completely impossible for part time workers. He said simply, "Since I'm a temporary employee I would just be let go. As simple as that . . . I wouldn't be compensated for my time gone, so I'd be going without work." In both of these examples, the men perceived that leaves of absence were not an option at all in their current positions.

Another interviewee explained that his company had vacation time and allowed accrual, but that there were negative connotations for actually taking longer blocks of time off. He explained:

> In other places, you can accumulate it over time and take a little bit longer leave. But even then, there's a culture around not necessarily doing that so that you're not gone for six months after saving up for a few years.

For this interviewee, the negative connotations around taking extended time off dissuaded him from considering leaves of absence. In a similar way, Henry explained where he thought negative leave associations began:

> The previous generation of men in particular, who were raised to sort of believe that a man's career defines him, and so taking time away from the career was somehow seen as not a noble thing to do, but a sort of shameful thing to do if he had to step away from his job. So I don't agree with any of it, but that's where I think it comes from.

Although Henry did not agree with the sentiment that leaves were shameful or not noble, he believed a number of men still subscribed to the idea that taking too much time away from their careers was bad.

Bruce saw the "it's-legal-but-frowned-upon" feeling about leaves of absence in his experience as well. He explained that he knew leaves were possible, but not always encouraged, and illuminated how messages about leave-taking practices are sometimes muddled:

> From what I've seen, [taking a leave is] a pretty common practice in my field . . . At smaller companies, while I can't say there's negative feeling, there's definitely a lot of pressure for the individual to get back to work as fast as they can. There's a general concern just to make sure everything is going well, whatever the reason for the leave of absence, to make sure everything is okay. But, at smaller companies, they definitely pressure you more to get back as soon as you can.

Although their explanations frequently illuminated conflicting details, the majority of the men interviewed felt that their current organization was highly supportive of leaves of absence. However, most of the men also viewed themselves as "lucky" or "fortunate" to have found such supportive environments. In many cases, men explained that they left unsupportive work environments or managers that are more typical of the industry.

OUTLIERS

While many men lamented that they would enjoy more time away from work to pursue their nonwork priorities, a majority of the interviewees made statements or briefly mentioned that they, personally, felt balanced, even though most other men were not. They perceived themselves as outliers because they achieved balance while others usually did not. They said things such as "I have to say that I'm quite a bit different from other guys" or "This is probably not a typical answer" to describe themselves as different from the stereotypical unbalanced worker. For example, A.J. explained,

"I don't know how my answer's going to measure up to everybody else, because my data, I'm probably going to assume, is going to be an outlier for your research." Another interviewee said, "I hope I don't throw off your project because I'm so different." Claiming outlier status helped the men gain positive face in relation to balance. It is likely that people do not want to think of themselves as unbalanced. As such, claiming outlier status suggests that many industries and work expectations are regularly unbalanced, but that the individuals have somehow avoided the pitfalls in order to remain personally balanced. The men attributed outlier status to two main functions: luck in industry position, and strategic move for balance, each of which is explained below.

Some of the interviewees mentioned that they felt lucky because their organizations supported work–life balance and categorized their organizations as outliers. These interviewees made comments such as "I've just been pretty lucky with the companies I've been in," and "I've been fortunate that my manager really supports my need for family time." Framing themselves as lucky or fortunate indicated not only that they recognized industry problems but also that they personally were able to avoid some of the negative traps of their occupation and were able to have or achieve balance. Thus, there is recognition of widespread occupational imbalance, but little direct blame on the individual's personal choices, organizational policies, or culture, which the men frequently labeled as outliers.

Henry, a movie reviewer, explained his unique stroke of luck in finding balance:

> Well, and this is where I get to be a little bit different 'cause I enjoy [movies]. I get paid for them, but their more almost hobbies. You know, reviewing movies has been something I've wanted to do . . . I always wanted to review movies, and so it's hard to kind of delay it because technically that's work, but I probably would be watching movies for fun anyway. It's as if I'm automatically balanced because it is so fun.

For Henry, his dream job made him believe he was unique from other men in finding balance. Another interviewee shared the following,

> It was just dumb luck, really. I have a great manager who gets it, and my manager's supervisor gets it. So even though most guys in my position are completely imbalanced, I have managed to get by quite well.

Outlier status by luck seems to be a way the men frequently gave credit to good managers. They usually explained that other managers in other divisions, in previous companies, or in general did not support work–life balance but that, by luck, their current managers did support them.

Other interviewees who claimed outlier status (either explicitly or implicitly) asserted that they had used strategic tactics to ensure their own balance. For example, one interviewee explained:

> You have to figure it out for yourself. I know that I'm different than most of the guys you're talking to, but that's because I figured it out when I was young. I left [a big organization] purposefully and went to work for a smaller firm so that I could have balance. I did the whole "workaholic" thing and I'm done with that. It doesn't have to be all work, but you have to be smart about that in your career choices or you can easily stay in the wrong place.

This interviewee's strategic career moves enabled him to achieve work–life balance. Another interviewee shared a similar ideology, albeit in a conflicting example:

> That's why I've stuck with big firms and never did a startup. Startups are the ones who have no balance. They may get more glory, maybe, but they are totally imbalanced. Working for a big company is a lot of work at first, but it also has some structures for you to gain more and more balance the longer you are there, and that is in writing. They guarantee you time off for balance.

In this example, organizational choice was also strategic for balance purposes, although it presents support for large organizations. This interviewee perceived his own career advancement and work–life balance were better facilitated in large firms.

Darrell, a music producer, explained his strategic plan to create balance in his life:

> It was very deliberate. I mean, it was like when we like looked at the pee stick that said we were pregnant. We called our parents and then I started drafting my letter to the band saying I'm not going to be on the road anymore because I have just seen it. And guys in the band have, I think almost all of them have, kids and they've got things they've missed from their kids, especially little kids. They'd be out on the road for four or six weeks in a row and you have a two month old. Six weeks later, it's like an entirely different child. You come home and you don't even recognize them. I saw enough of that go down and I knew that was not for me. And [I] was fortunate enough to be able to make something work that allowed me to not have to do that.

Darrell strategically modified his own job role and work environment when his family situation changed, based on his observations of the unbalanced lives of some of his peers.

These examples of strategically achieving balance despite industry or organizational demand suggest that most men believe other organizations do not accommodate "life." As such, individuals who want more free time away from work or who need leaves of absence must move to different kinds of organizations and must seek out the most supportive organizations amongst these.

WHEN LEAVES ARE ACCEPTABLE

Most of the men in this study believed leaves of absence were only acceptable for very specific reasons. In general, family leave was unacceptable beyond 1 or 2 weeks. However, leave for serious medical crisis, travel home for foreign workers, and time off to manage burnout were frequently presented as answers when asked when leave would be acceptable.

The men often cited serious medical conditions, for employees or for close family members, as acceptable reasons why men might leave work for a time. Pat shared the following:

> My mom um, got sick with cancer, and so I did take uh, a leave of absence to fly out to where she um, lived and um, I helped her go through some surgeries and operations and I was gone for about, I think, three weeks? So . . . I feel like I, I was very much supported. And they checked in and sent flowers and they actually just told me to just be gone as much as I needed to. I have a pretty strong work ethic, and I think I showed myself there. Which I do here as well, I just feel like probably in my current location it wouldn't be AS supported as it was there.

In a similar way, Rocket described the support he felt to take time away from work when he had medical issues:

> I felt very supported. It was actually kind of a unique circumstance because I was having health issues at the time, and I was trying to figure out what the health issues were, and I was going through a bunch of different tests, and so just saying all this just to set it up, that it wasn't like one single block of time. So [I]actually worked it out so that my leave of absence was dispersed across like three or four months, I think. Like I think I dropped to part time, and then part of that time was leave of absence time.

Although Rocket did not take a long leave at one time, he believed his absences were significant enough to explain in the context of our conversation about leaves of absence.

In a final example, one writer explained that major health crises are acceptable reasons to leave work. He said,

My supervisor's supervisor, who had switched positions, he actually was diagnosed with cancer, and they were really incredibly flexible and have maintained so, allowing him to take off months at a time, and then coming back and returning, and then coming back in part-time form, and then sort of working his way back into full-time.

This leave of absence arrangement served as a model for this interviewee, who believed that his company would support him should he ever personally need to take a leave of absence for health reasons.

A few men in this study shared examples of nonnative coworkers who gained permission to take 2 or 3 months off between projects to go home to see their families. Oliver explained:

We have a lot of foreigners working for us. So we've allowed them to, for example, go back home and spend a month or two in China or Russia or where they're coming from and work bimonthly and take some vacation in between. I've actually done the same myself. I grew up in Germany and I go there sometimes and just work bimonthly.

Oliver described this as a routine practice and a completely supported form of leave. He mentioned that foreign workers were typically under strict government rules and often cannot work while they are home. For example, workers from Iran are under strict policies because of international trade rules. Oliver speculated that it was perhaps one of the only true leaves of absence available, where workers did not work at all while they were away. Similarly, Desmond explained that

contractors who come from India and China and come work on a project in the United States [often ask] for a month leave or six weeks leave and they would visit their family, get married, or have a baby. So, the having the baby leave would be a couple weeks, but they [would] take that opportunity to have a much longer break to go home and visit their family. So, there's quite a bit of that [occurring], but that is very specific to people who come in from overseas.

Desmond also claimed that this kind of leave was perfectly acceptable and supported in his organizational experience. Management supported people who wanted to see their families at least once or twice a year and considered it an important reason to take a leave of absence.

The final reason the men in this study gave as acceptable for leaves of absence was burnout. Burnout is taken as a combination of factors that might push men to quit their jobs, such as divorce, alcoholism, or other "breakdown" points. More than half of the interviewees either concluded or began with a discussion of "burnout" and claimed that they knew they found balance when they were able to avoid burnout, regardless of how they personally chose to avoid it. For these men, the condition of burnout was real, and a valid reason to take a leave of absence. The interviewees described burnout as occurring when individuals feel emotionally and physically drained from working too hard. Interviewees attributed workers succumbing to problems (e.g., drug and alcohol addictions, divorces, and health problems) to burnout and strongly suggested that work–life balance was primarily about avoiding burnout. Interestingly, the men who talked about burnout overwhelmingly supported leaves of absence for men to support burnout avoidance, even when they did not support leaves of absence for births or deaths. This suggests that the reason for taking a leave of absence is critically important in the way in which others perceive the leave.

For example, A.J. explained:

> I have even seen people take a leave of absence because they are so stressed out from their job mentally and emotionally because they have been under a lot of pressure. They're about to burn out and they need that time off.

In a similar example, Christopher shared a story about a coworker with burnout:

> We had a guy that kind of got burned out, so he used up all his sick leave and all his vacation time and was gone for like three months and then came back. We all supported that. You gotta do what you gotta do.

A soccer coach interviewed claimed he knew a few men who took a leave when they felt burned out: "I've seen people take a leave of absence to clear their head, to see if this is what they really want to do, to think about if they can really handle it."

The men describing burnout seemed to understand that the pressures of work sometimes push people too far—a danger for the employee and his coworkers. An architect shared the following:

> Every person has to take it upon themselves to find [balance] or else you will end up losing it at some point. People can snap at work, I've seen people throw down models or go on a tirade because of the stress- they are ridden to a point where they break.

He shared that the firm considered implementing new practices after the first incident to keep other employees safe when one employee snapped. He was concerned that "snapping" seemed like a regular part of business.

No individuals in this study expressed taking a leave of absence solely for burnout, but they tended to frame this practice as excelling in balance. Greg explained:

> When people work 60 hours a week, they start to burn out [and] they become less productive, yada, yada, yada. My first year out of college, I was working like 65 hours a week for months and months at a time.

When it came time, after my one year anniversary, to give out raises, I got the same raise as one of my coworkers who, at the time, wasn't being very productive because he couldn't get a security clearance and was basically doing busy work. And, you know, we got the same raise and like, okay, that's when I realized that . . . I'm not going to kill myself and burnout for them.

Greg further explained that this early lesson in a near burnout experience led him to revise his work–life-balance practices. He now works mostly 40-hour weeks and takes periodic days off.

Terrence also mentioned burnout avoidance as the key to work–life balance:

Balance means being able to spend enough time with my wife [so] that she knows I know her. You know, it's that I know I'm in a relationship. Being able to be there for her, being able to take enough time for myself as well, to make sure that I don't get too stressed out, or—what's the word? I don't remember what the term is—but, don't get too overwhelmed basically by work. Oh, right. Burnout.

The men in this study drew on burnout more than any medical condition that might require people to leave work. Jerick, a lifestyle coach, warned that "unbalance leads to burnout in your 50s. Get sleeping pills and something to numb the pain."

In a poignant example, one interviewee explained that burnout avoidance is the point of work–life balance programs:

The entire point of having [work–life] policies and programs and whatnot is so we don't get burnout. I mean, if we are burned out, we can't work. If you let yourself burn out, you just aren't going to be productive, and then your work life is messed up, and everything else you have going on is messed up. Yeah, so balance is that: making sure that doesn't happen, making sure you work out, [and] take care of yourself, see your kids, travel, go to church, or whatever, play video games, sleep, whatever it takes to keep yourself in check.

For this interviewee, balance meant doing "whatever it takes" to avoid burnout.

Chip, a real estate advisor, explained how work–life policies functioned as reactionary to burnout:

In an real-estate company, its often either family life or work, and usually, unfortunately, [leaves of absence are] more reactive time off where either they kind of burnt themselves out and kind of blew off steam in probably not the most healthy ways . . . So I would say a lot of the times it was very reactive time off. Whether it was just dealing with a situation, most people, I feel, burned through their travel time with kind of transcend makeup for sleep deficit or just trying to just get back to normal . . . with guys it definitely has been more of a thing. You just work your butt off and you figure it out later.

Chip believed that work–life policies could be proactive rather than reactive to help protect workers from burnout.

Managing burnout as evidence of a balanced life presents some contradictions in the context of leave-taking practice. It almost serves as a way to bypass biases about leaves of absence while still making space for nonwork pursuits because it stands as an acceptable reason to take time away from work. However, supporting leaves of absence to avoid burnout disregards the notion that leaves of absence could be acceptable for other reasons. Additionally, approving leaves to avoid burnout expressly benefits organizations more so than the individuals granted the leave and who can claim burnout is ambiguous. Thus, casting burnout avoidance as proof of balance without contestation is problematic.

The perspectives set forth in this chapter lay the groundwork for understanding the cultural and opinion-based context for work–life policies and leaves of absence. It is important to emphasize that men are thinking about work–life balance and how they do and do not achieve it in their relationships with work. As described, although some men think about work–life in traditional conceptions of work and life as separate entities, the interviewees also gave their perspectives on balance and leaves as contested, contradictory, and muddled concepts. This chapter illuminated a "current status" of men and work–life, as presented by the interviewees. In the next chapter I begin an investigation into the causes of the glass handcuffs phenomenon by looking toward macro discourses about work expectations.

NOTE

1. As mentioned previously, *balance* is a highly problematized term because it implies balance is possible and can make individuals who feel imbalanced as if they are somehow to blame for not managing their lives in the right ways (Kirby, Golden, Medved, Jorgenson, & Buzzanell, 2003; Kunin, 2012).

REFERENCES

Cabral-Levesque, S. (2015, January 5). Is work-life balance part of your New Year's resolutions? [Blog comment]. Retrieved from http://www.teachingquality.org/content/blogs/paul-barnwell/work-life-balance-part-your-new-year-s-resolutions

Kirby, E., Golden, A., Medved, C., Jorgenson, J., & Buzzanell, P. (2003). An organizational communication challenge to the discourse of work and family research: From problematics to empowerment. *Communication Yearbook, 27,* 1–43.

Kunin, M. (2012). *The new feminist agenda: Defining the next revolution for women, work, and family.* White River Junction, VT: Chelsea Green Publishing.

Newman, K. (2014, December 30). 9 founders share their New Year's resolutions for work-life balance. Retrieved from http://tech.co/new-years-resolutions-for-work-life-balance-2014-12

Robinson, S. (2015). Five New Year's resolutions that will change your life. *Forbes.* Retrieved from http://www.forbes.com/sites/shanerobinson/2015/01/10/five-new-years-resolutions-that-will-change-your-life/

Part II

Causes for the Glass Handcuffs

5 Macro Discourses of Dedication, Passion, and Commitment

In his chapter about managing women in the workplace, *The Wall Street Journal* managing editor Alan Murray (2010) shared a story about Jack Welch, management guru:

> Speaking at the Society of Human Resource Management's annual conference in June 2009, Welch created a stir by declaring, "There's no such thing as work–life balance." Instead, he said, "There are work–life choices, and you make them, and they have consequences. If you take time off to raise children, and you miss a key promotion as a result, well, too bad." (p. 48)

Murray (2010) reported that the backlash from Welch's comments was quick and severe, with many calling Welch a male chauvinist because the ideology he espoused perpetuated discrimination of women in the workplace. However, the story is included in the section of Murray's book that talked about "managing women," and neither Welch, Murray, nor the people writing in to complain about the comments were concerned with work–life balance for men. The high profile businessmen in this example did not consider work–life as a men's issue, nor did they assume men might have care-work responsibilities or health issues that might require them to leave work for extended periods.

The words and actions of high profile men provide a context for understanding how employed men make sense of their work–life choices. This chapter presents an analysis of 34 texts written by or about high-ranking executives in *Fortune* 500 firms. It also includes men who are not in *Fortune* 500 firms but are listed on *Forbes*'s "World's Most Powerful Men" list for 2014.[1] The analysis of the popular texts forms a ground on which the interview respondents interpret their work and actions. For instance, many interviewees referenced the men profiled in these books when describing their own occupational expectations. These texts illuminated macro discourses that make possible the discursive resources other men use to construct their occupational identities, leave-taking, and work–life practices. They essentially lay a foundation for work expectations in a variety of occupations.

Conceptually, it is necessary to connect macro and micro discourses. Macro discourses are broad social narratives embedded in systems of representation. Ashcraft and Mumby (2004) present four frames that represent how scholars study gender and organization. Of particular relevance to this study are the second and fourth frames. Frame 2 describes "concrete identity performances [invoked by] popular discourses of gender and work" (Ashcraft & Mumby, 2004, p. 23). The fourth frame suggests that grand social narratives serve as textual guides that influence and shape identities. Ashcraft and Mumby suggest that there is a productive tension between these macro discourses and the micro discourses, as they both influence and are influenced by the other. These specific frames "hinge on a dynamic conception of power as a constitutive, productive element of gender and organizational discourse" (Ashcraft & Mumby, 2004, p. 26). Thus, looking at gender and organization from both frames, as I have done in this study, reveals the ways in which people *do* gender and work in accordance with grand narratives about how they should act.

The micro–macro relationship might also be understood as an agency–structure relationship, a concept that attempts to outline the connection between the conscious behavior of individuals and the limitations to conscious choice produced by institutions. Scholars frequently overlook the interplay between macro discourses and micro everyday practices as they privilege one over the other (Ashcraft & Mumby, 2004). In this chapter, I have tried to capture the way that grand narratives about how to work inform the everyday practices of individuals by drawing out relevant discourses from scholarly and popular literature. Unearthing powerful discourses reveals the available scripts by which individual social actors can act. It makes visible the myriad of ways that people might behave in "acceptable ways" and, consequently, the ways they might behave "unacceptably." However, pulling out discourses also presents an opportunity for transformation. By making visible the opportunities and constraints afforded to individuals through discourses, the chance for a reimagining of how the scripts are written is possible. This approach creates space for both the bodies that perform work and the institutional and social expectations that are available to people. This is the space from which the opportunity to rewrite the script occurs: where the flesh of actors meets the pressure of discourse.

For a feminist study, reaching this moment of possible transformation means that there is an opportunity for emancipation or a lessening of oppression. However, it is necessary to find the sites and spots of conflict and tension between expectations embedded in macro discourses and performances in micro everyday behavior. If a reimagining of social scripts is to occur, one must first be able to see how power and inequality runs through current versions of performance. Studying individual performances against the backdrop of macro discourses allows such a procedure to occur. For a standpoint feminist study, the implicated scripts include not only individual roles, but also how the expectations, opportunities, and constraints of those roles operate according to social location. In other words, macro discourses do not influence people in the same ways. The macro discourse of entrepreneurialism, for example, affects working-class people and knowledge workers in different ways, just as it moves in gendered ways through all organizational actors.

If grand narratives provide the possibilities of how one might act in accordance with his or her social location, the interplay of micro and macro discourses is also the site of identity construction. Identities are the ways in which people understand themselves. People have a variety of experiences, quite dependent on the particular bodies they inhabit. Factors of social location such as race, class, ability, and gender shape the ways that people view the world and, as such, how they view themselves. Discourses put forth narratives, however, that are applied across social locations. This is particularly problematic when discourses emerge from and for privileged bodies without consideration for the ways in which they would be applied to others.

Specific bodies that do not align with the expectations embedded in discourses experience conflict, which can create difficulties in enacting identities considered as "acceptable" according to discursive expectations. For example, these popular texts analyzed in this chapter evidence a macro discourse that one should almost always work and should not take time away from work. However, people with certain disabilities might need to leave work to care for their own health at unplanned times. These competing needs can create a disconnect in identity, as these individuals attempt to meet the macro-discursive expectations about how people should perform work. Thus, identity is constructed through these conflicts of micro and macro discourse and is dependent on social location.

The interplay between macro-discourses and micro-discursive resources used by individual men is important to unpack as there are striking similarities between the ways in which occupational identities, leave-taking, and other work–life practices are framed. One interviewee referred to "the greats" when explaining how he wanted to be as influential as Bill Gates and Steve Jobs. This interviewee not only mentioned the icons as men but also referenced their work–life practices as models for career success. A few men talked about the books reviewed for this study specifically by title and seemed to connect the practices in the books to their own "choices" at work. In this way, the men in this study largely performed their identities in accordance with the broad narratives presented in the texts. Others called on famous quotes and rumors about the men profiled in these books as evidence to support various points they made when describing their personal work–life practices.

My analysis of these books revealed five main macro discourses that served as guiding information for the interviewees: (a) good workers are passionate, (b) success requires excessive work hours, (c) dedicated employees sacrifice time with their families, (d) dedicated employees also sacrifice their health, and (e) negative events, such as executive coups, occur when employees are out of the office. In this chapter, I provide textual excerpts from the 34 books written by or about male CEOs and company founders that evidence these discourses. It is important to note that some of the men profiled were not directly responding to prompts about work–life balance. Sometimes they addressed such concerns while relating other stories, and others purposefully left out details about their work–life balance considerations or information about their families. Many others may have believed that the "life" part of work–life was irrelevant in a business strategy book. In part, this might be because some of the books were written before work–life came to be a defining concept for managers and executives. After reading about some of the men's passions for taking care of their employees and for corporate social responsibility, it is possible that, if directly asked today, some of them might speak out more strongly in support for various work–life policies. For others, work–life likely still does not figure into their experiences.

EXECUTIVE TALK ABOUT WORK–LIFE BALANCE AND LEAVES OF ABSENCE

Before analyzing the major themes from the books, I would like to present data about how the executives spoke about work–life balance and/or leaves of absence. Some of the men profiled directly addressed work–life balance or leaves of absence in their texts. Sometimes their examples were explicit discussions about work and life boundaries, and others shared implicit work–life examples. Many of the texts did not address work–life concerns at all—a silence that reveals little emphasis or thought put toward work–life management. The comments about work–life circled around three main themes. First, some of the men described work and life as interchangeable: Their work was their life, and their lives were through their work. Second, many men made supportive comments about balancing work and other aspects of their lives. Third, a few men directly spoke about not supporting work–life initiatives.

Work and Life Overlap

Many of the men profiled in the texts described work and life as heavily overlapping. In these examples, the division between work and life did not explain life for many of the icons profiled. For example, Steve Jobs said, "I sent emails to groups of people at 2 A.M. and batted things around . . . We think about this a lot because it's not a job, it's our life" (Isaacson, 2011, p. 532). As another example, one of Google's stated employee benefits includes the following: "Work and play are not mutually exclusive. It is possible to code and pass the puck at the same time" (Lowe, 2009, p. 170). While the men profiled in these examples worked excessive hours, they embodied a "work hard, play hard" ideology. Lowe (1998) asserted that "while Microsofties often work up to 80-hour weeks, they also play hockey in the hallways, trick each other, play their musical instruments at work . . . and have fun" (p. 65). Mark Zuckerberg of Facebook articulated this ideology. He claimed, "My goal is not to have a job. Making cool things is just something I love doing, and not having someone tell me what to do or a timeframe in which to do it is the luxury I am looking for in my life" (Beahm, 2012, p. 43)

Two of the men included in the textual analysis developed their complete business mission (in part) on the concept of work–life balance. Andrew Rosen, chairman and CEO of Kaplan, Inc., a global leader in diverse education, described the work–life benefits of online education modules. He claimed that his company could "create models that will be custom-designed to suit students' academic strengths and weaknesses, learning styles, goals, time availability, life challenges, and more. These models will enable institutions to deliver the precise education each student needs, when she needs it" (Rosen, 2011, p. 186). The time flexibility inherent in online education directly facilitates work–life balance and is often marketed as a way busy professionals or parents can fit education into their schedules. But perhaps no other influential executive has mixed work and life so completely as the infamous founder of Playboy Enterprises, Hugh Hefner. Hefner is credited with fueling the "ongoing shift from a work culture to a leisure culture" (Watts, 2009, p. 83). His entire company was founded on capturing "The Good Life" (Watts, 2009, p. 76), and the famed magazine features everything pleasurable. During the heyday of the Playboy Mansion, lines between pleasure and work blurred such that work included sex, parties, drugs, and travel (Watts, 2009).

Perspectives Supporting Work–Life

A few texts included examples of the executives taking time away from work. Pamela Isdell, who wrote the forward for her husband Neville Isdell's (Coca-Cola Company) book, shared: "Neville would insist on taking his holiday every year, come what may. This was very important to him and our family" (Isdell, 2011, pp. xiii–xiv). In another example, Ralph Lauren took a medical leave of absence for 3.5 months to recover from brain tumor surgery. However, amid rumors that he was dying, Lauren decided to start making social appearances during his recovery to protect consumer confidence in his brand (Trachtenberg, 1988). Larry Ellison of Oracle "had a reputation for being easily bored by the process of running a business and often took time off" (Symonds, 2013, p. 7). After he was fired from Citigroup, Jamie Dimon took some time off to relax before looking for a new job (Crisafulli, 2009). In the texts analyzed, the previously mentioned were the only examples of executives explicitly taking extended time off. These examples reflect data about larger leave-taking trends regarding support for medical leave and burnout recovery and occasional shorter vacations.

Although they may not have taken a leave of absence, many men described full or limited support for work–life balance in general. The strongest supporter was John Chambers of Cisco Systems, who implemented a host of work–life options and programs in his company. Some examples included telecommuting options, a day care center with technology for parents to watch their children from work, installing high-speed Internet in employees' homes, on-site dental services, paid sabbaticals, concierge programs, nursing rooms for new mothers, a car wash service, and a dry cleaning service, all "to help employees move seamlessly between on-the-job and off-the-job duties throughout the day" (Waters, 2002, p. 89). Chambers described the policies as necessary to attract and keep excellent employees (Waters, 2002). Alan Murray (2010) from *The Wall Street Journal* also made an economic argument for supporting work–life policies at work. He advocated giving middle-aged workers sabbaticals to help them "gain a fresh commitment to their jobs" (p. 46). Murray also recommended, in a section of his book titled "Managing Women," that employers "give people opportunities to take time off to raise their kids or care for an aging parent. It will pay off for your organization in the end" (2010, p. 49).

Other executives spoke out in support of work–life policies for more moral reasons. Howard Schultz's (Starbucks) father broke his foot when he was young. Schultz remembered, "Like so many others of his station in life, when Dad didn't work, he didn't get paid" (Schultz & Yang, 1997, p. 3). This early memory prompted Schultz to care deeply about the welfare of his employees, and after one of his close employees contracted AIDS and was unable to work, Schultz went on to provide generous health care for his team, including part-time workers (Schultz & Yang, 1997). In another moral example, Michael Dell explained why he hired others to help him do his job: "I wanted to grow and develop myself. And I wanted to maintain a healthy balance in my life, and spend time with my young and rapidly growing family" (Dell & Fredman, 1999, p. 64). However, other than this tidbit, Dell did not directly address work–life balance issues. These examples show executives directly speaking about making balance a priority for their employees. Other executives spoke about making balance a reality in their own lives.

Achieving balance as a busy executive often meant working through competing demands. Bill McDermott (2014) of SAP spoke about his wife Julie's cancer fight: "Two things I knew for sure: one, I would be by Julie's side for every doctor's appointment, every procedure. Two, I had to stay focused at my new job. I owed it to Gartner [his employer at the time]. I also had two hefty mortgages and, soon, medical bills" (pp. 183–184). After this experience, McDermott wrote his goals for life. The second is "balance between work and family" (2014, p. 194). In another example, Jeff Immelt (General Electric) shared his work–life management strategies:

"One company, one wife," he says. Outside of the office Immelt spends most of his free time, which he admits is not much, with his wife and

> college-aged daughter . . . Immelt keeps his Blackberry on seven days a week because important news affecting a global company the size of GE never stops, but he balances that demand by giving up hobbies . . . "I think it's important to have balance," says Immelt. I love my company, I love my family, and I don't think I have to compromise between the two. I think I can do both. But it means you're going to have to make other tradeoffs." (Magee, 2009, p. 70)

Immelt believed he could achieve balance by giving up outside distractions and focusing on work and family.

Some of the executives mentioned having to explicitly think about spending time with family. Lee Iacocca (Ford Motor Company and Crysler) explained:

> I've always worked hard during the week while trying to keep my weekends free for family and recreation. Except for periods of real crisis I've never worked on Friday night, Saturday, or Sunday. (Iacocca & Novak, 1986, p. 20)

Iacocca set aside weekends to spend away from work whenever possible. He later shared the following:

> I've seen a lot of executives who neglect their families, and it always makes me sad. After a young guy dropped dead at his desk, McNamara, then president of Ford, sent out a memo that said: "I want everybody to be out of the office by 9:00 P.M." . . . You can't let a corporation turn into a labor camp. Hard work is essential. But there's also time for rest and relaxation, for going to see your kid in the school play or at a swim meet. And if you don't do those things while the kids are young, there's no way to make it up later on. (Iacocca & Novack, 1986, p. 289)

Iacocca specifically made time to prioritize family in his attempts to achieve balance.

Michael Bloomberg (Salomon Brothers, Bloomberg L.P., and New York City) also spoke about how to strategically manage time:

> Having a business career and raising a family create inherent conflicts. Investment of time is the primary controllable determinant of success in both . . . When it comes to managing my time . . . I sleep less, combine my social life with business entertaining, and make my commute to work short. Rather than succumbing to the temptation to nap, I use my cellular phone to make business calls and read reports and newspapers while traveling. An understanding former spouse and kids help . . . Still, as you balance work and family, the inevitable either/or will invariable arise: the hockey game or the board meeting . . . Sometimes you go to

one and sometimes to the other . . . I've always thought much of my early career success wouldn't have been possible if I had been married at the time. Without the family responsibilities, I was able to channel my efforts toward business. (Bloomberg & Winkler, 1997, pp. 211–214)

Bloomberg explained that he had to give up some family events *and* some work events in order to achieve his version of balance.

In a final example of a supportive work–life perspective, Jamie Dimon explained his work–life priorities:

My children, my family . . . right next to that is humanity . . . And then way down here is JPMorgan. I don't mean that in a bad way, and it may seem contradictory as in "Okay, Jamie, you spend 80 hours a week at JPMorgan." (Crisafulli, 2009, pp. 212–213)

Dimon recalled a vacation during which he attempted to work and enjoy family time. When his children asked him to play with them in the ocean, he replied, "I only have 30 minutes" (Crisafulli, 2009, p. 216). This episode prompted him to work less during subsequent vacations, although he believed that through work, he could be a better father and humanitarian (Crisafulli, 2009).

Perspectives Against Work–Life Balance

Some of the texts contained passages in which the executives directly spoke out against work–life practices or policies. In an ironic twist, all of the men included in this section also spoke in supportive ways about work–life. This contradiction hints at the complicated ways men think about and enact work–life management.

Lee Iacocca described his outrage at union requests for paid personal days. He claimed, "I always think back to World War II: France was on a four-day week, and Germany was on a six-day week. Remember who got creamed?" (Iacocca & Novak, 1986, p. 308). He referred to paid personal days as an occasion "where each worker gets a certain number of days off a year just for the hell of it" (Iacocca & Novak, 1986, p. 308) and claimed that

all of these plans—unlimited COLA (Cost of Living Allowance); "thirty and out" [when a person works 30 years and can retire early]; unlimited medical benefits; and paid personal holidays—violate common sense. No matter how sophisticated something like paid personal holidays sounds, there's no logical way you can pay a guy just to stay home. (Iacocca & Novak, 1986, p. 308)

Iacocca believed work–life policies would result in drastic economic losses for his companies. In a similar way, Bill McDermott shared a story from his early days at SAP when he noticed the lagging company was nearly empty one Friday. He wrote, "Sorry, we all have families, but if we keep spiraling, we won't have customers, or our jobs. People should be on fire, on the phone, in conference rooms strategizing, writing, and rewriting contracts—doing *something*" (McDermott, 2014, p. 205). Although he absolutely valued family time, he also equated face time in the office with economic success for the company.

In a final example, Michael Bloomberg explained that he saw no substitute for long hours in the office:

> You can hope that "anti-exploitation" labor laws protecting workers with mandated coffee breaks, two-year maternity and paternity leaves, six-week minimum vacations, and a cap on hours you're allowed to work will keep your competitors down. The Communists tried to eliminate any form of meritocracy for seventy years and, in addition to wrecking their economies, they literally starved fifty million people to death in the process. (Bloomberg & Winkler, 1997, pp. 223–224)

By comparing work–life policies to Communists (and later Socialists), Bloomberg emphasized his democratic belief in meritocracy. He thought time away from work made less merited employees.

As presented here, the data reveal that some executives did think about work–life balance and some showed limited support for policies facilitating better balance. However, a few of the men blatantly opposed critical work–life policies, and many others did not address work–life in their books. The executives who did support work–life policies reveal a complicated picture about their understanding of these policies. Although they mentioned support for balance, many of them also shared expectations about excessive face time and may have had a distorted view of balance (e.g., believing an 80- hour workweek allowed for adequate balance). The next sections of this chapter flesh out some of these contradictions by highlighting the most pervasive ways the executives talked about work expectations.

GOOD WORKERS ARE PASSIONATE

One way that the popular texts discursively characterized good workers was through the notion of passion. Many of the icons profiled characterized themselves and successful others as extremely passionate, obsessive, or otherwise totally enamored with their occupations. Perhaps the most obvious example is Steve Jobs (Apple), who was well known for his passion for his job. Jay Elliot, an Apple employee hired by Jobs, claimed, "[Jobs's] obsession is a passion for the product, a passion for product perfection" (Isaacson, 2011, p. 83). As another example, musician Wynton Marsalis described Jobs as "a man possessed," (Isaacson, 2011, p. 402) explaining, "After a while,

I started looking at him and not the computer, because I was so fascinated with his passion" (Isaacson, 2011, p. 402). Jobs himself explained: "My passion has been to build an enduring company where people were motivated to make great products. Everything else was secondary" (Isaacson, 2011, p. 568). Jobs's passion for his work rigorously eclipsed other pursuits in his life.

In a similarly classic example, Bill Gates (Microsoft) was so obsessed with computers that "his parents ordered him to take a leave of absence from computers, which he did" (Lowe, 1998, p. 11). Gates stepped away from computers for some months at his parents' request, but returned with rigorous zeal after his "leave." Wallace and Erickson (1992) claimed that "even as a child Gates had an obsessive personality" (p. 12). They also noted that Gates could not explain his fascination with "his own 'wonder,' the computer. But it triggered a deep passion, an obsession, in him" (Wallace & Erickson, 1992, p. 22). This dance between passion and obsession was a characterization noted about in nearly all of the icons in the popular texts analyzed.

Chairman and CEO of the Dow Chemical Company, Andrew Liveris (2011), said, "I am passionate about manufacturing" (p. 26). He also stated that it was "not just a pleasure, but an honor to work [at Dow Chemicals] . . . Every day that I come to work, I do so with a feeling of great privilege. Serving as your CEO has been the greatest honor of my life" (p. xx). In a similar way, Larry Ellison of Oracle "always talked about technology and Oracle with passion and intensity" (Symonds, 2013, p. 7). The men deeply believed in their fields, companies, and products.

Examples of executives' passionate dedication to their jobs spanned a variety of occupations. At Ralph Lauren, Sal Cesarani, a designer claimed, "I was obsessed with what I was doing. My wife knew it was the most exciting thing" (Trachtenberg, 1988, p. 99). Lauren himself claimed, "My soul is in what I do. I give all my feelings, like a writer, everything, about what I love" (Trachtenberg, 1988, p. 280). Jeff Immelt of General Electric similarly claimed, "This is not a job. This is a passion. This is my life" (Magee, 2009, p. 39). Immelt did not distinguish between work and life because he felt such extreme passion for his job. Mark Zuckerberg also described his passionate drive for work, stating, "I just built a whole lot of different things. And that's just a passion of mine . . . You need to do stuff you are passionate about. The companies that work are the ones that people really care about and have a vision for the world, so do something you like" (Beahm, 2012, pp. 46, 53).

The men spoke of their love for their jobs as a driving force in their lives. Iacocca explained:

> My years as general manager of the Ford Division were the happiest period of my life . . . this was fire-in-the-belly time. We were high from smoking our own brand. (Iacocca & Novak, 1986, p. 61)

Iacocca described his passion as "fire in the belly" and a "high." In a similar way, Donald Trump claimed, "I like making deals, preferable big deals. That's how I get my kicks" (Trump & Schwartz, 2009, p. 3). Trump felt alive while making deals. In another example, a partner at Goldman Sachs explained why people worked so hard: "There is nothing else in their lives that gives them nearly the charge work does" (Cohan, 2012, p. 231). For most of the executives included in this analysis, work encompassed most of their lives. Hugh Hefner described an extreme, passionate, dedication to his work. His "personal identification with *Playboy* became almost total" (Watts, 2009, p. 81).

Some of the men referred to their jobs as "callings" or "destiny" and referenced a higher power as guiding their occupational lives. For example, George W. Bush (2010) explained his decision to run for president of the United States by saying, "I felt a calling to run" (p. 36). He later explained, "My most solemn duty, the calling of my presidency, was to protect America." (Bush, 2010, p. 155). He and wife, Laura, referred to his time after his presidency as the "afterlife" (Busch, 2010, p. 475). In another example, Neville Isdell (Coca-Cola Company) explained his passion for Coke. He said, "I have a belief system that when the Good Lord created the world, he created Coke number one and Pepsi number two" (Isdell & Beasley, 2011, p. 66). Bush and Isdell both believed that God had a hand in leading them to their occupations. In comparable moves, Alan Murray (2010) of *The Wall Street Journal* claimed that "management is a higher calling" (p. 169), and Warren Buffet's wife referred to Buffet's work as "a sort of holy mission" (Schroeder, 2008, p. 206). Finally, Bill McDermott (2014) called his promotion to CEO of SAP as "destiny unfolding" (p. 256). These examples demonstrate the executives' tendency to see God's will or destiny in their occupational roles.

In a similar way, Howard Schultz explained his calling to Starbucks: "I believe in destiny. In Yiddish, they call it bashert . . . I could feel the tug of Starbucks. There was something magic about it, a passion and authenticity I had never experienced in business" (Schultz & Yang, 1997, p. 36). Schultz mentioned his passion for good coffee, and for Starbucks—the company— throughout his book. He identified himself strongly with his position in the company, stating, "I identified so closely with Starbucks that any flaw in Starbucks felt like my own personal weakness" (Schultz & Yang, 1997, p. 48).

While nearly all the executives spoke about their own passions for their work, many also described passion as a quality they seek in employees. Drawing on Jack Welch, management guru, Alan Murray (*The Wall Street Journal*) recommended his hiring managers evaluate "candidates for their 'passion.' By 'passion' . . . I mean a heartfelt, deep, and authentic excitement about work" (Murray, 2010, p. 37). Bill McDermott (2014) of SAP agreed and claimed, "The best people for a role, I knew, would be those whose ambitions and passions fit the job" (p. 234). Howard Schultz of Starbucks seeks passion in his employees as well. He explained, "Their passion and devotion is our number-one competitive advantage. Lose it, and we've lost the game" (Schultz & Yang, 1997, p. 138). Comparably, Hugh Hefner "expected everyone to share his passion for the magazine and created daunting standards of achievement" (Watts, 2009, p. 100). These excerpts reveal how macro discourses shape culture. The executives feel extreme passion and commitment; they then seek to hire and promote passionate employees.

A. G. Lafley, former Chairman and CEO of Procter & Gamble (P&G), shared a story about how P&G promoted passion. Chip Bergh, then P&G's president of men's grooming, directed his team to "spend two weeks in India . . . [wanting them] to live with these consumers . . . to go into their homes . . . [in order] to understand how shaving fits into their lives." After doing so, one senior scientist was so moved by the work immersion that he "designed the first razor on a napkin flying back to London . . . The man . . . had tears in his eyes as he told the story" (Lafley & Martin, 2013, p. 109–110). Supposedly, the senior scientist felt such passion for the purpose of his company and belief in the importance of product development that emotions bubbled over as he thought about it

One way the executives promoted passion was to engage employees in the overall vision of their companies. David Novak of Yum! Brands described this strategy:

> It's not just you who has to care about your vision for your business; it has to appeal to everyone involved in making it happen. In order to do all this, your vision has to inspire. Every employee, whether it's someone working a shift for minimum wage or a high-level executive, wants to be a part of something bigger. (Novak, 2012, p. 114)

Novak believed that employees were a part of making his company a success, and wanted to include them in his passionate vision. In a similar way, Michael Dell shared, "My goal has always been to make sure that everyone at Dell feels they are a part of something great—something special—perhaps something even greater than themselves" (Dell & Fredman, 1999, pp. 107–108).

In many cases, employee passion developed into a corporate culture of passion. Sculley and Byrne (1987) asserted that Apple employees exhibited "so much passion in their eyes [that] they were mesmerized, possessed almost, by what they were doing; they were universally young, passionate, idealistic, and brilliant" (p. 85). This kind of passion was considered a desirable trait for employees at all levels of the organization.

Sometimes, corporate cultures of passion were compared to cults. For example, John Whitehead wrote Goldman Sachs's "12 commandments," which drove the success of the company. The "Goldman Way" guided a "new generation of highly paid Wall Street soldiers, who have been called everything from 'cyborgs' to 'Stepford wives' to the 'Manchurian banders'" (Cohan, 2011, p. 207). Part of the Goldman way was to recruit people who were passionately ambitious and driven toward success (Cohan, 2012).

Another company widely regarded as cultlike is Disney. Capodagli and Jackson (1999) explained:

> To ensure that employees at all levels would be guided by his beliefs and his visionary sense of purpose, Walt Disney fostered what amounted

to an almost cult like atmosphere. His passionate belief in the need to instill complete company culture led him to set up a formal training program that has come to be known as Disney University. (p. 40)

Many corporate training programs now exist and feature sections to inspire passion for particular companies.

A few icons mentioned "drinking the company Kool-Aid"[2] to describe their complete dedication to the company. Bill McDermott of SAP previously worked at Xerox for many years. During his SAP hiring interview, the interviewer noted Bill's tremendous passion. McDermott (2014) stated that, throughout his career, people looked at him "as if [he'd] downed the entire pitcher of Xerox's Kool-Aid" (p. 79). In another example, those living the "Goldman Way" at Goldman Sachs often described their fervor as "drinking the Kool-Aid" (Cohan, 2012, p. 363).

The discourse of occupational passion complicates work–life balance. The icons described their passion as what drove their excessive hours and the reason they sacrificed their health and families. They also pointed to their passion as an important reason for their success. By extension, they wanted to hire employees who were also totally committed to and passionate about their companies, and believed that the employees who would be successful should show this extreme passion and dedication at all times. Taking time away from work signals less passion and less dedication to work. Thus, the strong influence of work passion makes the support of work–life policies tenuous and directly contributes to the glass handcuffs. Passionate employees do not want to leave their work places. Passionate employees value their jobs above nearly all else.

SUCCESS REQUIRES EXCESSIVE WORK HOURS

The passion the executives felt for their jobs culminated in excessive time commitments to work. Nearly all of the icons referenced extremely long hours per day and described an intense pace throughout the day. They spoke about working through meals, arriving early, staying late, and working on evenings and weekends, and most of the icons did all of these activities for years.

The incredible time commitment and work ethic demanded from Goldman Sachs employees resulted in long shifts at work. In 1984, one employee explained his commitment to the firm he helped build: "I work until 2:30 in the morning and then come back for breakfast at 8:00 A.M. almost every day" (Cohan, 2012, p. 231). In the ultimate display of commitment, on the Friday of Memorial Day weekend, 1991, a time when many employees planned to head out of town, 40 employees were required to meet in a conference room. They sat for hours waiting for their manager to come. Three employees left. At 10:00 P.M., the partner who demanded the meeting appeared, took attendance, and dismissed them. The three dissenters were fired when they returned on Tuesday (Cohan, 2012). Face time and excessive commitment to the firm are still central tenets of Goldman Sachs's culture.

Other executives also regaled tales of long work hours. Iacocca described his years during the development of the Mustang as a time "when I thought nothing of grabbing a hamburger for dinner and staying at the office until midnight" (Iacocca & Novak, 94). Trump described a similar time commitment, writing,

> I wake up most mornings very early, around six . . . There's rarely a day with fewer than fifty calls, and often it runs to over a hundred. In between, I have at least a dozen meetings . . . I rarely stop for lunch. I leave my office by six-thirty, but I frequently make calls from home until midnight, and all weekend long. It never stops, and I wouldn't have it any other way. (Trump & Schwartz, 2009, p. 3)

Trump presented a typical timeline of events in his life. Each minute seemed taken up with work.

When asked to come out of retirement to run the Coca-Cola Company, Neville Isdell struggled with the decision. He claimed he was "finally finding time to spend with [his] family after decades of moving all over the world and working countless fifteen-hour days" (Isdell & Beasley, 2011, p. 3). Although Isdell famously came out of retirement to run Coke, he and his wife worried what returning to nonstop work would mean for Isdell's health and family.

Multiple other examples illustrate this tendency to work countless hours. Walt Disney "began nearly every new project with eager and enthusiastic participants, an enormous advantage in a process that often involved long hours of work seven days a week" (Capodagli & Jackson, 1999, p. 18). Although this particular example does not give a numerical representation of hours worked, other examples about Disney referenced night, signifying that the "long hours" mentioned here lasted well into night, seven days a week (Capodagli & Jackson, 1999).

In a similar way, Larry Ellison of Oracle was also known to work incredibly long hours. Symonds (2013) wrote,

> Ellison was working harder than he'd ever imagined, to the extent that it probably contributed to the breakdown of his second marriage . . . [Ellison explained,] "I'd arrive home around midnight most evenings . . . That was the second wife I'd managed to drive away . . . My personal life had fallen apart, and work was the only thing left that mattered. So I worked even more–until the hours of the day ran out." (p. 64)

Ellison admitted to putting in 14- to 16-hour days regularly (Symonds, 2013). At Ralph Lauren, Jeffrey Banks, a designer and onetime protégé, described working for Ralph Lauren while attending school. Trachtenberg (1988) explained, "The hours were exhausting . . . Banks lost thirty pounds in three months, his grades suffered, and finally his teachers told him he would have to choose between Polo and school" (p. 89). Sal Cesarani, another Ralph Lauren designer, shared a similar experience: "I lived morning, noon, and night at Ralph Lauren . . . I didn't have time to breathe" (Trachtenberg, 1988, p. 99).

Alan Mulally of Ford Motor Company also demonstrated this practice of excessive work hours. Hoffman (2012) described

> a friendly competition [that] developed between Mulally and two of his executives, Don Leclair and Michael Bannister; to see who would be the first one into the office each morning. Getting there first had long been a badge of honor for the finance guys—a way of establishing that they were the ones who really ran the place . . . Mulally was always at the office first. Bannister gave up when he realized that 5:30 A.M. was still too late . . . [Leclair] had to get up at 4:30 A.M. at the latest. (p. 114)

Mulally "got to the office early each morning. He was already answering e-mails by 6 A.M. He worked until dinnertime, then went home and spent the rest of the evening reading reports, retiring early. He worked seven days a week" (Hoffman, 2012, p. 198). Mulally's work ethic is often credited as part of his success in turning around the company.

Other executives cited working seven days a week. For example, Hugh Hefner's work ethic was described as "compulsive" (Watts, 2009, p. 6). He worked a "frenzied pace" (Watts, 2009, p. 81)—"Playboy consume[d] seven days of every week, more than a dozen hours a day, and [he] knock[ed] off at 1:30 or 2:00 in the morning" (Watts, 2009, p. 81). Hefner "frequently slept [at the office] and his family saw him less and less. Quite literally, he lived his work" (p. 98). His iconic bathrobe wardrobe began because he slept at the office so frequently and did not have time to dress before starting work. In another example, Bill McDermott (2014) of SAP described his years at Xerox:

> I worked a lot. By 5:50 A.M., I was on a train . . . Every week, I worked the equivalent of 24/7, but still tried to be home on weekends. But even on Saturdays and Sundays, I answered most emails within minutes, although now I was also texting, and I answered those pretty fast, too. (p. 290)

Even when McDermott was home with his family, he continued to work through the evenings and weekends.

In another example, Jamie Dimon of JPMorganChase is well known for working long hours. He "casually mentions working an 80-hour week" (Crisafulli, 2009, p. 20). In turn, James Crown (JPMorganChase executive) observed that

> he was hard on people because he was very demanding—demanding in terms of hours, demanding in terms of performance . . . But no one

worked harder than he did. It was not a question of telling people that they should work all day Saturday. (Crisafulli, 2009, p. 106)

Later, despite significant pushback, he changed branch hours to accommodate customers. He claimed, "You are going to be open in every single market equal to your competitors, whatever that is . . . I don't give a sh— about employee morale" (Crisafulli, 2009, p. 127). Face time to accommodate customers was a high priority for Dimon.

Michael Bloomberg recalled his feelings when he was asked to leave Salomon Brothers. He claimed, "This, after fifteen years of twelve-hour days and six-day weeks" (Bloomberg & Winkler, 1997, p. 1). Bloomberg shared his excessive face time philosophy throughout his memoir:

The more you work, the better you do . . . I always outworked the other guy . . . Still, I had a life. I don't remember being so driven or focused that my job got in the way of playing in the evenings and weekends. I dated all the girls. I skied and jogged and partied more than most. I just made sure I devoted twelve hours to work and twelve hours to fun— every day. (Bloomberg & Winkler, 1997, p. 30)

Bloomberg did not address other ways he might use his time outside of work and fun (such as sleep), but presumably he spent 12 hours a day on work, and the rest of his time sleeping and doing other "fun" activities. Bloomberg extended his work-hard expectations to his employees. He explained that he expected longer hours and less vacation time for employees higher in the organizational hierarchy and cautioned those who disagreed with his philosophy to turn down offered promotions. He explained,

The rewards almost always go to those who outwork the others. You've got to come in early, stay late, lunch at your desk, take projects home nights and weekends. The time you put in is the single most important controllable variable determining your future. (Bloomberg & Winkler, 1997, p. 223)

Bloomberg's passion for long work hours radiated through his book. He believed it was the most important factor in determining career success.

Amazon employees were also required to work extremely long hours with high productivity; customer service representatives dropping below seven e-mails a minute were regularly fired. Amazon employees would work until two or three in the morning in the early days, and in general, the Amazon staff was considered overworked (Brandt, 2011). CEO Jeff Bezos, however, had

no empathy for employees who complain about working long hours in pursuit of his quest [and] often pushed his people . . . It was not uncommon [for his employees] to work twelve hour days, seven days a week. (p. 168–169)

The pattern of intense time dedication across occupations is striking; nearly every industry leader expects excessive face time.

Other firms also demanded hard work and long days. For example, Lowe (1998) described the following:

> Microsoft is infamous for working its employees hard—but few work harder than Bill Gates himself. Between 1978 and 1984 Gates took only 15 days off work . . . The cafeteria at Microsoft headquarters in Redmond is open until midnight to allow for people who work late. (p. 37)

Accommodating people who worked late hours reflected Gates's expectations for long work hours. Indeed, Gates asserted, "If you don't like to work hard and be intense and do your best, this is not the place to work" (Lowe, 1998, p. 37). Gates's words indicate that employees who do not "work hard and be intense" are not good employees at Microsoft.

Wallace and Erickson (1992) also described how Gates perpetuated the intense face time requirement. They claimed that he would regularly sleep in the office and that employees were often required to work 20-hour days. They also shared a story that Gates required employees to park in the order they arrived, and as a result, employees did not want to be seen leaving before the person who arrived before them. Additionally, Wallace and Erickson (1992) claimed that

> beginning in 1984, Microsoft managers secretly began using the E-Mail system to determine which hourly employees were working on weekends . . . This information was retrieved and then used by the company to determine employee bonuses. (p. 276)

Maxwell (2002) corroborated this account of Microsoft and noted that "during the Windows Death March, it wasn't unusual to have programmers sleeping in their cubicles" (p. 109).

These, and many other, stories and examples of an intense time commitment filled the pages of the popular texts. In a final memorable example, Apple employees made T-shirts that said "90 hours a week and loving it!" (Isaacson, 2011, p. 124). Although their time requirements were extreme, workers typically expected long hours as part of their occupation. The texts did not address whether or not such hours were necessary, only how workers pushed beyond their human barriers (e.g., sleep and hygiene) to work around the clock.

This discourse of excessive time commitment is purported throughout the texts. However, there was no significant consideration of employees who might have trouble meeting excessive face-time requirements. As discussed earlier, employed women carry a disproportionate responsibility for care work, which may make excessive face-time commitments at work impossible. However, expectations of time, communicated to employees through macro discourses, do not account for employee differences.

DEDICATED EMPLOYEES SACRIFICE TIME WITH THEIR FAMILIES

Without question, the men featured in the texts expected to sacrifice at least some, if not the majority, of their time with their families. They spoke often about divorces, missed childhoods, and struggling to make time for their partners, parents, and children. For example, Alan Mulally of Ford Motor Company reportedly "rarely saw his family, though he scheduled regular telephone calls with his wife, children, and mother" (Hoffman, 2012, p. 198). The physical absence of the executives from their families frequently resulted in negative outcomes.

Most of the executives experienced at least one divorce. L. Jay Tenenbaum, a highly paid partner at Goldman Sachs, decided to leave unexpectedly in 1975 after 22 years with Goldman because he wanted to make sure "his second marriage did not go the way of his first, which it very well might have had he stayed at Goldman Sachs" (Cohan, 2012, p. 186). Goldman employees reportedly had the highest divorce rate on Wall Street and were encouraged to fit life events (such as marriages) around work (Cohan, 2012). Married couple Sandra K. Lerner and Leonard Bosack started Cisco Systems because of their passion for technology. Eventually, however, "the business had taken a toll on their marriage, and they soon split up. Lerner blames years of overwork, financial struggles, and making the company a priority instead of the marriage" (Waters, 2002, p. 37).

While they never divorced, Warren Buffet's wife Susie moved to a different state after years of frustration at her husband's excessive work. A friend of the Buffets "described Susie as 'sort of a single mother'" (Schroeder, 2008, p. 217). It seems "Susie [thought] that Warren would be more attentive to her and the family if he quit working" (Schroeder, 2008, p. 256). Yet "as one put it, Warren's 'real marriage' was to Berkshire Hathaway" (Schroeder, 2008, p. 374). Years later, he would try to undo the damage he caused by not spending time with his family.

The texts revealed many examples in which the executives relied on their spouses to take a disproportionate responsibility for care work. As the examples presented so far illustrate, sometimes the arrangement worked out. However, quite frequently the executives' spouses tired of playing second fiddle to work. Bloomberg (1997) described gaining commitment from his wife when he desired to start his own company. However, she later decided the long work hours no longer suited her. The couple divorced (Bloomberg, 1997). Although the families may have agreed to support the executives on their journey to power, they did not always come out unscathed.

The absence of their fathers caused stress for many children of high-ranking executives. In the forward she wrote to her husband's book, Pamela Isdell recalled, "The one person in our family who suffered from all our globe-trotting was our darling daughter, Cara . . . poor Cara was moved to so many different countries (she has lived on five continents and attended six schools), she found it very disruptive during her early life" (Isdell & Beasley, 2011, p. xiii). The Isdells moved around the globe constantly for Neville Isdell's career with the Coca-Cola Company.

John Scully of Apple described certain times when it was difficult for him to spend time with his family:

> I left Leezy and our daughter, Laura, back east for the first five months . . . because I knew I had to immerse myself in the new job . . . I would get up at 4:30 A.M. every morning, run along El Camino Real, and work at Apple from 7:00 A.M. until 10:00 or 11:00 P.M. . . . Because it was a seven-day-a-week job, Leezy left for our home in Maine for the summer. She realized she would see little of me over the next few months. (Scully & Byrne, 1987, pp. 130–131, 288)

Scully decided to leave his family in another state because he knew he would not be able to spend any time with them while starting a new job. In a similar way, Larry Ellison believed that some work periods made it more difficult to spend time with family. He explained, "If I disappeared from the kids' lives for a while, like in 1991, something bad must be happening. During those times I became so focused on work and survival that I locked everything else out—even the kids" (Symonds, 2013, p. 342).

A few of the men included in this analysis viewed children as a distraction from their work. For example, Hugh Hefner did not want children during his first marriage. Watts (2009) described how

> he had agreed to a family because of social pressures to have children, and the arrival of daughter Christie . . . delighted him. But at heart, Hefner was no family man, and in his words, "All this togetherness seemed meaningless. I went through the motions, but my heart wasn't in it." (p. 58)

Although family was not an important consideration for Hefner in the early years of Playboy, he did go on to enjoy an engaging family relationship with the children from his second marriage and eventually built a relationship with his daughter from his first marriage (Watts, 2009).

In another example, Steve Jobs (Apple) abandoned his pregnant girlfriend and ignored his daughter on her birth because of his dedication to work. He felt that technical innovation was his destiny—not parenting—and initially did not want anything to do with his firstborn daughter Lisa (Isaacson, 2011). In fact, Jobs's relationships with all his daughters were distant, as he would often ignore them completely. Jobs's wife, Laurene Powell, explained,

"He focuses on his work, and [as a result] at times he has not been there for the girls" (Isaacson, 2011, p. 283). These examples illustrate the power of the executives' occupational identities, which superseded their identities as fathers.

It was not simply distant relationships that caused difficulties for the children of executives. In some cases, families were at risk because of their fathers' occupational positions. For example, after killing two of Saddam Hussein's sons, George W. Bush learned that "Saddam had ordered the killing of [daughters] Barbara and Jenna in return for the death of his sons" (Bush, 2010, p. 263). Although death threats on the children of high-profile men are rare, some of the children were at risk of kidnapping. Neville Isdell (Coca-Cola Company) explained the dangers of his job in Germany:

> This was the era of a German terrorist group called the Red Army Faction, which killed and kidnapped leading business figures . . . I was reliably informed that my name was on the list. Our home was equipped with a panic button . . . We were also provided with a company driver who would take Cara to and from school each day, always by varied routes. (Isdell & Beasley, 2011, p. 95)

Coke provided extra security for its executives abroad, but the danger for Isdell's family was real. In a similar example, Ralph Lauren explained his reluctance to talk about his family, stating, "'I'm not saying a thing' . . . He was concerned about their security; some years back Calvin Klein's daughter was kidnapped" (Trachtenberg, 1988, p. 231).

Despite the challenges the executives faced in juggling their work roles with family life, many of the men believed they had strong family ties. In general, they attributed the strength of their family relationships to supportive women. For example, Howard Schultz (Starbucks) shared the following:

> I always try to make time for family and friends . . . But keeping up those personal relationships is stressful, too. Sheri has been able to gauge the pressures on me as the business matured, and during times I was distracted she somehow managed to keep the family on an even keel. I can't imagine that I could have built Starbucks . . . without having a strong, secure wife like Sheri. (Schultz & Yang, 1997, pp. 198–199)

Schultz regularly consulted Sheri about business decisions, and shared how he sometimes disappointed her because of his focus on work (Schultz & Yang, 1997). In another example, Gus Levy, a strong promoter of rigorous work, acknowledged the pressure and intense work expectations at Goldman. He credited his success in life to his very understanding wife (Cohan, 2012).

Lee Iacocca (1986) also credited his wife with facilitating good balance. He described working around the clock at Crysler. He said, "Thank God

I had a wife who understood me" (Iacocca, 2008, p. 182). Iacocca's wife understood when he had stressful times at work. In a similar way, Ricky Lauren, Ralph Lauren's wife, stayed home to manage the family affairs while supporting her husband's career. Trachtenberg (1988) claimed, "Ricky became accustomed to having [Ralph] come home near midnight; he would try to make it up to her on weekends" (p. 117).

Bill McDermott's (SAP) wife understood her husband's schedule. He explained, "Julie already understood my pace, having witnessed the time I put into other people. We both knew I would not be as successful, or as happy, without that same level of intensity" (McDermott, 2014, p. 115). Julie accepted her husband's rigorous schedule and stopped working herself to manage their family. McDermott had similar support for his work from his mother. Even when his mother lay on her deathbed, she encouraged McDermott to leave the hospital to deliver an important speech. His mother insisted he go, and when she could no longer speak, his family convinced McDermott to leave the hospital for work, stating that it was what his mother would want (McDermott, 2014). He took a few days off to be with family after her passing. He noted, "I did not stay away [from work] long, however, so as not to interrupt our momentum. Mom would have wanted me to get back to work" (McDermott, 2014, p. 278).

Men frequently positioned sacrificing time with their families as a necessary evil on the way to occupational success. They mostly described deep love and affection for their families and praised the women in their lives[3] for raising their children and withstanding long periods of isolation. Some of the men spoke wistfully about lost or strained relationships with their children, ex-wives, and parents. Most recognized the struggle of (and some experienced guilt from) putting their families' needs behind the needs of their companies. However, the executives did not oppose the widespread practice of family sacrifice. Rather than challenge the status quo, the men described their strategies for working within it and accepted the loss of family time as a price tag for their rise to power.

These examples point to one of the most consequential outcomes of the glass handcuffs phenomenon: keeping men out of the home and less engaged in care work responsibilities. The glass handcuffs not only keep men at work but also away from care work. The data presented here show a few versions of fatherhood, yet all of them, no matter how much they love their children, remain somewhat detached. The candor (and sometimes regret) the men expressed about their need to often sacrifice family time reveals that the expectation to sacrifice all other aspects of life except work is real. The men here mostly described this sacrifice as unavoidable, a necessary step in order to achieve career success.

These examples translate into a powerful discourse that suggests family is in opposition to, and not as important as, work. Because employed women continue to take on the lion's share of care work, discourses that de-prioritize family directly contribute to discrimination for all women (who managers may assume will have family responsibilities at some point, whether this is true or not) and fathers who might take time away from work for family.

DEDICATED EMPLOYEES SACRIFICE THEIR HEALTH

Family was not the only aspect of life the icons sacrificed. Many of the men shared examples of times they sacrificed their personal health for work. The most prevalent health risks for the executives were those related to stress and exhaustion. Many of the texts mentioned stress-related health problems as part and parcel of high-ranking jobs. Gus Levy (Goldman Sachs) suffered a stroke during a work meeting, which caused his early death (Cohan, 2012). In the management meeting after his death, Bob Munchin said to his team,

> There'll be time to discuss [Levy's] contributions at a later time. Right now, as he taught us so well, it's important that we all get on with our work and the job to be done today. That's what Gus would have wanted. (Cohan, 2012, p. 190)

Michael Bloomberg described how Levy's death had an impact his own expectations about working at Soloman Brothers:

> You thought of it as a job for life. You would work your way up, eventually become a partner, and die at a ripe old age in the middle of a business meeting (that's how both Cy Lewis and Gus Levy left this world). (Bloomberg & Winkler, 1997, p. 20)

The stories of men passing on in the middle of a work meeting were retold in many of the texts, always with an air of respectability, as if dying at work symbolized truly great commitment to the company. According to one story, Alan Mulally (Ford Motor Company) demoted Mark Schultz, then head of Ford's international operations. Schultz was angry and decided to retire. His wife thought it was a stroke of luck, considering both Schultz's grandfather and father both died of heart attacks before age 60 while working for Ford (Hoffman, 2012).

Hugh Hefner's health also suffered considerable during his life as head of Playboy Enterprises. Hefner had a "habit of working to the point of physical exhaustion" (Watts, 2009, p. 103). In order to put the magazine issues out, Hefner slept very little. In 1957, he found it difficult to continue working his exhausting schedule. A colleague recommended Dexedrine to keep Hefner alert. He quickly was able to say awake for 3 to 4 days at a time, without any sleep and with very little food (Watts, 2009). Hefner developed a serious addiction but needed the drugs to help him work around the clock. Ultimately, Hefner beat his addiction but still worked under immense stress. Investigations of drugs and deaths at the Playboy Mansion ultimately pushed him to the edge of stress and exhaustion, and he suffered a stroke in 1985 (Watts, 2009).

In another example, Paul Allen of Microsoft became seriously ill with Hodgkin's lymphoma and began to reduce the hours he put into Microsoft. Allen (2011) claimed,

> Instead of doing the sane thing and taking a leave, I went into the office a few afternoons a week, just to keep my hand in. That was the no-excuses Microsoft culture: relentless commitment to work. (p. 162)

That Allen would take some days off work went against the work ethic of Bill Gates and Microsoft. Although he was receiving radiation treatments at the time, Allen was criticized by his peers and employees for slacking off (Wallace & Erickson, 1992).

Some of the executives often acted quite casual about their health issues. For example, Lee Iacocca (Ford Motor Company and Chrysler) claimed, "I've seen a lot of men die only a few months after they retire. Sure, working can kill you. But so can not working" (Iacocca & Novak, 1986, p. 178). George W. Bush refused to leave Washington when intelligence suggested there was a direct threat to his safety. Instead, he wanted to stay and do his job for the American people. He explained: "If it was God's will that I die in the White House, I would accept it" (Bush, 2010, p. 159).

Neville Isdell of the Coca-Cola Company demonstrated a similar casual attitude toward his work-related health issues. He recounted a story of a time he conducted an interview while traveling:

> When I interviewed Joe for the job, I was in the Makati Medical Center, with a drip in my arm, weak and emaciated, having lost ten pounds from a bout with typhoid fever and a recurrence of the malaria I had as a child in Africa. I looked like a skeleton. Such was life on the road. Both before and after my recovery, King King, Tony, and I worked almost every weekend. (Isdell & Beasley, 2011, p. 74)

While some men might have taken time off for typhoid fever and malaria, Isdell continued to work at a frantic pace around the clock. Later, he admitted that work stress caused his elevated blood pressure, and that his wife "did not want [him] to take the chairman's job, worried that it would seriously damage [his] health" (Isdell & Beasley, 2011, p. 3). Pamela Isdell's fears were not unwarranted as her husband regularly risked his health for work.

Many executives experiences work-related health issues. Warren Buffet sometimes struggled with excruciating back pain, which was likely caused by work stress. Sometimes the pain left him bedridden for days (Schroeder, 2008). In a final and extreme example, Hoffman (2012) recounted a long, tense negotiation meeting with the Ford executives and the United Auto Workers: "At 3:20 Sunday morning, Ron Gettelfinger and Alan Mulally shook hands in Joe Layman's office. Joe Hinrichs, who had not even taken a nap since Thursday, found he could not stand up. He had to call for a driver to take him home" (pp. 234–235).

The examples presented thus far demonstrate negative health outcomes related to stress and exhaustion. However, the men also risked their health in other ways. For example, Ralph Lauren discovered he had a brain tumor that required immediate surgery but decided to delay the surgery. Trachtenberg (1988) described the situation:

> Why did he put off his operation? Because Ralph wanted to work on his fall 1987 collection. What he wanted to do was have his show in April and then take a vacation. Ralph thought he could have his operation in early April and be back at work so quickly nobody would notice. (p. 238)

Lauren's doctor allowed him to postpone the surgery, and Ralph finished the show before taking care of the tumor. In another example, Larry Ellison of Oracle shared a story about living through the 6.7 earthquake that hit Northridge, California, in 1994 from his hotel. While workers desperately attempted to clear the hotel for safety, Ellison refused to leave his room because he needed his sleep for an important work presentation the next morning (Symonds, 2013). Ellison believed the presentation was more important than his own safety during the earthquake.

Finally, some of the men profiled in this book talked about the threat of violence in boardrooms. Magee (2009) described multiple times when company men came into physical altercations over work-related decisions: "[Jeff] Immelt [from General Electric] and the GM [General Motors] executive almost came to physical blows at the meeting" (p. 25). Later, Jack Welch, former General Electric CEO said he would "get a gun out and shoot [Immelt] if he [didn't] make what he promised [earnings] in the future" (Magee, 2009, p. 146). The threat of physical violence is related to the deep passion that many of the men felt for their occupations. Tense business deals, firings, succession plans, and other negotiations sometimes pushed the executives to violence to protect their own occupational interests. Violence, of course, carries a risk to the participant's individual health.

Executive coups, surprise firings or restructuring, and impactful changes to employee projects, sometimes happened while employees were away from the office. These stories seem to warn that leaving one's post, even for a short time, might result in the loss of a job. Taken together, and these stories contribute to a macro discourse that leaving work is problematic.

When Paul Allen took time some days off to recover from the radiation treatments he received to treat his Hodgkin's lymphoma, he overheard Bill Gates and Steve Ballmer talking about him. Allen (2011) described the following:

> One evening in late December 1982, I heard Bill and Steve speaking heatedly in Bill's office and paused outside to listen in. It was easy to

get the gist of the conversation. They were bemoaning my recent lack of production and discussing how they might dilute my Microsoft equity by issuing options to themselves and other shareholders. Steve and Bill both formally apologized . . . Sometimes it seemed that Bill so utterly identified with Microsoft that he'd get confused about where the company left off and he began. I didn't feel quite the same way. (p. 168)

This moment was a turning point for Paul Allen and marked one reason why he left Microsoft. This example quite clearly shows that Microsoft was intolerant of leaves of absence, and Allen quit the organization he loved before he was officially pushed out.

Another telling example emerged from the Apple texts when Andy Hertzfeld, Jobs's friend and a software engineer on the Macintosh team, took an approved and supported leave of absence to recover from a near burnout after the push for the Macintosh roll out. Isaacson (2011) explained that while he was gone, Hertzfeld

learned that Jobs had given out bonuses of up to $50,000 to engineers on the Macintosh team. So he went to Jobs to ask for one. Jobs responded that [Hertzfeld's manager] had decided not to give the bonuses to people who were on leave. Hertzfeld later heard that the decision had actually been made by Jobs. (p. 190)

Jobs seemed to be disciplining Hertzfeld for taking a leave of absence. However, in later years, Jobs would take many medical leaves when fighting cancer, although he routinely worked during his leaves and continued to be very involved in the company. These, and other, stories in the popular texts make clear that organizational environments unsupportive of leave are a commonplace.

In 1999, Jon Corzine, the CEO of Goldman Sachs, was ousted, a victim of a coup which voted him out while he was away from the firm on vacation. Time away from work did not fit into the culture of Goldman Sachs. In 2010, a former vice president was fired for taking a maternity leave and asking to return to work part-time. Her lawsuit, however, was reported as if she had made a choice to off-ramp rather than explaining the elimination of her position after her leave (Cohan, 2012). In another example, Lee Iacocca was fired from the Ford Motor Company. Henry Ford first held a meeting while Iacocca was out of the country and took away funding for one of his projects. Iacocca returned to find himself out of a job (Iacocca & Novak, 1986). An executive at Oracle faced a similar power shift while on vacation. Larry Ellison decided he wanted to be the president of Oracle (taking the title back from Ray Lane). He called Lane while Lane was on vacation to tell him, likely an effort to avoid an uncomfortable face-to-face confrontation. Lane recalled reading the press release in the paper with his family on vacation, a move he called "totally below the belt" (Symonds, 2013, p. 137).

These examples reveal a different cause for the glass handcuffs: fear that one's rivals might make a move during an absence. The competition for power at the upper echelons of the organizations profiled made the threat of a coup quite real for many of the men. Losing money, position, or employment was a risk many of these men did not wish to take. They left only when absolutely necessary and often stayed connected while away.

Leaving work also made employees vulnerable. Bill McDermott of SAP recalled an experience from high school while he was managing a deli. His boss hired someone to run the deli short-term while McDermott went away for vacation with his family. Sadly, the replacement robbed the deli completely clean. All the stock, equipment, and anything else in the deli was gone, and, thus, McDermott was out of a job[4] (McDermott, 2014). Howard Schultz recounted how he missed one of the worst days in Starbucks's history while on vacation (his first in 10 years). Believing Starbucks was strong enough to leave for a short time, Schultz finally took a vacation he had been promising his wife for years. However, on the third day of his vacation, he received an urgent call that a freeze in Brazil sent coffee-bean prices skyrocketing. Schultz immediately returned to Starbucks and spent the next 2 years recovering from the problems that occurred while he was gone (Schultz & Yang, 1997). While Schultz's vacation did not cause the freeze in Brazil, his confidence that Starbucks would be fine in his absence proved wrong.

Collectively, the examples presented in this section serve as a warning to men thinking about taking time away from work. The experiences of these iconic men demonstrate that job loss or other disaster can happen to anyone who is not present to defend his position or company. This logic also contributes to the glass handcuffs because it reminds men that they should not leave their work for extended periods.

MACRO DISCOURSES AND THE GLASS HANDCUFFS

In summary, the profiles of iconic business and world figures serve as a context from which individual workers make sense of their everyday work–life practices. The popular texts analyzed here revealed important macro discourses that provide data for how decisions and policies about leaves of absence are settled, including (a) good workers are passionate, (b) success requires excessive work hours, (c) dedicated employees sacrifice time with their families, (d) dedicated employees also sacrifice their health, and (e) negative events, such as executive coups, occur when employees are out of the office. Each of these macro discourses directly contribute to the glass handcuffs, and serve to keep men locked into work.

Individual men thinking about how to act in organizations draw upon these macro discourses to justify why they do not leave work. The expectations of business leaders inform middle-level managers about what it takes to succeed at work. Managers purport this information and evaluate employees based on their ability to live up to the expectations. Often, the expectations of executives drive entire organizational cultures so that all employees are expected to conform to individual executive's practices. As Charles Koch of Koch Industries, Inc. explained, "Because we want Koch Industries to succeed over the long term, we cannot afford to select or retain individual whose core values are inconsistent with our MBM Guiding Principles" (Koch, 2007, p. 89). Executives hire and promote employees who meet and exceed their personal expectations. Mission statements and job roles conform to executive practices. Furthermore, when companies compete with each other, the "best-of-breed" practices (Lafley & Martin, 2013) span occupations and industries, and are often written in strategy books meant to guide the individual actions of all employees in a field. Thus, macro discourses are a central cause to the glass handcuff phenomenon because they instruct men—explicitly through strategy guides and training and implicitly through stories and role modeling—to forgo time away from work.

NOTES

1. See Appendix B for a full list of the individuals and firms profiled, as well as the methodology for collecting these data.
2. "Drinking the Kool-Aid" is a phrase which refers to the 1978 mass suicide by members of a religious group. Jim Jones, the leader, commanded the members to drink Kool-Aid laced with cyanide. Currently, the phrase indicates complete and total dedication to a leader or a group.
3. None of the men profiled described a same-sex family arrangement, and the very deliberate use of the term *wife* reflects the executive's typically traditional conformation to the male-breadwinner, female-homemaker family model.
4. He later went on to purchase and revive the deli (McDermott, 2014).

REFERENCES

Allen, P. (2011). *Idea man: A memoir by the cofounder of Microsoft*. New York, NY: Portfolio/Penguin.

Ashcraft, K. L., & Mumby, D. K. (2004). *Reworking gender: A feminist communicology of organization*. Thousand Oaks, CA: Sage.

Beahm, G. (Ed.). (2012). *The boy billionaire: Mark Zuckerberg in his own words*. Evanston, IL: Agate Publishing.

Bloomberg, M., & Winkler, M. (1997). *Bloomberg by Bloomberg*. New York, NY: Wiley.

Brandt, R. (2011). *One click: Jeff Bezos and the rise of Amazon.com*. New York, NY: Portfolio/Penguin.

Bush, G. W. (2010). *Decision points*. New York, NY: Random House.

Capodagli, B., & Jackson, L. (1999). *The Disney way: Harnessing the management secrets of Disney in your company*. New York, NY: McGraw-Hill.

Cohan, W. D. (2012). *Money and power: How Goldman Sachs came to rule the world*. New York, NY: Random House.

Crisafulli, P. (2009). *The house of Dimon: How JPMorgan's Jamie Dimon rose to the top of the financial world*. Hoboken, NJ: Wiley.

Dell, M., & Fredman, C. (1999). *Direct from Dell: Strategies that revolutionized an industry*. Harper Business.

Hoffman, B. G. (2012). *American icon: Alan Mulally and the fight to save Ford Motor Company*. New York, NY: Random House.

Iacocca, L., & Novak, W. (1986). *Iacocca: An autobiography*. New York, NY: Random House.

Isaacson, W. (2011). *Steve Jobs*. New York, NY: Simon & Schuster.

Isdell, N., & Beasley, D. (2011). *Inside Coca-Cola: A CEO's life story of building the world's most popular brand*. New York, NY: Macmillan.

Koch, C. G. (2007). *The science of success: How market-based management built the world's largest private company*. New York, NY: John Wiley & Sons.

Lafley, A. G., & Martin, R. L. (2013). *Playing to win: How strategy really works*. Boston, MA: Harvard Business Press.

Liveris, A. (2011). *Make it in America, updated edition: The case for re-inventing the economy*. Hoboken, NJ: Wiley.

Lowe, J. (1998). *Bill Gates speaks: Insight from the world's greatest entrepreneur*. Hoboken, NJ: Wiley.

Lowe, J. (2009). *Google speaks: Secrets of the world's greatest billionaire entrepreneurs, Sergey Brin and Larry Page*. Hoboken, NJ: Wiley.

Magee, D. (2009). *Jeff Immelt and the new GE way: Innovation, transformation and winning in the 21st century*. New York, NY: McGraw-Hill Professional.

Maxwell, F. (2002). *Bad boy Ballmer: The man who rules Microsoft*. New York, NY: William Morrow.

McDermott, B. (2014). *Winners dream: A journey from corner store to corner office*. New York, NY: Simon and Schuster.

Murray, A. (2010). *The Wall Street Journal essential guide to management: Lasting lessons from the best leadership minds of our time*. New York, NY: HarperCollins.

Rosen, A. S. (2011). *Change.edu: Rebooting for the new talent economy*. New York, NY: Kaplan.

Schroeder, A. (2008). *The snowball: Warren Buffett and the business of life*. New York, NY: Random House.

Schultz, H., & Yang, D. J. (1997). *Pour your heart into it: How Starbucks built a company one cup at a time*. New York, NY: Hyperion.

Sculley, J., & Byrne, J. A. (1987). *Odyssey: Pepsi to Apple: A journey of adventure, ideas, and the future*. New York, NY: Harper & Row Publishers.

Symonds, M. (2013). *Softwar: An intimate portrait of Larry Ellison and Oracle*. New York, NY: Simon and Schuster.

Trachtenberg, J. A. (1988). *Ralph Lauren: The man behind the mystique*. New York, NY: Little, Brown.

Trump, D. J., & Schwartz, T. (2009). *Trump: The art of the deal*. New York, NY: Random House.

Wallace, J., & Erickson, J. (1992). *Hard drive: Bill Gates and the making of the Microsoft empire*. New York, NY: Harper Business.

Waters, J. K. (2002). *John Chambers and the CISCO way: Navigating through volatility*. Hoboken, NJ: Wiley.

Watts, S. (2009). *Mr. Playboy: Hugh Hefner and the American dream*. Hoboken, NJ: Wiley.

6 "But I Was a Programmer before I Was a Dad"
Occupational Uniqueness and Occupational Identity

We live in a culture of America where you are defined by your job. Now that can change. It changed for me that I'm defined, in part, also by my family now, but still I drive my identity, or a lot of my value, by the work that I do. When I was younger and I was unemployed for a while, I felt worthless . . . I felt depressed because I was raised to work . . . It is me, and I was lost without it.

—Christopher, technical engineer

In the United States, occupational identities are important markers for individuals. It is customary to ask others the question, "What do you do?" by way of introduction, because of an emphasis placed on the importance of work. Workers develop occupational selves very early in their careers, often during training or socialization through specific languages, meanings, skills, and values (Kuhn et al., 2008). As one interviewee explained,

[My job is] my identifier. It's who I am, you know? For a guy it's like what do you build? If you say, "Oh, I'm an IT guy," "I'm a finance guy," "I'm a this or that," if you ask them what do you do, who comes up and says, "I'm a father?" And that should be your first 'cause that's the most important job you can do in this world. "What do you do?" "Well, I'm a father." "No, no. What do you do for work?" "Oh, for work, oh that, I do this," but men will identify more because it's really who we present ourselves as. It's who we want the world to see us as. Whether we're a dump truck driver or CEO of a company it's definitely what we are, and so it's very important.

Occupational identities create coherent narratives which unify individuals in particular occupations (Larson & Olson, 2008). The men in this study drew upon their occupational identities to explain why they could or could not take time away from work, and claimed their occupations dictated work–life "balance" options. They did this in two primary ways. First, the men spoke about their *individual occupational identities*, and second, they talked about *occupational uniqueness*. They believed their individual identities as workers in a particular occupation precluded them from taking too much time off from work, because they possessed specialized skills or because they wanted to protect their occupational reputation. They drew out occupational uniqueness to justify their work–life "decisions" by claiming their occupations required unique time commitments, or required unique scheduling consideration.

Almost every participant in this study made occupational arguments and mostly claimed their occupations were unique and somehow different from other occupations in the barriers to taking leaves of absence. Most of the men believed work–life was possible but perceived their own occupations as having unique constraints from other occupations. It is ironic that men from multiple different occupations claimed this; clearly, the sentiment is not unique to each occupation but, rather, a discursive move that all the men in this study made. When looking across occupations in this way, overcoming individual occupational obstacles is less relevant than the institutional impacts of an entire workforce that believes there are special and unique reasons as to why work–life policies simply cannot work.

In this chapter, I first provide some framing comments about occupational identity and occupational discourse. Next, I share some examples of the ways in which the men in this study talked about their individual occupational identities and their perceived uniqueness of their occupations. The chapter closes with an analysis about why this matters and what it means when half of the U.S. workforce believes they cannot leave work.

OCCUPATIONAL IDENTITIES

People make sense of others and themselves by placing people in particular occupational categories. As each occupation carries specific expectations and stereotypes, gleaning occupational information about others seems like a simplistic way to understand what kind of person one has met. Macro-occupational discourses educate people about what kind of person should work in a particular occupation, how work should be accomplished, how workers should act and behave, how workers should feel and what they should value, where power exists, how much pride they should feel about their occupations in relation to others, and so on (Cohn, 2000; Tracy, Myers, & Scott, 2006). Occupational discourses are so prescriptive that one can imagine what it would be like to have several different occupations. When children play "school," they know the teacher has power over the students and the principal has power over the teacher. They know that teachers are generally nice and soft-spoken and that they can get justifiably angry toward unruly kids. Individuals draw on these available occupational discourses to make sense of their work lives and to constitute their personal identities, and select (consciously or otherwise) their occupational identities from the available predetermined occupational discourses.

In this way, occupational identity is an ongoing discursive exercise that cuts across time and space, institutions, and individuals, in response to necessity, desire, and material concerns (Ashcraft, 2007). Occupational discourses are "master-narratives" (Larson & Olson, 2008, p. 25), which interact with the competing, multiple, fragmented, fluid, and local micro narratives that make up individual identities. Identity construction is the constant effort to negotiate competing discourses, including occupational discourses. However, individual agency is not as influential as the strong discursive constructions that guide occupational cultures. As workers engage in accepted occupational moves, they continually reify occupational identities for themselves and others (Erickson, 2008). Although master occupational discourses dictate the parameters for the ideal-type worker in each occupation, counternarratives are possible within the occupational space (Hiestand & Buzzanell, 2007) and frequently become part of the occupational identity. For example, the McShit movement sold millions of T-shirts to disgruntled McDonalds workers to wear under their uniforms in protest of the intense emotion labor required in their jobs. Thus, the "disgruntled but smiling" worker emerged as an available identity for some workers.

Of course, this basic understanding of occupational identity overlooks some significant issues with the ways occupations and occupational discourses form. Occupations always emerge in historical contexts that developed around particular groups of workers. As such, occupations are political, constructed, and articulated in inequitable terms. However, occupations frequently become so regimented that people rarely stop to question the historical conditions upon which occupational assumptions stand (Ashcraft, 2005a, 2005b, 2007; Greene, Ackers, and Black, 2002). Because most occupations developed for white, hetero-partnered, able-bodied men, considering how they might otherwise unfold is necessary. For example, Cohn's (2000) work about men's opposition to women's equality in the military (aptly titled "How can she claim equal rights when she can't do as many push-ups?") shows how deeply ingrained occupational and organizational identities are structurally gendered and dependent on assumptions of social categories. In her analysis of equal standards, Cohn revealed the constructed and arbitrary nature of which standards are used to measure competence in the military. Cohn noted,

> Since upper body strength and running speed are areas where most women will not be as strong as most men, they become the standard for proving [equality]. You do not hear, 'How can they ask for equal rights when they can't fly, or drive a tank, or lead, or do the job competently?" because women can. (2000, p. 138)

However, arguments about equality in the military largely focus around women's ability to compete with men in physical performance standards, such as push-ups.

Ashcraft's (2005a, 2005b, 2007) ongoing work with male commercial airline pilots is another example of this historical occupational development. Through her work, Ashcraft revealed the explicit and purposeful gendering of pilots. She traced how gender, race, class, and sexuality worked together to organize the airline pilot's professional identity. The aviation industry strategically worked to establish commercial flying as an activity for a privileged few and worked to establish a hierarchy of labor that limited occupational membership to all but a select few. While pilots were originally daring ladybirds on display to prove that flying was safe, the industry ultimately changed the public persona of pilot to a dependable male commanding officer. Heavy occupational discourses of becoming "the man" and "working up through the ranks" helped to naturalize occupational identities in aviation so that the historical *construction* of pilot as patriarch is not visible. Cohn's and Ashcraft's examples illustrate how occupations develop historically and often intentionally for *particular kinds of workers*, which makes possible the development of occupational ideal types.

The crux of the problem for modern U.S. workers is that not all employees in particular occupations conform to the historically developed ideal type. This disjuncture makes possible discrimination, hostile work environments, inequitable policies, and a host of other issues that frequently result in oppression, discrimination, and general lack of equality at work. Rigid occupational discourses do not typically allow for intersections of other identity markers such as race, class, gender, and ability, which inherently create different identities. These intersections create vastly different lived experiences within occupations and can create multiple, competing identities within an occupational category. Recognizing where some of these intersections incite inequality is an important goal in understanding occupational equality. Of particular interest in this study, the historical purposeful and political gendering of occupations influences how individual workers understand and act in relation to leave and other work–life policies.

INDIVIDUAL OCCUPATIONAL IDENTITIES

The first way the men in this study explained their difficulty in taking time away from work was by expressing their individual occupational identity uniqueness. They did this in three primary ways. First, the men shared their perception that people in their occupations were a "special breed,"[1] were "destined" for their occupation, or otherwise had a "natural" talent for their particular occupation. A second way they spoke about occupational identity was their perception that they possessed specialized skills that precluded them from taking time away from work. These two justifications, destiny and specialized skills, mostly came from knowledge workers. The third theme that emerged about individual occupational identity was about individual occupational reputation or the value of one's "word." This theme emerged primarily from workers who did not perceive themselves as irreplaceable but rather considered their occupational identities as emergent from hard work, honesty, and loyalty. Men from a variety of occupations talked about reputation, but nearly all the men from working-class jobs made these kinds of arguments when describing how their occupational identities precluded them from taking too much time away from work. Each of these rationales contributes to men's propensity to feel a strong dedication to their work.

Occupational "Types"

Many workers believed their occupations drew in a specific "type" of person. Workers described being a specific personality type, a certain kind of mind, or loving their work passionately or obsessively. Put simply, the data revealed that some people believed in occupational destiny and that there is an inherent, possibly biological, explanation for people who excel in some careers as compared to those who do not. For example, technical worker Adam explained: "The industry draws people of a certain personality or certain personalities that tend to forgo work–life balance." Shawn, an engineer, made a similar argument. He claimed, "There really are very distinct types of people that go into different fields of engineering. And that's because it requires a different approach to thinking and a different perspective on the way that we see things around us." Similarly, Jeff, an engineer, explained, "We are a very unique breed. You're going to find there's a personality factor that some of *us* have and some of *you* don't."

Knowledge workers in particular, discussed particular "types" of people throughout the data. In many cases, the assumed naturalness of a "detail-oriented" mind, a "creative brain," a "natural inclination for management," a "technical mind," or a "particular personality profile" remained unchallenged assumptions in much of the talk. For example, a small-business owner explained, "Some people are born for this kind of leadership," while Pat, an accountant, explained, "You have to have a financial type mind to be successful in this kind of work. It requires a certain attention to details, commitment to deadlines, and a thoughtful approach to finding errors and remembering specifics." In another example, one interviewee explained the natural occurrence of a technical type:

> There are certain people born for this kind of work. It isn't for everyone. [Either] you are born with a technical mind or you aren't. [Either] you are born to tinker and fix things, or you might be born to be a banker. Not everyone can do what I do. We all have our given strengths and weaknesses. I was lucky that I was born with an aptitude for this kind of work and that I like it.

This interviewee explained the need for a "natural aptitude" throughout his interview, and suggested that technical prowess was a "given strength" for some people, but not for others.

Men working manual labor jobs also made arguments about the unique nature of their occupational identities. For example, Tom, a ditch digger, explained:

> When I got out of the service, I started applying at all the big companies around the city. Since I didn't have a college degree, I was looking more at the labor careers. Most of the guys are in a similar boat. We knew what kind of jobs we could get.

Tom saw a wide divide between college-educated men and men without college educations and viewed these groups as different "types" of men who took up different occupations. He explained later:

> It is hard. Hard physical labor. It is getting better now because we've got a lot more equipment, technology, but most of the years it was throwing around a 100 lb. jackhammer, digging holes by hand . . . it is not work just everybody can do day in day out. Not everyone can take it. You had to get peace in your mind and keep your body from falling apart.

For Tom, not all men could numb their minds to find peace with the intense pain and monotony associated with digging ditches. Tripp, a driver, also believed that his occupation required a distinctive personality type. He explained, "I was born for the road. I get too jumpy if I'm in one place too long. Not everyone is like that, so it's a good job for me."

Jake, a law enforcement officer, drew a similar argument. He shared the following:

> If you're, you're working in a law enforcement job . . . the kinds of things that you have to deal with . . . the things that you have to witness . . . you have to be, um more or less immune to on the job, um causes you to be a very different person than the rest of the world. Um a lot of people, a lot of uh normal, other people judge us. We see crazy shit and, and then go pretend to be a normal human being, just like everybody else. Like, just like uh John Q that just works in an office.

This officer perceived law enforcement officers as unique "types" of people who are different from "normal human beings."

In a final example, Ryder, a driver/liquor deliverer, believed he was uniquely suited for his work:

> I mean it's hard work, you're basically moving anywhere from, you know, 200 to 500 cases a day and you have anywhere from 20 . . . to

38 stops every day. So you have to be a hard worker, you have to be self-motivated, and you have to be in pretty good shape. It's not for everyone, that's for sure.

For Ryder, the very physical demands of his job precluded many men from finding success in liquor distribution. The idea that occupations require special kinds of people to perform the work contributes to a second theme the data revealed about personal occupational identity: Individuals have specialized skills that make their absence at work problematic or impossible.

Specialized Skills

Another way the men interviewed for this study claimed that their occupations prevented them from taking leaves of absence was to reference the specialized skills required for their work. Because many jobs require highly specialized and inimitable skills, the men believed it would be difficult to replace them at work. Computer engineer Jarvis explained, "You kind of get into this position as an engineer where you specialize, specialize, specialize, specialize and now all of a sudden you're trapped." Jarvis described men who took leaves of absence "confident" because he perceived that these men risked their jobs by taking the time away from work. A mechanical engineer, A.J., provided an analogy to describe the burden of taking a leave of absence from technical work:

> Think of engineering like a sports team. You've got a star football player or a star basketball player and they got out for an injury. Now one minute they're Super Bowl prospects, and the next thing you know, you don't even know if they're going to go to the playoffs.

That the absence of one person could have an impact on the success of the entire team, project, or company was evident throughout many of the interviews. When asked what skills he would look for in a person he would hire to replace him, Ben, a construction worker, answered, "Someone to replace me? Gosh I don't know if you could." Ben explained that his specific and varied skills could not be quickly or easily replaced. In a similar way, Joel said,

> Of course, it's impossible for me to leave, because, you know, if I'm gone, the business doesn't run. If I'm not there, it just doesn't run. It's like if the head coach isn't there, his team doesn't get coached by him.

Interviewees used these kinds of analogies to justify how their skills were necessary for the success of their workplaces. Seth, an environmental tester, explained, "You have specific licenses, so not everybody can do it. I got 4–5 weeks of vacation, but you can't take it all at once. You are lucky if you get a week in a row 'cause they might need me personally, and nobody else can cover."

Having an impact on the team members by forcing them to cover individually specific job tasks concerned many of the men. Trevor, a member of the Coast Guard, explained:

> It kinda depends on . . . what do you bring to the unit, more or less. Like if I leave for a week, and I'm the only one who can do my job, how many other people am I screwing over when I leave kinda thing. If it's nobody, then it's a little different. If it's when you leave there's a lot of people that get screwed over because of it, then there's a little more backlash. So um it just depends on your skills and what you bring to the table for the team. Um for me um, I know uh, I've gotten negative backlash for [taking longer leaves].

Many of the men making arguments about their specialized skills worried about how their absence would have an impact on their coworkers, their managers, employees, clients, or the success of particular projects. In another example, Oliver explained how difficult it was to replace technical workers during their temporary leaves:

> I've been here when people have taken leave and it's hard. There's no way around it. You can't hire someone new for that time. It's just impractical in those scenarios, because the training takes too long for someone [to complete], and so other people are left to pick up the slack.

Oliver's notion that many workers cannot be replaced during their leaves of absence was also described by Doug, who explained, "Right now in my company, if any of us on the team take a week off . . . it does slow us down, and speed is by far the biggest advantage in a startup . . . We have complementary skills." In this case, Doug perceived the extended absence of a team member, each with a unique skill set, as an impediment to the company's success.

Not all men believed their skills were completely unique. Noah, a nonprofit worker, explained:

> I think that it is entirely possible to take a leave of absence from my work, to trust my supervisor and my coworkers to either absorb my workload themselves or to bring somebody on a temporary basis to get them through the period when I was on leave. Having said that, I know many people that worked in nonprofits and have moved on, who have said it wasn't possible to take a leave of absence—that nobody could do their work for them. And I think it's self-imposed, that barrier. And say it's not possible, my work is too important—but I don't think it's true (laughing). . . . Everybody's replaceable.

In a similar way, Ken, an accountant, explained, "People think their presence is mandatory, but most of us can be replaced." Even though they disagreed with the truth of the "not replaceable" discourse, both Noah and Ken pointed to the popular notion that individuals—particularly those who perceive themselves to be unique from other workers because of their passion, their "type," or their skills—were not easily replaceable.

Reputation

A final way the men in this study drew on their *individual* occupational identities to describe how and why they chose to forgo leaves of absence and other kinds of work–life policies was the protection of their occupational reputations. Describing the importance of their "word," work ethic, trust, and integrity, many men believed they spent years building a good occupational reputation and would not want to risk their reputations by taking too much time away from work. Vincent, an accountant, explained: "The most important characteristic is integrity. Without integrity, in our role, you've got nothing because you lose the confidence of your clients if you don't have that." Vincent mentioned integrity and keeping his word throughout his interview and believed that his personal reputation was the reason for his career success.

In another example, Miguel described the most important characteristic for a coach: "People need to be reliable. If they say they are going to do something, they do it. You can't do that when you're gone." Miguel believed that his coworkers and players would question his reliability if he were to take a leave of absence during recruiting or the season. Tyler, a CEO in manufacturing, described his public persona as an important consideration for his occupation: "You have a social responsibility, if you will, that at times can be a little bit tough because you are always in the eye of the public. It can make it tough to live your life." Tyler believed that the public perception of his integrity and intent was a vitally important component in his ability to retain his position. In a final example, Pat the accountant described his view that leaves of absence could interfere with a successfully built reputation:

> I think successful performance in your job breeds more responsibility . . . you're promoted and you can find yourself on a career path that's moving upward, but it's very contingent upon being able to handle the new tasks that are given to you and completing your job responsibilities in a timely fashion successfully, and if you take a leave of absence, it has a different connotation from taking a vacation. If I take a vacation, I've earned it, it's my break. If I take a leave of absence? It's just that my workload is too much for me. At least that's how I would consider it. I could see how that could quickly derail you from your career path. It could ruin your reputation and really hamper future success.

Potentially ruining one's reputation was a risk too great to take for many men.

While men from a variety of occupations discussed integrity and reputation as a reason to avoid leaves of absence, all of the men from working class jobs used this argument to explain their work–life "choices." Sam, an energy worker, astutely explained this phenomenon. He shared, "In this kind of work, your word and your reputation are all you have." In a similar way, Max, a courier, explained, "You could train a monkey to do what I do—It's basically just driving a car. But I worked my way up so they trust me. I wouldn't want to ruin that." For Max, building up trust resulted in him getting more commissions than other independent courier, and had an impact on his bottom line.

THE UNIQUENESS OF *EVERY* OCCUPATION COMPLICATES WORK–LIFE

The second way men linked their work–life practices with their occupations was through casting their occupations as unique from other kinds of work in ways that precluded them from being able to take leaves of absence. However, when linked together in a data set, the actual uniqueness of each occupation seems precarious. Nearly every interviewee claimed occupational uniqueness in some way. For example, one owner of a family business explained:

> Family business can be very challenging on a personal level. Much different than other jobs . . . it is up to you to create boundaries, but I didn't know how to do that. For the times I wasn't conscious of that, I really struggled. I can see how my brothers also struggle with that.

In this example, the business owner characterized family businesses as a type of occupational position that is different from other kinds of work.

In another example, Coast Guard member Trevor explained how military occupations are different from civilian jobs:

> Some civilian jobs you get a certain amount of sick days . . . we don't. So if you were to, you know, get sick and needed to take off from work . . . uh, depending on your uh unit and the uh command uh philosophy and their kinda way they deal with their subordinates, [but you] can't just call in one day and be like "hey I'm sick I'm not coming in." (laughing) . . . the coast guard's a very small organization . . . we don't have many people to spare . . . So um, so when I leave, like if me or someone else of the unit leaves, when they leave since we are such a minimally manned unit um people will have to pick up that slack, it's noticeable. It's not just kind of a dead body that like ah whatever you know if he leaves it's not a big deal. People feel it . . . So that's why you do kinda get that negative backlash.

In this example, Trevor believed the unique size of the Coast Guard, coupled with the militaristic constraints of his occupation, made it quite different from civilian occupations and different from other branches of the military.

Men from many occupations made these kinds of uniqueness arguments. Jake, a law enforcement officer, shared the following:

> If you're not in the law enforcement profession, a lot of people can kinda, they view cops in this kind of negative connotation, where you know "oh well, you know, they're assholes" . . . but they don't realize what they actually have to do. What kind of stuff they see every day. We, you know, you see the worst of humanity every day, virtually.

For Jake, the extreme scenes of violence he witnessed everyday was different from and unimaginable for people in other occupations. He believed this made it hard for men in his occupation to balance work and other areas of life. He explained:

> You see this really, really big spike, and uh you know shattered families and uh divorces within law enforcement. Uh I know the annual for uh, for divorces in general is the base line is fifty percent. If you go specifically into the law enforcement side you're looking at more like seventy, eighty-five percent divorce rate in law enforcement . . . it's just because of that job. The specific things that you have to deal with and stuff and then you bring it home with you, and then it causes all kinds of issues. So the biggest thing, especially with law enforcement is kinda maintaining that balance. And so with other jobs it may be a little easier, it may be a little more difficult, but again it depends on that specific job that you're working in.

Jake found law enforcement to have a unique occupational nature that influenced the ways that he could accomplish work and life.

In another context, Tom, a ditch digger, explained how the union determined the work–life options for his occupation:

> Because I'm union, I get a generous sick and vacation package. It is standard. So many people are going away; they are trying to change it. It depends on the number of years you've been with the union. It is all written out.

He explained that in order to work, he must belong to the union, and that the powerful union made clear decisions about the policies that affected his work and time. Tom did not feel much agency in regards to leaves of absence because the unique influence of the union determined how, when, and how much he could spend away from work. In a final example, Antonio also drew on occupational uniqueness to explain why he could not easily take a leave of absence from work, and described how occupational related stress made him feel that taking a leave of absence was difficult in his research job. He shared the following:

> We're all really stressed out here because it is research oriented. It seems like we have way too much workload. So, when one person is gone, it just kind of trickles down, it has to get done. Um. And I think that's a big factor, and a reason why they would frown against [taking a leave] here.

As the previous examples illustrate, the men in this study claimed that their occupations had unique conditions that determined whether they could take a leave of absence. Certainly, while occupations do have unique qualities that makes work distinct, the overarching theme that these examples demonstrate is a consistent justification for why men feel handcuffed to their work. These general comments linking occupation and work–life options spanned the interviews. However, the interviewees also drew explicitly on two specific patterns to explain how the uniqueness of their occupations had an impact on their work–life practices: (a) claiming their occupations had a unique requirement for hours worked and (b) citing unique scheduling issues that made leaving difficult or impossible.

Unique Commitment of Hours

Many of the men in this study talked about the unique extreme face time requirements of their occupations. In response to my recruitment e-mail gathering participants for this study of work–life balance, one college professor replied simply, "100% work; 0% home, no time for an interview." Clearly, this potential interviewee did not have time even to give an interview. Reports of an excessive time commitment came from many men across occupations. For example, Richard, an information technology (IT) executive, explained:

> I personally worked generally twelve hours a day. [It is] very exceptional [for me] to not work at least 60 hours a week. In fact, one time I put the whole organization on mandatory 12 hours a day, 6 days a week because they weren't exerting a sufficient effort from my observation. Well, they come back and said, "We just can't do 6 twelves. Can we leave Saturday at noon?" So I said sure. We in management had to back off to only getting 66 hours a week out of them.
>   During the [decades of] the sixties and seventies, the company expected you basically to be at work when[ever] the rest of the organization was, and for not doing that, it was basically almost viewed as insubordination and reason for termination. So, in our cases, people really worked hard. We put in a lot time. Personally, when I was on the

technical side, we pulled a lot of 24-hour turns. We would have some cots set up in the lab and basically [we would] take 2-hour power naps and we'd work around the clock trying to get the project done.

I'd say things started changing around the mid-'80s. There was some major shift going on that people just wouldn't sign up, [that] they wouldn't do that anymore. But back in the '60s and '70s there was an understanding that [employees would do] whatever it took to get the job done.

Richard noted that he personally maintained the high work ethic throughout his career, even as employees began to push back against working so many hours.

Technical occupations, in particular, seem to inspire excessive hours. Phillip, a computer programmer, explained that maximum hours are sometimes required. He said, "If a site needs to launch then that definitely could be an 80 hour work week. So it just depends . . . we all sort of worked off the clock a lot." Similarly, Christopher, a computer engineer who described long shifts and little sleep, also spoke about working around the clock or "off the clock":

Once, I had to be gone for over a month. I got 12 hours of sleep every 4 days . . . When I travel, it's different. When I travel, I work until the job gets done. There have been times where I've been on a specific trip and in 4 days, I'll get 12 hours' worth of sleep. But those are rare, [and] I do get paid for every hour that I work, up to a cap.

Working beyond the "cap" would qualify as unusual, because such caps are frequently set beyond 16-hour days by management. Quentin, an IT consultant, also mentioned a 16-hour expectation. He claimed, "If you're working 16 hour days for a few days straight, that's to be expected."

The notion that 16-hour days could be normal, expected, or natural indicates that the extreme time requirements make many employees feel that they must work most of the time. Computer scientist Michael exemplified this ideology and admitted, "In the past five years, I've taken one day off sick. I've got like 500 hours of sick leave saved up." Most participants in this study proclaimed that they were reluctant to use their personal time because they understood expectations to perform around the clock. This expectation for long hours and extreme commitment is evident in one technical marketing director's description of how he worked through the birth of his children:

I had two babies in the last two years and so, I'll be honest, I did work in the hospital. I mean, they had Wi-Fi both times, so I was on my laptop, you know, up until like an hour before [the delivery] and then after.

These technical workers' expectations of long work hours were used to describe how technical work is unique from other occupations and that this factor of mitigates workers' potential to easily take leaves of absence.

However, men from other occupations also drew on the discourse of excessive hour requirements to describe their occupations. For example, Rhett, an architect, shared his experience managing time expectations during periods of layoffs:

> People with families started getting laid off first. They can't stay late. In architecture, the field changed rapidly with the onset of computers and technology. I saw the tail end of that change, and I'm not sure how that changed the whole field. You can work all the time and that is expected now, when it wasn't before. So people who can't work all the time were the first to go. With day care and having to pick up your kids by 5 or 6 o'clock, when some people stay until 7. They maybe got there at 9 and they didn't see that I was there at 7. They just see me "leaving early." My advice now would be to start late and leave late.

Rhett's experience working with face-time expectations and assumptions of 60- to 70-hour weeks resulted in additional stress which he thought would be absent in other occupations. He perceived these expectations as particular to architecture.

In a similar example, Coast Guard member Trevor described the excessive time commitment required for his job:

> You know you could be working depending on your, your shift work and stuff like that and um depending on the case and stuff you're working on you could be working twenty-four hours straight. You know, forty-eight hours straight you know at the same time you maybe get an hour or two nap in between that's it. So it just depends on what kind of operation you're involved in, um what kind of hand you have in it, but um again the hours are pretty, pretty rough.

Trevor characterized his experience working long stretches of time as unique to the coast guard. However, Brent, a government worker, expressed that most "people in the higher levels of government . . . work a lot of hours," and Remy, a dealer at casino, shared, "At the executive management level, they will tell you they care about work–life, but they really want you to spend as much time as possible at work."

Stanley, a graduate student, explained: "Time is constantly an issue, time and exhaustion. When I finally do have time for something besides work, I'm too tired to do something and then otherwise I don't have time." Stanley mentioned excessive hours many times during his interview. Another graduate student shared Stanley's opinion. He claimed, "There's a big thing in academia where there's no such thing as downtime or off time, so you're never off from work . . . like weekends don't mean anything. It being Friday night doesn't mean anything." In a final example, Regge explained, "I'll work 20 hours a day . . . I woke up at 4:30 this morning and started typing notes as to what I needed to do for the day, so to take a day off seems far-fetched right now." As these examples illustrate, men from a variety of occupations believed their excessive time commitments were part of the occupations in which they worked.

In a similar way, Chip, a real estate consultant, described the never-ending supply of work in real estate, which gives the perception that hours are continual and endless in the industry:

> Well, real estate is tough, and that's kind of one of the things I see often with realtors—that real estate is never-ending. I mean you can always be doing something more . . . Pretty much most of the people I know in the industry just are always, "Should I be following up with this person?" "Should I be reaching out to these people?" And there's always more and more and more, and you can always be picking up more and more clients.

Chip perceived real estate as unique in the way work could be continually demanded with no perceived end.

As these examples illustrate, although many men believed their occupations demanded unique hour expectations, the uniqueness of excessive time expectations was actually *not* a unique characteristic of the men's occupations, but rather quite common among many occupations. Therefore, the assumption that excessive time commitments are occupationally specific is problematic. Instead, the widespread expectation that men, in particular, work excessive hours crosses occupational lines and more accurately describes work expectations for most men.

Unique Scheduling Constraints

Many of the men interviewed for this study explained work–life constraints as dependent upon unique occupational scheduling issues. Many spoke specifically about project-based work. For example, Shawn, an engineer, described project-based work as incompatible with leaves of absence and explained, "The nature of the work because projects are so performance- and schedule-driven—makes it such that leaves of absence in the midst of the project are very difficult to take." The project-based nature of his work lead Shawn to believe that it was the particular structure of his work that made taking a leave of absence difficult. Shawn later elaborated that jobs that were not based on projects might be more flexible. In a similar move, A.J. a mechanical engineer, explained:

> We have to work, work, work, because . . . once a project is done, if there's not any work . . . they'll just lay you off until they want to hire

you back [when they get more work]. So, during that work, work, work hard period, if you want to take a leave of absence, it's like, "Oh, see you later, you're out of here!"

There's also the idea among men that [you've] got to work—come hell or high water—because all these projects are time oriented and quality oriented. In this field, to be successful, you've got to put in the time, the hours, the thought, the energy . . . [many] careers are project-driven, and a lot of times, if you're a key contributor to that project, the other people on that team need you to be present and active consistently [in order] for that project to be successful, [which] has direct impact on the bottom-line of the company. And so, [it is] a little less friendly to leave of absences.

As his quote illustrates, A.J. did not perceive support for the notion that employees might take a leave of absence during a project and believed that most engineers would face termination rather than given leave.

In a similar way, Howard, a contractor, agreed the project-based nature of his occupation precluded him from taking time off during a project. He explained, "Three months off? No. That would mean quitting. You can't take three months off on a six-month project. You lose too much, can't get caught up." Another interviewee, Bruce, an electrician, suggested that project-based work changed his own ideas about whether he would want to take a leave:

Everything is project based, so the longer I'm gone, the more my projects get backed up. The work doesn't go away. Your projects are still there when you get back, so that, I think balances any desire to leave. Leaving will just create more stress, which then reduces my work–life balance. So taking an actual leave is not helpful.

The tight scheduling and deadline-driven nature of his project-based work created stress for Bruce, who explained that he found balance by avoiding stress and by simply not taking leaves. Because getting behind on deadlines caused Bruce additional stress, leaving work for too long a time would not assist him in achieving balance.

Rocket, a marketing director, also described the project-based design of his work as a limiting factor in his ability to take time off:

[I can't leave] during big projects. So we're rebranding the library so there is a lot of work that has to be done leading up to that so I can't take time off for that. So it's more kind of project campaign, and during this time I couldn't take an extended leave of absence.

Leaving his leadership position during an important project period would be difficult for Rocket, and potentially detrimental for the project. In addition to project-based work, Rocket also explained that certain months of the year would be difficult time to take a leave of absence:

> Budgeting, that's another thing for us. So the budget process here, unfortunately, is pretty long, but I would say September, October is our budget planning cycle here, so it's difficult for me to take that time off as well.

In Rocket's case, taking extended time away from work would be quite difficult for a few reasons. Although he expressed commitment to his family and other life pursuits, the constraints of his job made it a challenging scheduling effort for him to make space for everything he wanted to do in life.

Other men explained unique occupational scheduling through the concept of busy times or seasons. For example, Vincent, an accountant said,

> We have horrendous responsibilities, especially during tax time . . . You have to consider your pressure times—in the tax world, it is March 15, April 15, Sept. 15 and Oct. 15. As a result, each one of them have certain deadlines that have to be met. Those deadlines can't be changed. They're statutory. As a result, you have to budget your time, you have to budget your information flow to accommodate those deadlines . . . So when it comes to vacation, when it comes to that schedule, those times don't allow for vacation, or you have to finish it before the vacation. One year, I had one that started April 9th. So, my April 15 was April 8th that year. I just adjusted everything.

For Vincent, working around tax season was a scheduling constraint unique to accountants and part of his job that he accepted and worked around throughout his career.

Drawing a similar argument, casino dealer Remy described the "blackout" dates of his occupation, during which no employees can take time off:

> If you plan ahead, it is easy [to take a leave of absence]. But we have blackouts. No vacations between Christmas and New Year's. In the summer, if you want, and you can be flexible with your dates, you can go, but you have to book it in January . . . We celebrate the holidays when we can. The biggest example is Christmas. We are off on Christmas day an average every 7 years. So, we celebrate when we can. If we are off, we try to take it off. But I get every Thanksgiving off. It is the one family holiday in the year.

Remy's description of the unique scheduling requirements of casino work extended to the typical scheduling required for jobs that never sleep:

> Casinos are open 24/7, 365 days a year, so you are subject to working whenever. After you've been there a while, you'll settle into a regular

schedule . . . In general terms of work–life balance, any business that operates 24/7 is going to create obstacles for work–life balance. It creates a problem for some more than others. A mom with a teenager, who has to work during the witching hours. Every parent strives for the ideal 9–5, but they rely on family, they work opposite shifts from their spouse, they try to create continuous supervision. There was a time in my life when I had kids at home and I had these issues.

For this worker, achieving and maintaining balance was attainable; however, it required early planning and the occasional sacrifice.

One coach interviewed for this project explained that taking time off from work during his "season" would be detrimental to his career. He shared the following:

I generally have to take my time of in the summers, like in July, beginning of August if I want to do anything. Because I'm just busy all year round. And if you take time off, especially with coaching, you know, it about, soccer's about rhythm, and practicing, constantly to get better. If you take time off, kids aren't doing that, you see the fall off when you do get back out there. So, I try not to take time off during season. I try to do everything I have to, you know, when we do get breaks because I don't like losing that rhythm . . . I try to set my schedule and be organized and just have in my mind that when the season is going on, I'm not going to do any extracurricular activities. I only do it when it's necessary or when it's possible. So it does make it hard to take time off when you coach. You have to adhere to a set, a certain schedule, you know, games are already planned out, and you can't miss a game because you want to go to Daytona Beach, or something.

The notion of a perpetual succession of seasons, including preseason, recruiting, plus actual games, made this coach believe that he could only take time off or "do extracurricular activities" for two months out of the year.

Regge, the baseball consultant, also described the importance of a succession of seasons. He said,

The most important time for me is the baseball winter meetings here in about a month. Like I could not take those three days off. Those are the most important three days of my entire year . . . there are times of the year where I, under no circumstance, could go, no matter what's going on, I have to be there. Spring training is very important time for me, obviously the World Series is very important. But who would want to leave during the World Series anyway?

Regge described a continual occurrence of mandatory times in his industry during which he would have a difficult time taking a leave of absence.

A debate coach explained a similar experience around competition season. He explained, "If I were to ask for a leave of absence right now, it would probably be a disaster 'cause we're right in the middle of the season." He explained that his hectic travel and competition schedule would make taking a leave of absence impossible, or at least detrimental to the team.

Ryder, a driver/liquor distributor, also explained a "season" during which leaves were impossible:

> Normally, in the month of November and the month of December, nobody—not even supervisors—nobody gets any time off in December. That is just the entire month is blacked out because we are so busy. An in November, only one person per week gets off in November.

Ryder's busy time coincided with the prominent U.S. holidays, and because his organization was busy, Ryder did not have the option to take time off in November or December. In a similar way, two interviewees spoke about busy seasons that would preclude them from taking leaves of absence. Ben, a construction worker, explained:

> In our market where it's freezing cold during the winter time, we work primarily during the summer. So I would say that's when we're trying to be the breadwinner so to speak. So if someone had to leave in June, that would be [more] detrimental than taking time off in December or January when there's not a whole lot going on anyway.

John, who owns a window tinting business, explained a similar phenomenon:

> It's challenging mainly because it's seasonal, it's feast or famine. We're fishermen of sun, so when that season's on and we have to fish, then it's pretty demanding. It's overwhelming at times, and there's really not a lot of personal time. It's sleep, eat, and work. So for four months out of the year or so, it's kind of all consuming, the downside. I would never leave during our busy season unless it was a real emergency.

These examples highlight the ways in which men characterize their work as having unique scheduling requirements.

However, many of these same men claimed that taking time off was, in fact, quite possible and even likely outside of their "crunch times," seasons, and busy times. For example, interviewee Quentin, an IT consultant, explained:

> A nice thing about this job is that since you go from project to project, there are a lot of times when you might not have a real heavy commitment. So, if you can get things to work out, especially with clients, and say, "Hey, I'm done with my work, here. I don't have anything starting

for a while," they're really supportive of that type of stuff, as long as you're willing to sacrifice being paid for a while, I guess.

As Quentin's example evidences, taking unpaid time off in between projects was a regular practice for men in his occupation. Most of the interviewees in this study perceived the ability to take time off between projects as a benefit of their work. Another project-based interviewee, a graphic designer, explained:

> In between projects, everything kind of changes. If the project is over, if you're in between things or if you're just waiting on work to start, then you know, you might be able to take off [with] no problem[s]. But, if someone is leaving kind of in the middle of their job, then it's not quite as well received, or if they dump a bunch of stuff on other people. You know, again, it really depends on company culture, and how people work, and how valuable you are to the project. But, it is great that we can take off in between [projects].

Many men interviewed explained that well-planned leaves of absence occurring between projects or seasons were appropriate, although none had actually scheduled particular life events that required leaves of absence directly around project schedules.

CONCLUSION

In general, most of the workers believe they are uniquely suited for their occupations and that their work is not suitable for everyone. At the same time, they perceive their occupations to provide unique constraints to work–life practices, particularly taking time away from work. These assumptions, however, are problematic. When people naturalize and institutionalize occupations, the opportunity for change is nearly impossible and, as such, increasing diversity and equality is subsequently unlikely. Ashcraft's (2013) *glass slipper* theory revealed that occupations do not materialize magically or naturally, but instead develop specifically for certain bodies. The glass-slipper theory explained how occupations appear to be natural, innate callings for some workers and, by extension, as highly implausible or improbable career choices for others. The glass-slipper metaphor illustrates the near impossibility of slipping on an occupation that was not designed for you. The "natural fit" seems like an innate privilege. In effect, "there is nothing natural about slipping comfortably into a shoe designed exclusively for your foot" (Ashcraft, 2013, p. 17).

Recognizing that the *nature* of work and the *natural* worker are *not* fixed or "natural" entities, but, rather, are constructs developed over time, makes change possible (see, e.g., Ashcraft, 2012; Britton, 2000). Indeed, occupational identity is only temporarily fixed and is thus open for (re)negotiation. Renegotiation, then, presents an opportunity for increased social justice and equality in all occupations. Reimagining the ideal types for all occupations makes equality more possible. Grasping the constructed nature of work and the ideal worker is quite essential to the goals of this project. In order to increase equity for white women and workers of color, it is necessary to dispel the myth that certain work is only suitable for particular people. In addition, it is also necessary to recognize the ways in which the work itself developed historically to suit its ideal worker, which has an impact on work–life policies.

Most occupations, structured specifically for ideal type workers, developed such that work hours and time expectations suitable for workers without responsibilities outside of work. However, as workplaces and workers have changed, occupational structures have yet to change in response. Work–life policies largely reflect this ideology, and these policies mostly fit into existing occupational structures with little, if any, thought to revising the work structure itself. Most jobs developed for white, heterosexual, partnered, and abled men who did not need to take leaves of absence. Thus, taking a leave of absence is a stigmatized practice, because it is outside the purview of ideal-type worker. Occupational cultures solidified around the notion that work should occur as an around-the-clock endeavor, so leaves of absence and other kinds of work–life initiatives have been slow to gain traction. Leave-taking is not an option that fits with either the structure, hours required, or scheduling for most work. Children (including their arrival, school activities, and illness) often come with no notice for strategic scheduling of leave. In a similar way, illnesses (self or that of a loved one) do not allow for prescheduling and many disabilities to not allow workers to prepare to take time off from work. Characterizing leave as possible only when strategically scheduled, around a season or a busy time, is problematic, and complicates many workers' surprise needs to take time away from work.

Despite their certainty that leaves of absence either would hurt their careers or required strategic scheduling, most men also said that leave-taking practice *is* appropriate for women. Drawing from traditional conceptualizations of gender, most men believed that women have more of a "right" to leave work because of "natural" care work responsibilities. How these gendered assumptions about male and female roles have an impact on work–life policies is the drawn out in the next chapter.

NOTE

1. Tracy et al. (2006) found employees used dark jokes to characterize themselves as a "special breed of individuals capable of coping with the occupations' stress" (p. 291).

REFERENCES

Ashcraft, K. L. (2005a). Resistance through consent? Occupational identity, organizational form, and the maintenance of masculinity among commercial airline pilots. *Management Communication Quarterly, 19*(1), 67–90. doi:10.1177/0893 318905276560

Ashcraft, K. L. (2005b, May). *Resisting gendered threats in the meeting of occupation and organization: The case of airline pilots.* Paper presented at the meeting of the International Communication Association Conference, New York, NY.

Ashcraft, K. L. (2007). Appreciating the 'work' of discourse: Occupational identity and difference as organizing mechanisms in the case of commercial airline pilots. *Discourse & Communication, 1*(1), 9–36. doi:10.1177/1750481307071982

Ashcraft, K. L. (2013). The glass slipper: 'Incorporating' occupational identity in management studies. *Academy of Management Review, 38*(1), 6–31. doi:10.5465/amr.2010.0219

Britton, D. (2000). The epistemology of the gendered organization. *Gender & Society, 14*(3), 417–434. doi:10.1177/089124300014003004

Cohn, C. (2000). "How can she claim equal rights when she doesn't have to do as many push-ups as I do?" The framing of men's opposition to women's equality in the military. *Men and Masculinities, 3*(2), 131–151. doi:10.1177/10971 84X00003002001

Erickson, K. (2008). Historical change, technological innovation, and continuities of gender in three occupations. *Work and Occupations, 35*(3), 358–368. doi:10.1177/0730888408322230

Greene, A., Ackers, P., & Black, J. (2002). Going against the historical grain: Perspectives on gendered occupational identity and resistance to the breakdown of occupational segregation in two manufacturing firms. *Gender, Work and Organization, 9*(3), 266–285. doi:10.1111/1468–0432.00160

Hiestand, A., & Buzzanell. P. (2007, November). *Counseling careers: (re)constructing occupational identities, narratives, and identifications.* Paper presented at the meeting of the National Communication Association, Chicago, IL.

Kuhn, T., Golden, A., Jorgenson, J., Buzzanell, P., Kisselburgh, L., Kleinman, S., & Cruz, D. (2008). Cultural discourses and discursive resources for meaning/ful work: Constructing and disrupting identities in contemporary capitalism. *Management Communication Quarterly, 22*(1), 162–171. doi:10.1177/089331890 8318262

Larson, G., & Olson, A. (2008, November). *Constructing occupational identities on the last frontier: Masculine, high-tech, entrepreneurial work in Montana.* Paper presented at the annual meeting of the National Communication Association 94th Annual Convention, San Diego, CA.

Tracy, S. J., Myers, K., & Scott, C. (2006). Cracking jokes and crafting selves: Sensemaking and identity management among human service workers. *Communication Monographs, 73*(3), 283–308. doi:10.1080/03637750600889500

7 "It Is My Responsibility to Find the Right Balance"
Entrepreneurialism as a Constraint

Entrepreneurialism describes the "take-care-of-yourself" ideology and discourse that characterizes the beliefs, attitudes, and expectations of most U.S. citizens. Iconized by the American Dream, where any individual can be *what* they want to be with enough hard work, U.S. Americans, in particular, live by the guiding principal that the individual is responsible for making good "choices"[1] and that individuals are largely responsible for their own destinies. Evidence for the pervasiveness of entrepreneurial discourse is found throughout common language to guide life, such as "play the hand you were dealt," "pick yourself up by your bootstraps," and other phrases that capture the very individual responsibility U.S. Americans place on themselves to create their destiny. It captures beliefs and expectations across myriad facets of life, such as child rearing, dating, health, emotions, and, importantly, work. Du Gay (1996) explained that the enterprising vision of excellence provides a novel image of the worker, positioning him- or herself as entrepreneurial. He claimed that the term *entrepreneur* no longer simply implied the founder of an independent business venture; rather, it had traversed its traditional limits and now referred to the application of entrepreneurial practices to the everyday work practices of employees. This *intrapreneurial* or *postentrepreneurial* (because it takes entrepreneurship a stage farther) revolution therefore provides the possibility for every member of an organization to express individual initiative and to develop fully their potential in the service of the corporation (Du Gay, 1996).

In this chapter, I explain how the discourse of entrepreneurialism is a major cause of the glass handcuffs phenomenon. I argue that entrepreneurialism is at the heart of work–life balance and choice and keeps men locked into a cycle of continuous work. Analysis of the interview data reveals the stronghold of entrepreneurial discourse, because the men consistently articulated their feelings about individual responsibility for their work skills and career success. They framed work–life balance decisions, including leaves of absence, as choices for which they were responsible depending on how much success they wanted to achieve in their careers. This chapter unfolds with samples of the ways in which men drew on entrepreneurial discourse to describe the personal responsibility they felt in a number of career areas. The examples begin with broad assumptions about personal responsibility for acquiring skills and for controlling one's career trajectory. Next, the examples narrow to demonstrate how work–life choices are made within an entrepreneurial frame. From here, it is easy to see how and why men cast leaves of absence as choices that are either detrimental to career success or aspects of work that must be strategically managed individually. Finally, I discuss implications stemming from entrepreneurialism, including mis-recognition (Lacan, 1966/1977) with the entrepreneurial ideal, extreme careerism, the gendering of work–life practices, and ultimately, the glass handcuffs.

THE PREVALENCE OF ENTREPRENEURIALIST DISCOURSE

Evidence of entrepreneurialism threaded through the interviews for this study and resonated through almost every work-related discussion. All of the men spoke about their careers either as completely individual endeavors or as requiring significant independent action to achieve success. One pervasive theme was the broad way men spoke about their individual responsibility for acquiring skills necessary to obtain jobs, promotions, and job security. Liam, a professor, explained: "Producing high quality is really important, but quality isn't something they teach you in school at all. Rather, it sort of had to do with independent studies. You have to teach yourself." For Liam and many other interviewees across occupations, the quality of work is critical, and employees felt responsible for learning how to produce "high-quality" work independently. In a similar example, a technology specialist claimed, "I taught myself most of my skills. You can't learn it all from a book, in most cases, we know more than the books anyway." For this interviewee, even advanced classes were not sophisticated enough to teach him what he wanted to know, so he taught himself through trial and error. One architect interviewed shared his experience developing his own skills through his own ambition. He said, "A lot is based upon what you're willing to put forward—what you're willing to learn. A lot is based upon your expectations for yourself." As these examples demonstrate, the men interviewed here spoke frequently of engaging in significant self-teaching in order to learn the skills required to be successful in their careers.[2] This finding is important because it demonstrates the pervasiveness of entrepreneurial thought in achieving success at work—often before the men even secured positions in their desired occupations.

In addition to self-motivating in order to acquire work skills, the men interviewed in this study felt completely responsible for the entire trajectory of their careers. They asserted their career success hinged upon the choices they made in life, and their ability to take charge of their destinies. For example, Jeff, an engineer, explained what makes people unsuccessful in his line of work:

> What makes people unsuccessful are the people that sit back and wait for direction from their manager. They'll sit at their cubicle and they won't do, they won't be proactive to look for things that they could be working on new ideas for a company. An unsuccessful person at a company is a person that just sits at their cubicle, an eight-to-five person, and does nothing unless their manager mandates them. That's an unsuccessful person.
>
> A person that goes above and beyond is looking for ideas, looking for new applications, [and] is putting in the extra effort to think outside the box, and think for the company as if it was coming out of their wallet instead of the company's wallet. That's the person that's successful in business . . . I'm a very entrepreneurial person [and] I'm very pro individualistic, you know. It's like you're responsible for your own destiny [and that] your future is in your hands.

Jeff believed that workers in most fields need some entrepreneurial gumption to succeed. He applauded individual effort and claimed that individuals who must "wait for direction" would not be successful. This is evidence of a heavy reliance on individual responsibility for career success. Hence, according to Jeff, to be successful is to be independent and able to manage oneself with little supervision. Drawing a similar argument, Max, a courier, explained how he felt responsible for creating his own path through work:

> You need to make your own policies and make your own success. I don't do very well in situations where policies are made for me. Chances are, where there are too many policies, I wouldn't be in that situation because I wouldn't be in control of my own life. I've taken control of my own life because I'm not very materialistic and I've made good choices. I can drive an old car instead of a new one that needs payments. Those thoughts have probably held me back a bit in life, but in the end, I think I'm happier for it.

As these examples demonstrate, entrepreneurialism is at the root of thoughts and feelings about work skills and career success. Indeed, references to individual responsibility, individual drive and motivation, and personal choices were present to some extent in every interview.

ENTREPRENEURIALISM, CHOICE, AND BALANCE

Through entrepreneurial discourse, work–life decisions are positioned as choices selected by individuals, amid their own motivation for career success.

In this version of entrepreneurialism, workers not only strategically select their work–life choices, but they also have training, guidance, and a plethora of materials to help them learn to successfully balance what organizations deem as important for them. This is not to say that employees completely lack autonomy; rather, the invisible hand of entrepreneurialism has already specified limited options that are or are not available for specific kinds of workers. Part of the ideology of entrepreneurialism is the notion of self-surveillance, monitoring, and control.

The work of Michel Foucault is extremely useful in analyzing entrepreneurialism. He claimed that power defines the conditions of possibility that underscore the way individuals experience themselves as people or their *potential self*. Foucault looked specifically at social institutions to understand the ways in which institutional discourses impact the actions, attitudes, learning, and talk of everyday life. His notion of discipline is influential here, as individuals regularly act in ways that coincide with organizational goals. Individuals internalize surveillance and monitor themselves and their peers. The discourse of entrepreneurialism is a particularly salient area for critique because it explicitly aligns individual subject positions with organizational benefit. Individuals deeply internalize entrepreneurialism, and as such, it is a nearly invisible means of power and control. The entrepreneurial worker is able to self-monitor, work long hours, and, in general, do "whatever it takes" to succeed and achieve in the workplace and at home. Through this discourse, the accomplishment of work and career "balance" are squarely the responsibility of the worker.

When employees feel tension around multiple roles, it is readily regarded as mismanagement in work–life decisions. The men interviewed for this study cast work–life balance completely in entrepreneurial ideology. For example, Greg, another architect, explained how all employees are responsible for their own balance:

> Some people are fine working all the time. Some people want cats. Some people are married to their jobs because they don't have anything else or want anything else. Those people might have issues, but they do have extra time to commit to their jobs. It's what kind of balance makes you happy. Every person has to take it upon themselves to find it or else you will end up losing it at some point. People can snap at work, I've seen people throw down models or go on a tirade because of the stress—they are ridden to a point where they break. Other people lose sight of what is important—sucked into the routine and forgetting about what is important. But every person has to think about their own lives and their own things and try to figure it out.

For this man, personally balancing work and life was necessary—not only for personal fulfillment but also for managing an unhealthy amount of stress at work. Vincent, an accountant, also positioned work and life management as an individual responsibility. He explained his views on work–life balance in this way:

> You must allocate your time between your responsibilities in your work life with your responsibilities in your personal life. The demands on those responsibilities which change over time. When the kids were younger, I coached each and every one of them. I would be home by 3/3:30. Once they've grown up, I'm not needed there, so that time is now filled with work. I look at my needs on the personal side and weigh what is important to me and attempt to carve out my business time to meet those needs. No matter what you do, you have to make sacrifices. I actually like golf. But I haven't golfed since college. I can't take 8 hours from either home or work. If I did, I would have problems with one or the other. People have to choose that for themselves . . . No matter what you do, no one's ever going to be happy with their allocations. It is different for everybody. You can't go back and redo what you did, you can only write the future. It is a difficult choice to balance your responsibilities, to your family and to the unknowns you are going to have in the future.

While Vincent believed he was able to achieve the "right kind of balance" for himself, he adamantly expressed his belief that each individual employee had to individually choose *what* to balance, and *how* to balance his or her time. Quite a few men believed that work–life balance required individual strategic planning. For example, Mark, a technical engineer, explained:

> It was a conscious effort on my part and my wife's [part] to, you know, not necessarily go after the highest paying job or anything like that but to have a steady job with a good company and forgo in the luxuries to balance [our] life.

In Mark's view, he strategically sought out a job which would allow him to maintain a balance that included more family time—a decision he considered in opposition to a higher paying job.

In another example, Remy, a casino dealer, described work–life balance as

> finding enough time to balance the demands on your business life while still reserving enough time for your personal time. No matter which decision you make, you are always going to be making compromises. But it is a decision you make carefully, based upon your personal desires for life.

Casting work–life balance as a strategic decision was the most common way the men spoke about work–life, and managing the "right" choices seemed an imperative skill for career success.

ENTREPRENEURIALISM AND LEAVE

Putting together their personal responsibility for their own career success with their individual responsibilities to manage their work–life balance, the men in this study explained that in order to be successful, they made individual choices to forgo leaving work for more than a week or two in order to strengthen their careers. The themes of presence and individual responsibility for career success were directly linked to leave-taking practice by a number of interviewees. This pressure to manage the entirety of one's career can create an acute tension for men thinking about taking a leave. For example, one field engineer explained:

> It wouldn't be great for my career if I left. You try to be indispensable, especially now when lots of people are getting laid off, so it's kind of like not a good idea to take a leave. I knew a guy who took two weeks off when his wife had a baby. He was laid off like two weeks later or something like that. So you have to think about your own career and really think about what is important: having a job or not?

The fear of losing his job was acute for this interviewee. He mentioned that leave is never a good idea in his occupation, but particularly so in the current economic situation.

Similarly, one computer scientist explained that taking leaves of absence just is not a smart career move for men:

> It kind of makes some sense that women are paid less, you know? Because many times—not all the time, obviously—they don't work as much. I mean, if you only work three-fourths of a year, because you are spending time with your family or whatever, you are going to make less and you are going to probably have less or outdated skills. I'm not faulting [women] by any means. But for men, it is more of a choice. [Men] can say, "Hey, I care about my career and advancing" and then they wouldn't want to take a leave. Or they might say "I don't care about my career, so I'm going to take a month off to bond with my kid." Either way, it is a matter of personal decision.

For this interviewee, an individual's decision of whether or not to take a leave of absence was directly correlated with his or her career success, and was completely an individual responsibility. The assumption that taking a leave of absence means "not working as much" points to some of the difficulty in gaining support to take a leave of absence. Furthermore, the assumption that people who take time away from work *should* earn less money evokes gendered assumptions about care work and home responsibilities. That these responsibilities are positioned as individual choices for men (but not women) provides evidence of how taking a leave of absence can be difficult and can generate biases. In another example, Tripp, a driver, explained:

> Anyone who takes time off from work, if it is significant, it eventually hurts their career. When one takes off, the other workers don't take a rest. It gives other people an opportunity to shine and take over. You could go back to work to find yourself misplaced. The fear of that is huge.

For Tripp, the pressure and competition from coworkers was enough to ensure he made "good" choice about not leaving work for extended periods. His perception that he was replaceable created a fear about leaving work.

In another example, Zed, a nonprofit worker, explained: "If you're not taking leave, then you're working. So the more you work, obviously, the more productivity you get, the more successful you will be." Zed's impression that time at work equates to productivity made him feel as if taking time away from work would hurt his career success. Remy also shared his view that taking time off could have hurt his career:

> If you are working in the same company, taking a vacation can be a problem. One time, I was planning to go to [my daughter's] graduation. I was also required to be at a meeting with a bunch of chief executives. It was discouraged that I take the time off. The powers that be wanted me to take the meeting. It could have affected my promote-ability.

Remy shared that this experience caused him stress and frustration and tested his commitment to his job because he did not want to miss his daughter's graduation. In a similar way, Jack, a marketing coordinator, expressed his frustration about the way his coworkers and manager perceive time away from work:

> Life isn't just freakin' black and white, there's grays. It's a whole gray scale. You have to decide which side you're on. You know which part of the gray scale you're at. So you know and I think that is kind of a shitty thing. I think it is kind of a realization that um, people do, you know, always, always at work, compared to the guy, "oh he's always on leave." Therefore the guy who's always on leave is a shithead and the other guy isn't. Because he's always here. But in reality, you know again life's more complex than that.

Jack explained that his girlfriend lived out of state, which necessitated his absence from work more often than other workers and prevented him from working overtime on weekends. He believed his absence was keeping him from promotion and felt extreme frustration about his situation.

MANAGING LEAVE

While many of the examples presented thus far suggest men do not think leaves of absence are good for their careers, not all the men thought leaves of absence were impossible. Some of the men, particularly those with more control over their day-to-day work (mostly in higher paying jobs), explained that they could take leave if they carefully managed their time away. Liam explained:

> [Whether you take leave is] really up to you. You get to manage how you get paid during that time. So, you sort of have to negotiate with the [manager], [and] if they deem you as essential, really, they only have to give you 12 weeks because of federal law, but if you are essential and you can negotiate well, you can get more. But it's really your negotiation that matters.

These interviewees asserted that negotiating how long leave would last and whether it was paid was the responsibility of the individual employee.

Vincent explained his thoughts on the ability of individuals to manage time away from work: "If you are dealing with a workload that takes 60 days and you want 7 days off, you have to do the work in 53 days. It would be hard, however, to make up more than a week or so." For Vincent, it was possible to leave work for a week at a time, but more than this would be detrimental to his career and his work objectives. Still, he believed that time away was possible with minimal impact to his career success. In a similar way, Oliver, a computer scientist, speculated that time away from work was possible, with additional individual effort:

> I think you can still take leave as long as you kind of independently continue to educate yourself. I think that's what I've seen people do is, even if they take leave. They still go and read and are interested in what they're doing and there's many ways now to keep up just by reading stuff on the internet or playing around.

In this example, Oliver believed that leaves of absence were not detrimental to career success but that he could manage his time away from work in a particular way to have less of an impact on his career. In a similar way, Jake, a police officer, explained how managing time away from work was an important individual responsibility:

> If you're just constantly always at work and stuff, that shows good work ethic and everything, but how is that, how is that affecting you on the back end. Either with your family, or with your spouse or with whatever else. So, so you know even though, yeah, it does look, you know "oh he's always at work" or "he's always on time" that's great

but how's that for the, the people on the back end for your family's side. You know and I think a lot of people have to look at that um, from that angle instead of just looking at it as oh well you know this work crap needs to get done. If you wanna be with whoever—your family—*you* gotta make it happen.

Jake believed that his time with his family (including his sister, his nephew, and his mother) was a high priority in his life. He also felt that his organization devalued his family compared to officers with children, and believed he had to fight his occupational demands to make time for his family. Still, he believed it was possible to strike a healthy balance with constant attention to time devoted in each area of life.

IMPLICATIONS OF ENTREPRENEURIALISM

Because entrepreneurialism is both widely prevalent and deeply engrained in individual workers in the United States, the implications for work–life practices are incredibly complicated. For the purposes of understanding how entrepreneurialism intersects with work–life practice, there are four main implications that bear discussion. First, entrepreneurialist discourse causes employees to experience mis-recognition and false identification with the entrepreneurial ideal (Lacan, 1966/1977; Nadesan, 2002; Nadesan & Trethewey, 2000). Second, entrepreneurialism can cause extreme careerism, particularly when set in the context of increasing consumption (Wieland, Bauer, & Deetz, 2009). Third, casting work–life practices as entrepreneurial choices contributes to harmful gendering of work–life policies and policy use. Finally, taken together, when workers shun work–life policies to protect occupational success, the glass handcuffs phenomenon emerges.

Mis-Recognition and False Identification

Mis-recognition is the false impression that the self is a unified, coherent bodily agent (the *I*). It is an ongoing process in which individuals understand the self and others through discourse (Lacan, 1966/1977). For example, individuals might assume they rationally "choose" to focus on work or life at any given time, and the choice presented can be determined internally. People assume they choose their careers, for example, or identify as the kind of person they wish to be. However, no one can ever actually make these choices individually because the *I* is always influenced by the opinions of others (the *me*). As such, society prescribes choices—the person one *wants* to be is only a choice in that individuals select identities from a handful of predetermined options (Nadesan & Trethewey, 2000). Individuals can only express identities that they know, which have already been presented in predetermined and predictable ways. Discourse helps accomplish this misrecognition by generating preferred subject positions with which the self can identify.

The *entrepreneurial ideal* represents the ideal organizational type (Acker, 1990), the preferred subject position which serves as a model for employee behavior. A number of facets of organizational life, including, for example, job roles and skills, occupations, and organizational policy, were developed around an ideal employee. The *ideal type* in U.S. organizations is a white, able-bodied, young, heterosexual, partnered, and unencumbered man. This man can dedicate his life to his occupation and organization and does not have responsibilities outside of his work life. To this, the entrepreneurial ideal must also be clever enough to manage his own career, motivated to move up, savvy enough to navigate organizational hierarchies, and attain economic success through his own hard work and efforts. The entrepreneurial ideal may also be a risk taker (Ahl, 2004), aggressive, manipulative, tough and domineering (Mulholland, 1996), adventurous and fulfilled through work (Gill, 2013), and innovative (Schramm, 2006).

The entrepreneurial ideal is promulgated through discourse to frame the ways employees believe they are expected to act. For example, the ideal entrepreneurial computer programmer works very hard and does not get much sleep during times of rapid innovation. This overarching discourse leads individual computer programmers to act in predictable ways. They work very hard and get little sleep during development "sprints." This practice not only solidifies the subject position of programmers, because new individuals in the field are indoctrinated into the profession in the same way; it also prevents alternative ways of enacting "computer programmer." These predetermined subject positions are styled so that they overwhelmingly act in ways that benefit organizations. Computer programmers working endless hours are good for the bottom line of the organization for which they work. While individuals believe they are consenting to construct their identities (or performing their authentic selves), they are actually selecting to identify with organizationally preferred selves engineered by the discourse. In this way, individuals are less autonomous and do not have as much agency as assumed. Thus, choices are not choices at all. Predetermined positions limit possibilities in ways that are not readily identifiable. Hegemony persists as individuals routinely perform the same identities in predetermined subject positions that do not provide the same possibilities for all (Nadesan & Trethewey, 2000).

Entrepreneurial discourse functions to create the preferred subject positions of "autonomous," "consensual" individuals who are responsible for their own self-surveillance and success. Nadesan and Trethewey (2000) claimed the entrepreneurial ideal serves as the basis of mis-recognition because the entrepreneurial ideal is impossible to achieve. Therefore, identifications with it are imaginary. The individual success required to adopt the entrepreneurial identity is a myth that is contingent on many factors, including race, class, and age. Put simply, individuals do not all have the same opportunities to identify with specific subject positions. The choices available are predetermined and largely reflect gender, race, class, age, abilities, and so on. When individuals assume that everybody can embody the entrepreneurial ideal, they overlook the power dynamics that make the possibilities for self-reliance *different* for some people. As discussed, the entrepreneurial ideal is healthy, young, without family, has endless energy and consistently acquires new skills, and never stops innovating on behalf of the organization (Nadesan & Trethewey, 2000). Any singular individual could in no way maintain this ideal forever, but some individuals cannot maintain it *ever*. Critical examination reveals the ways in which entrepreneurialist discourse presents possibilities that are *impossibilities* and proves false the idea that choice is a controllable phenomenon. Failure to embody the entrepreneurialist ideal is a probability for most. Both men and women will experience mis-recognition, but the failure is more likely for women, who must try to mold both their minds and their bodies to a masculinized, patriarchal symbolic order (Nadesan & Trethewey, 2000).

Extreme Careerism

A second implication of entrepreneurialism that impacts leave and other work–life policies is extreme careerism. Entrepreneurial culture deeply pervades the self, such that it makes possible extreme careerism and consumerism. These practices have destructive implications for organizations, families, and individuals who are "colonized" further when entrepreneurialism turns workers into producers (Wieland et al., 2009).

An increased consumption leads to an increased need for entrepreneurialism. Entrepreneurial ideology and consumption work hand in hand to have an impact on how much individuals need to work in order to live. As people consume more, they must work more to support an increased standard of living (Wieland, et al, 2009). Higher levels of consumption can force the "need" for a two-paycheck family. Conceptions of work, of how it is performed, of who performs it, and in what quantities are all determined, in large part, by levels of consumption. How consumptionism drives and constrains individuals, organizations, and society at large impacts work–life arrangements.

Emerging from both the American Dream ideology and the more modern, fierce individualism, materialism, consumptionism, and capitalism, entrepreneurial employees embody the ideals of enterprise. As Gill (2013) explained, entrepreneurialism is

> the American Dream for those who are already privileged. The dimensions of bootstrapping and hard work endemic to the self-made man have taken a back seat to wealth creation, technological innovation, and elite networking. In that the entrepreneurial man archetype meshes long-standing US ideologies of work and identity with neoliberal

individualism, he is familiar, but novel; within our grasp, but just out of reach . . . In this, we see the underpinnings of entrepreneurial capitalism as an organizing logic. (pp. 350–351)

Entrepreneurialism turns all workers into producers. Consumption increases to match production so that constant production is necessary. Continuous achievement and careerism allows for the combination of consumption and production to continue endlessly. When workers engage in this cycle of production at work for consumption at home, boundaries between work and life are blurred and cemented. The worker must continue producing to maintain his or her life outside of work. This practice can blur work–life lines, as continuous or increased consumption requires further production, which can then take the worker away from home for increasing lengths of time.

Entrepreneurial Selves and Gendered Organizational Behavior

A third important work–life implication that emerges from entrepreneurialism is the unhealthy gendering of work–life policies and policy use. The ways in which gendering occurs through the discourse of entrepreneurialism is critically important to understand how it operates to manifest material consequences for both men and women in organizations. Entrepreneurialism is widely recognized as a masculine discourse by scholars (Kerfoot, 1998; Miller, 2002; Mulholland, 1996) yet pulses, unseen, through organizational thought.[3] However invisible, the privileged masculine ideal of entrepreneurialism is possible for only elite, wealthy men. The entrepreneurial discourse is not available to women because it is rooted in masculinity and expectations that are unattainable for most women in organizations. As Gill (2013) explained,

> although entrepreneurial discourse seemingly forwards an egalitarian ideal, it ultimately both obscures and legitimizes inequality. In that neoliberal entrepreneurialism places success in the hands of the individual, it maintains that all individuals stand an equal chance of "achieving" entrepreneurship. Yet, the archetype of entrepreneurial man has been shown to be one that legitimizes white, male, and/or otherwise privileged entrepreneurs at the expense of women and entrepreneurs of color. (p. 336)

Hegemony continues, unchallenged, and women in organizations struggle to live up to masculine expectations.

Once the masculine attributes of entrepreneurialism are clear, implications can be unraveled for women in and out of organizations.[4] Under entrepreneurialism, women and men are responsible for taking care of their own success. The material reality of the wage gap typically means that if one parent is to forgo paid work, it will likely be the woman. This becomes particularly problematic for single parents and for families that cannot afford to "choose" to stay home.

If men think using work–life policies hurts their chances for career success, they do not use them. This creates a double bind for employees who need to use work–life policies in order to manage their careers and additional care work responsibilities. Because it is most often women who shoulder the burden of care work and other private sphere responsibilities, workers regularly cast work–life policies as feminine. This makes the option of using policies even more remote because such use carries a feminine stigma that can materially result in fewer promotions and lower wages.

THE GLASS HANDCUFFS PHENOMENON

Taken together, the data presented here and the implications from the interviews create conditions for which the glass handcuffs phenomenon can occur. All employees attempt to enact the entrepreneurial ideal, achieving personal success individually. They engage in extreme careerism in order to survive in a society that is constantly increasing its consumption practices. Policies and programs which might have alleviated these constant, high-pressure work conditions are cast as feminine and carry a stigma and material price tag for use. Thus, most employees try to minimize the use (or the visibility of their use) of work–life policies. Leave is also subject to heavy gendering because it is associated with pregnancy. As such, men often feel they cannot or should not take time away from work. To do so would indicate they are not the entrepreneurial ideal, and could very seriously jeopardize their ability to achieve material success, which could be detrimental to their family income. Thus, most men continue to engage in nonstop work, essentially locking themselves to their jobs for real and perceived financial sustainability.

A deconstruction of entrepreneurial discourse reveals that it is at the heart of the current conception of work–life balance. The gendered nature of entrepreneurialism works to reproduce and reify the binary of public–private by engaging in traditional domain practices, pushing women out of organizations and keeping men in. Lewis's (2006) study of women entrepreneurs found that the women's commitment to entrepreneurship was one way to achieve *better* work–life balance. In this way, the discourse of entrepreneurialism is an alternative discourse: Women embrace entrepreneurialism as a way to subvert organizational control over their private lives, not as a force that subjugates them. Whether women leave traditional organizations to start their own business or because they are unable to "balance" work–life commitments in the same way as their male counterparts in entrepreneurial organizations do, the effect is the same: women draw upon entrepreneurialist discourse to inform their work–life practices.

Even if women are "choosing" to leave organizations, entrepreneurialism reinforces the men-as-public/women-as-home binary. For this reason, the deconstruction and analysis of entrepreneurialism as they influence conceptions of work–life "balance" are critical for moving beyond the binary of work–life, which itself may not be very productive. Entrepreneurialist discourse makes available specific choices for workers managing work and nonwork concerns, but the discourse embeds in individual identity such that its shaping influence is difficult to see. Because of the gendered nature of entrepreneurialism, choice and balance also work in gendered ways, putting unequal pressure on women and men to conform to entrepreneurialist ideals both in and outside of organizations. While women are pushed out of organizational spheres, men are locked in. This binary gridlock of public–private hurts both men and women as they attempt to manage their work and nonwork lives. The masculine entrepreneurialist discourse prevents men from engaging as fully as they might like in their private lives. For example, fewer than 1% of all men in the United States are stay-at-home fathers (U.S. Census Bureau, 2013). Understanding the powerful, invisible, and masculine discourse of entrepreneurialism is to create an opening for emancipation for both men and women. Women could potentially achieve equity in organizations and home while men could unlock the invisible handcuffs that hold them at work.

NOTES

1. *Choice* is a problematized term, particularly with regard to work decisions. Put simply, many employees do not have choices regarding how and when they perform work (Buzzanell & Lucas, 2013). However, like *balance*, I do not use quotation marks to offset the word throughout the remainder of the text.
2. Labeling workers for the skills they possess began in World War I, when the United States introduced a specialized personnel system that registered people by skill set. This allowed for strategic planning that used individual skills and capacities in the organization of war. The theory of registering people by skill transferred to business and translated as using individual skills to maximize production/profit for organizations. Employees wanting mobility or the opportunity to advance in an organization started individually seeking out ways to add skills to their repertoires. This individual enterprising effort ultimately benefitted the organization. Individual employees took the burden of getting the right skills, or worked to improve themselves based on their "type," and organizations benefited from their efforts. (Rose, 1989)
3. In her study of female entrepreneurs, Lewis (2006) pointed out that masculinity is nearly invisible in entrepreneurial discourses, an "unmarked category" against which otherness is constructed.
4. Medved and Kirby (2005) revealed the use of traditional work terms by stay-at-home moms. Referring to themselves as the "family CEO," stay-at-home mothers believe that "motherhood is a career" (Sanders & Bullen, 2002, p. xi, from Medved & Kirby, 2005, p. 448). By commodifying stay-at-home mothering in entrepreneurialist language, notions of choice and balance begin to take traction. Families measure the choice to stay home with children or to return to work by the hourly wage worth of the woman compared to day care costs.

REFERENCES

Acker, J. (1990). Hierarchies, jobs, bodies: A theory of gendered organizations. *Gender & Society*, 4(2), 139–158. doi:10.1177/089124390004002002

Ahl, H. (2004). *The scientific reproduction of gender inequality: A discourse analysis of research texts on women entrepreneurship*. Malmö, Sweden: Liber.

Buzzanell, P. M., & Lucas, K. (2013). 1 Constrained and constructed choices in career: An examination of communication pathways to dignity. In E. L. Cohen (Ed.), *Communication yearbook 37* (pp. 3–31). New York, NY: Routledge

Du Gay, P. (1996). *Consumption and Identity at Work*. London: Sage Publications.

Gill, R. (2013). The evolution of organizational archetypes: From the American to the entrepreneurial dream. *Communication Monographs*, 80(3), 331–353. doi:10.10 80/03637751.2013.788252

Kerfoot, D. (1998). Managing masculinity in contemporary organizational life: A managerial project. *Organization*, 5(1), 7–26. doi:10.1177/135050849851002

Lacan, J. (1977). *Ecrits: A selection* (A. Sheridan, Trans.). New York, NY: W.W. Norton. (Original work published in 1966)

Lewis, P. (2006). The quest for invisibility: female entrepreneurs and the masculine norm of entrepreneurship. *Gender, Work & Organization*, 13(5), 453–469. doi: 10.1111/j.1468-0432.2006.00317.x

Medved, C. & Kirby, E. (2005). Family CEOs: A feminist analysis of corporate mothering discourses. *Management Communication Quarterly*, 18(4) 435–478. doi: 10.1177/0893318904273690

Miller, G. E. (2002). The frontier, entrepreneurialism, and engineers: Women coping with a web of masculinities in an organizational culture. *Culture and Organization*, 8(2), 145–160. doi:10.1080/14759550212836

Mulholland, K. (1996). Entrepreneurialism, masculinity and the self-made man. In D. L. Collinson & J. Hearn (Eds.), *Men as managers, managers as men: Critical perspectives on men, masculinity and management* (pp. 123–149). London, England: Sage.

Nadesan, M. H. (2002). Engineering the entrepreneurial infant: Brain science, infant development toys, and governmentality. *Cultural Studies*, 16(3), 401–432. doi:10.1080/09502380210128315

Nadesan, M.H, & Trethewey, A. (2000). Performing the enterprising subject: Gendered strategies for success (?). *Text and Performance Quarterly*, 20(3), 223–250. doi:10.1080/10462930009366299

Rose, N. (1989). *Governing the Soul: The Shaping of the Private Self*. New York: Free Association Books.

Schramm, C. J. (2006, January). *Entrepreneurial capitalism and the end of bureaucracy: Reforming the mutual dialog of risk aversion*. Paper presented at the 2006 meeting of the American Economic Association, Boston, MA. Retrieved from http://www.aeaweb.org/assa/2006/0107_1015_0304.pdf

U.S. Census Bureau. (2013). Profile America: Facts for features, Father's Day 2011. Retrieved from http://www.census.gov/newsroom/releases/archives/facts_for_features_special_editions/cb11-ff11.html

Wieland, S. M. B., Bauer, J., & Deetz, S. (2009). Excessive careerism and destructive life stresses: The role of entrepreneurialism in colonizing identities. In B. Sypher & P. Lutgen-Sandvik (Eds.), *Destructive organizational communication: Processes, consequences, and constructive ways of organizing* (pp. 99–120). New York, NY: Routledge.

8 "It's Kind of . . . a Man Thing"
Gender, Economics, and the Impossibility of Leave

Perhaps one of the most pervasive causes of the glass handcuffs is gender. Deep rooted assumptions about the relationship between men and work function to keep men working outside the home for wages and create broad cultural expectations about what *men* should do. This chapter begins with a historical overview of the public/private sphere division, the middle-class ideal, and the exalted role of motherhood, all of which frame the way men's relationship to work has developed. Next, I present interview data that illustrate how men used gendered rationales to explain the impossibility or limited availability of leaves of absence, including their roles as breadwinners, assumptions about "natural" caretaking roles, and acknowledgment of gender bias in organizations. After fleshing out the gendered rationales related to leaves of absence, I move into a discussion about the material impacts of gendered organizational bias. The interviewees described the economic impacts of taking unpaid time away from work and explained how their roles as breadwinners or significant economic contributors made taking unpaid time off difficult or impossible.

PUBLIC AND PRIVATE SPHERES

The historical separation of public and private spheres shaped the rise of gendered work roles and the unequal valuation of work. The deep division between the public and private worlds served to make the family patterns of the middle class a sort of ideal model for which occupations developed, elevating the role of stay-at-home mothers while devaluing care work at the same time. Perceptions and expectations about the public and private spheres shape cultural ideologies that continue to affect people's relationships with work in gendered ways, and although the exact parameters around public and private spheres oscillate slightly over time, the gender alignment with particular spheres remains unchanged.

UNEQUALLY VALUED WORK AND
THE MIDDLE-CLASS IDEAL

Manufacturing and the capitalist influence on production changed conceptions of work. Necessities, such as soap, candles, and cloth, moved from home production to factory production by 1830 (Kessler-Harris, 2003). This shift in production prompted a shift in the valuation of work. Previously valued home production moved into the public spheres and became detached from the private sphere and women (McCarver & Blithe, 2014). Women's labor in the home continued in the form of care work—tending to children, elders, home, and community. However, the economic valuation of their work left the private sphere with the production of market-valued products. Cultural valuation of products over care strengthened with advancements in manufacturing and ultimately created a shift from a gendered division of labor to a gendered definition of labor (Boydston, 1994). Work tasks became associated with gender, such that jobs and roles would be socially acceptable for either men or women. Care work, which lacked a market-valued product, was absent from the public sphere and was assigned to women. Men were disassociated more and more from the private sphere and care work as market-driven production rendered their work as more important in the public sphere.

Young and low-income women went to work in manufacturing jobs in the early to mid-1800s, and made up nearly half of the manufacturing workforce, earning 25% to 30% of male wages (Kessler-Harris, 2003; The Women's Studies Work Group, 1975). Although work in the public sphere for women was considered patriotic during this time, they were expected to return to the private sphere upon marriage (Kessler-Harris, 2003). At the same time, society measured men by their ability to keep their wives away from the public sphere of work.

This ideology reflected the new capitalist ideology and promoted the male-as-sole-breadwinner family model. Men who could afford to maintain a family and home without the economic contributions of his wife, and women who took sole responsibility for having and raising children while her husband provided became deeply ingrained middle-class ideals (Kessler-Harris, 2003). The far-reaching impacts of this family model continue to pervade gender work expectations today.

By 1970, middle-class women's primary identity was firmly tied to motherhood and housework—even for employed women—which stunted women's identification with paid work and subverted their occupational identities (Smuts, 1971; The Women's Studies Work Group, 1975). Working class women did not have the same experience with work, but rather identified as both workers and mothers (Cobble, 2004). Although the middle-class ideal was not attainable for women working out of necessity, it still shaped the policies and gendered expectations about work, which would have an impact on working-class women in the following decades.

MOTHERHOOD AS WOMANHOOD

The cult of domesticity exalted the role of mother, capitalizing on assumptions about women's moral superiority and virtue, which solidified women's place in the home. Rigid Victorian expectations about women's responsibilities, roles, and place distanced women (either ideologically or in actuality) farther and farther from paid work. The simultaneous focus on work for men kept the development of fathering largely out of cultural ideology. These gendered assumptions about the gendered nature of work and the general nature of women and men followed women into the workforce in the 1960s and 1970s. Thus, on their entrance into the paid, public sphere of work, women remained primarily, if not solely, responsible for the private sphere as well.

Currently, women are still expected to maintain the private sphere. Men are increasingly welcomed into parenting and other care work; however, men who take their primary identities in the private sphere are rare. There has been very little reform effort regarding the home and family, and conservatives, traditionalists, and the Far Right have taken up much discussion about the private sphere (Okin, 1999). These groups frequently cry for a return to rigid gender divisions of labor, which would keep men at work and women solely in the home. These ever-present gender ideologies strongly contribute to the glass handcuffs phenomenon. For any study looking at work–life balance, the divide between the public and private spheres is inherent. Work–life balance as a concept and work–life policies are attempts to bridge the spheres in order to make life livable both for men and for women. However, as the data show, gender and separate sphere ideologies consistently frame how work–life is accomplished and how individuals feel about their work and home responsibilities.

GENDERED EXPECTATIONS AND LEAVES OF ABSENCE

About one third of the men in this study drew on gendered discourses to explain their leave-taking practices. Specifically, many interviewees claimed that *men* do not take leave and that their breadwinner role is theoretically and/or metaphorically important to their identities. The gendered role explanations described in this section refer specifically to three kinds of arguments the interviewees made about gender roles. First, many claimed their breadwinner roles (and often the "homemaker" roles of their partners) are important as part of their identities *as men*. Some of the interviewees extended their gendered assumptions to include the view that women should not work at all, while others described that working men did not need to or should not take up care-work responsibilities that would require them to take a leave of absence from work. A second claim about gendered roles from the interviewees was about the "natural" tendency of women to take up care work, particularly for breastfeeding, birth recovery, or "natural" caring tendencies. Most men making these claims believed that working women required or deserved time away from work to take care of their children. The final claim the interviewees made about gender roles was more "objective." They recognized the prevalence of gender bias at work and assumptions about the breadwinner roles and believed men could not take leaves of absence because of stigma attached to violating gender expectations at work. The interviewees did not necessarily make these claims exclusively or neatly, but rather drew on some or all of these logics when describing why they did not think men could take a leave of absence. This discussion was often an uncomfortable part of the interview, because the interviewees sometimes struggled to describe the unwritten gendered rules about time off or worried that traditional perspectives would be unwelcome. Overall, the interviewees *all* supported the notion that women can take leave for care work, but *men* do not often, or should not, take longer leaves of absence, particularly for care work. They believed that men taking leave for family would have a more difficult time than would women in the same position.

Men who drew traditional arguments about gender roles harkened back to times when women stayed home. Although a majority of these men did not take issue with other women working, they did not believe that a working woman—particularly a working mother—would be appropriate for their own family. As such, they did not believe that men should take leaves of absence, specifically for care work. For example, Jesse explained:

> It's kind of like, I don't know, a man thing . . . I don't know how to explain it. It's a male thing. It's kind of like . . . I was brought up to take care of what you need to take care of, no matter what.

Jesse's hesitation suggested that he was uncomfortable discussing what might have been perceived as traditional gender roles. Jesse elaborated that he did not want to be perceived as "old-fashioned," even though he felt compelled to avoid a practice that he characterized as typically feminine. In a similar way, another interviewee said, "A woman really should have more time off for family than would a man, if that makes sense. I'm trying not to sound too sexist, but, you know . . ." The men in these examples recognized the biased nature of their comments and tried to explain why a biased perception "made sense."

Although many interviewed men were cognizant of gendered expectations, some were entrenched in such roles more explicitly. For example, one interviewee said, "Why would men need to take a maternity leave? If I was just sitting home watching ladies' talk shows, after about two or three days I would go crazy." In another example, Jeff claimed,

> I have never seen anyone pull the FMLA card . . . I agree [that] women should get time when they have children. I think that's part of the deal. It should be, but I don't agree with men getting time off, the same amount of time off. And I haven't seen it [being taken by employees]. And I don't approve of it. I haven't heard of it either, [men] getting the same amount of time off, other than maybe [in] Europe.

Throughout the interview, Jeff emphatically disagreed with paternity leave beyond saved vacation time and noted the gendered assumptions that shaped his opinion. He called himself "traditional," believed mothers should not engage in paid employment, and worried that his traditional perspective would not be recognized in this study about gender.

However, other interviewees also preferred traditional approaches to gender roles. For example, one interviewee described how he would just not leave work, because men do not leave work:

> I don't know, it's less socially acceptable for a guy. Because I know me, come hell or high water, I'm going to work, no exceptions. I don't care if I'm feeling bad or anything. Even if I don't like my job, I'm going to look for a job, [and] I'm not going to take a leave of absence, I'm just going to continue to work come hell or high water.

This interviewee also noted that he believed women and other (less traditional) men could take leave if they wanted to go against the typical gender expectations, but that he personally would not. Vincent agreed:

> Male coworkers taking a leave of absence are rare. Ummm. I think about the most I've ever heard from male coworkers is taking off a week because of the birth of a new child. But in the business environment, it is pretty much frowned upon for men taking that much time off.

Pat echoed Vincent's belief that men taking too much time off is a "frowned-upon practice":

> Anyone who takes time off from work, if it is significant, it eventually hurts their career. When one takes off, the other workers don't take a rest. It gives other people an opportunity to shine and take over. You could go back to work to find yourself misplaced. The fear of that is one thing . . . If they need to take care of a new baby, if somebody is sick, I think those are good reasons, and if one can financially work through things or rearrange their job responsibilities, they should be encouraged to do that.

At the same point in time, they've got to remember that when it comes to work, their primary responsibility is to their employer and they can't fall down to those responsibilities any more than they can fall down on the responsibilities to their family. The responsibilities of both support each other. Businesses cannot and should not be in the business of accommodating a minority number of workers who would like this. They would show favoritism to one group of people rather than another. People used to say I want more money because I have a family. You can't have someone in today's society saying I want time off and let other people work harder because they are single.

Many interviewees expressed their alignment with, or pressure to, conform to the traditional breadwinner role. Jeff explained:

I think a lot of men inherently feel like a provider. It may be a very stereotypical and old, old thinking that the guy provides for the family or, if not, maybe it still has the embedded thought that, you know, "Hey, I'm the one that needs to be providing." Maybe that's why [men] feel more inspired to be there and work.

Richard felt a similar responsibility to be a breadwinner and to perform traditional gender roles:

Well, I think most of us view [that] we're the chief breadwinner and it goes back this out of sight, out of mind thing that hangs in the back of our mind. I love what I do, I just don't want to take the time off and come back and not have what it is that I love doing. Something might change, you know, the program might get cancelled, or new people coming in . . .

While I was working, then, my wife had basically become the chief child rearer. We had four kids: two girls [and] two boys, and her job was to raise the kids . . . and the four kids grew up great. I mean, they all got masters degrees and everything else, all very successful. So, she did a great job and I can't take any credit for that. And working the hours I did, I just was not as much involved with family time as I, you know, in retrospect, probably should have been, but the results turned out great. And, I was busy providing them financial support.

Richard claimed that he might have liked to spend more time with his children but that he felt pride that he financially put them all through college and carried the mortgages on some of his children's and grandchildren's homes.

Zed, a nonprofit worker, felt pressure to take on the role of breadwinner:

Well I think it's the stigma . . . it's kinda, you know, the fact that, you know, society says that men have to be the breadwinner and have to make, you know, make the money and so I think it's just that pressure and just the pressure just to maybe work up the ladder and um you know, prove not only to yourself but to the organization that your worthy of the pay that they give you perhaps?

Zed believed that societal pressure to be the breadwinner contributed to gender inequality at work and made him personally feel responsible to work as hard as he could to provide for his family.

Many interviewees described how they grew up expecting to be breadwinners. One interviewee explained: "I'm 55 years old, and when I was a kid, women didn't even work. My mother didn't work. And most of the mothers in my neighborhood did not work." Another man also described this kind of experience:

> I didn't take leave because I didn't need to. We have 4 children, and each time we had family here. In each instance, when [my wife] came home, my mother was here or she had some other kind of support. I think I worked less during that period of time because she needed extra help, but I wouldn't consider it time off.

For this interviewee, the women in his family took up the additional care work necessary around the time of a new baby. Christopher also explained the link between women and care work:

> Evolution and natural selection you know: it's the women who tend to have the babies, [and], you know, possibly hundreds or thousands of years ago, were the most loving, the ones who liked it the most, and men provided for them.

In a contradictory move, however, Christopher also claimed, "If my wife made my money, I would very seriously consider being a household dad, because I enjoy spending that much time with my daughter." Christopher shared that his desire to spend time with his daughter was different from how he perceived his peers' interest in parenting. For Christopher, traditional roles were important in the "natural" order of gender, but he would be willing to break from his natural breadwinner role given the opportunity.

Describing gendered roles as natural was an unchallenged assumption about breadwinner roles. Gabriel shared, "Men aren't naturally inclined to be stay-at-home parents. The majority might enjoy being a father, but they don't seem to have the nurturing that the mother has." Desmond also shared this perception. He shared his thoughts about why men don't take leave:

> The perception of the individual themselves is that if [a man] comes along and asks for leave because his wife is having a baby, people expect that leave to be short. Where it's perfectly acceptable for a female to

say, "Well, I wanna take two months off, three months off, four months off." I think we tend to think that kind of natural [and] take for granted that for women, it is more natural to take a longer leave. And that's perfectly, perfectly acceptable. I think it boils down to attitude. [When] men come in and say, "I want to take three months off because I'm having a baby," we may say, "Well, why do you need so much time off?" So, it's just like a natural perception, if you will.

The men regularly called on the "natural" division between women as nurturers and men as breadwinners to describe why they did not take leaves of absence. In another example, Liam, who was planning a partial paternity leave, explained:

I know with our family, we are looking to breastfeed, and really, there is only one of us who can do that. So, it's not really a question of who's gonna stay home first. If I didn't have such a generous employer, I wouldn't be able to take that time off.

Liam's statement about breastfeeding as a more acceptable explanation for taking leave hints at the perception that leaves of absence for newborns is less acceptable for people who do not breastfeed. Rhett also believed breastfeeding was a core explanation for gender inequality in leave-taking practice:

Because the woman is actually attached to the baby. I can't breastfeed, so there isn't really an excuse. If you aren't really going to breastfeed, but send your kid to day care, that isn't really fair. Men can never breastfeed.

Another interviewee, Tripp, explained why women could take leaves of absence while men could not:

It's necessity. Raising the kids, and being in that role in the family? They are usually the care providers for the children. If they are pregnant, they are going to need to be nursing and what not, as children get older and get sick, they are usually the ones to take off to take care of them.

In a similar way, Michael explained gendered assumptions about leave-taking that were evident in his experiences:

I think frequently women are more likely to feel that it's their responsibility and/or something that they want to do to take care of people who need taking care of, and that's either their very young babies, or sick relatives, or elderly parents. It tends to be women, I think, more than men, who do that. Men don't seem to feel that as much, but it is not necessarily a clear-cut division.

In this case, Michael referenced the stereotypical gender division of care work and pointed out that many women feel a responsibility for engaging in care work that men might not feel. Michael supposed that the assumption of care work was responsible for inequalities that exist in leave-taking practice. These kinds of arguments about the "nature" of women as caring, or the natural connection between women and leave because of breastfeeding made many men feel as if leaves of absence for care work were not acceptable for men.

Other men in the study articulated a more detached relationship to the gendered order of work. They shared their awareness about gendered expectations, and sometimes mentioned it was not fair. However, they believed that the stigma around violating the gendered order was frequently enough to deter them from personally taking a leave of absence from work.

For example, A.J. discussed gendered assumptions about leave-taking:

> I think sometimes it's almost easier if a girl needs to take a leave of absence for something, [that] it's a little more accepted than for a guy to do that. Guys just kind of have it known amongst themselves . . . I think that you see a lot of women who are [as] dedicated [as men] and have that same mentality [as men,] but I just think that the nature of having a child, I think of just a couple other examples. There are some women I know that they have, like, an ailing grandparent or parent and they're caring for them [but] you don't see too many guys taking care of their ailing parents. I mean some guys do, but you just don't see it as much among men as you do among females. And, if a guy's doing, that usually he's married, usually there's a woman in his life. But just a single guy? No, not as much.

A.J. was quite aware of gendered expectations of care work, and extended these to expectations about partner status. His thought that single "guys" do not engage in care work harkens the image of the ideal worker: one without responsibilities outside of work.

Another interviewee, who took 3 weeks of vacation time for the birth of his child, described some of the teasing he received from his coworkers and boss for his gendered digression:

> It was all in good fun . . . It was like, "You're not gonna want to be home that long with your wife and your kid, you're gonna want to come back" and, "Um, are you having the kid or is she having the kid?" And it was in good fun and I laughed at it and they certainly did not mean that in a mean way. It was good, it was appropriate.

Although this interviewee's coworkers' and boss's teasing was "all in good fun," it nonetheless reveals a reprimand for violating gendered assumptions about men taking leaves of absence, and parental leave in particular. This interviewee believed that 3 weeks was quite a long leave in his organization, and although his time away was supported by his manager and team, he heard many "teasing" comments before and after his time at home. Another interviewee, Joel, shared a similar sentiment:

> Men are embarrassed to ask for the time. It's hard to admit that that's what they're doing; a lot of guys just don't want to be vulnerable in that way and they just don't want to do it . . . people don't and nobody will say, because they don't want to sound like an asshole, but you know, guys think it, they're like, "Oh, well, what's your wife doing? If she's just sitting there, shouldn't you be out working?"

Nathan expressed that societal expectations and the way people are raised creates gendered norms in the workplace:

> Mothers and children are probably expected to be more together than a man would, although I certainly know plenty of men who have taken paternity leave. But [these men] typically come back sooner, and they come back full time. A woman might come back after a longer maternity leave, and maybe come back at some part-time status, to spend more time with her children. I think this is because that's just how women are brought up, and that is how our society still sees things, that the woman is the caregiver primarily.

Nathan explained that he liked the idea of men taking time off for personal and family time, but believed that it probably would not be supported in most organizations. Arie, a graduate student, articulated the gender bias around leaves of absence he witnessed in his organizational experience:

> I largely think, you know, it's part biology where they're the ones who happen to be carrying the children, and you know, that is definitely a toll, a physical toll, so leave is necessary in those instances. And a lot of it is cultural. Where you know, women have largely been associated with taking care of the family through history, so it's more acceptable in a lot of occupations for them to step out to take care of the family in that case. So you know, part necessity and part cultural things that have just evolved over time.
>
> And I think, you know, that taking care of the family or being the nurturing role that [is] imposed upon women, I think that may make it you know, easier for them to take leave for, you know, other family illnesses or things like that where they need to take care of some personal business with their family. Or tak[ing] care [of] someone in their family is likely more acceptable across the board for women to do a goal like that.
>
> Where men, you know, are culturally the breadwinners or viewed as the breadwinners more so. So it seems strange to people who are, you know, socialized in that manner to even think of men taking off time,

even though in the research it's pretty clear that that's beneficial in a lot of different ways.

Arie was supportive of women or men taking leave, but he understood that there were cultural restraints, biases, and differences in the ways men and women can take "acceptable" leaves.

Another interviewee explained a similar disconnect between organizations and individual employee beliefs about gender roles:

> [Organizations in my industry] are actually rather conservative on the inside. Employees are rather open in terms of traditional roles . . . It's in our cultural make-up. American social make-up. Even with dual income families, it is still in our psyche. Our parents still clung to that. Like owning your own home. [Traditional roles] are so engrained in our society even through in many homes it doesn't reflect that, it is accurate in some sense.

This interviewee also believed that men should theoretically take leaves of absence for care work and for self-care but thought it would be impossible for most men to keep their jobs. Tripp shared a similar vision:

> I think guys should take paternity leave, personally. It probably wouldn't go over so good. They might take you back when you got back, if you worked your way up again. In [my previous industry], it probably wouldn't have gone over well there either. Nobody likes it when you're gone. But you know, nobody likes it when women leave either. It just gets tolerated more.

In a final example, Trevor took some longer stretches away from his job in the military. During his interview, he was clear that any "unearned" time off would be reason for dismissal but that he should be allowed to use his "earned days" however he wanted. For this interviewee, he wanted to visit his girlfriend who lived out of state but felt serious backlash from his colleagues when he left. He explained the "harassment" he experienced:

> Um, because it was long chunks. It was big chunks of it and, and when I left there was other people that had to pick up a lot of my slack. So, um, there was a lot of negative, um, kinda back lash or harassment from that, from me taking big chunks of leave.

Although this interviewee expressed anger at the way he was treated, he did not believe the harassment was labor specific. Like some of the previous examples, this interviewee believed that women would also experience backlash for leaving. He continued:

> I wouldn't say necessarily it was gender specific. I would say it's more job specific, I think is really what it is. Um, because again in the Coast

Guard we have, you know, a whole different rank section of jobs. So [leave is] more or less kinda almost tied in with what your job is how much backlash you would get. (Laughter) . . . Females . . . there was actually even more backlash for them when they took leave.

As these examples demonstrate, assumptions about gender influence men's perceptions about the feasibility and acceptability of leaves of absence.

In this subsection, I outlined the ways that interviewees talked about how gendered expectations complicated leave-taking for men and frequently served as a justification for why leaves—particularly family leaves—are completely unnecessary for most men. By specifically explaining that leave is not a masculine practice, and that their roles as breadwinners were important, many men in this study presented a complicated picture of the ways in which gendered role assumptions complicate leave-taking practices. Although the gendered assumptions about work presented here were often described in terms of organizational, occupational, or societal culture, sometimes these ideologies crystalized into actual material constraints that made leaves difficult. In the next section, I present some data that lay out the ways in which the men in this study believed economics, sometimes related to their roles as breadwinners, constrained them from taking leaves of absence from work.

ECONOMICS

To this point, much of the data have presented discursive reasons for the inequality in leave-taking practices. However, actual economics also figure greatly in the ability of men—or any paid workers—to take leaves of absence. This split is what scholars call the symbolic-material divide. Although a focus on the invisible, discursive constraints is necessary, it also eclipses tangible, material aspects of organizing (Adler & Borys, 1993; Ashcraft, Kuhn, & Cooren, 2009). Organizations do emerge through communication, because practices are enacted in specific discursive moments. At the same time, they are filled with "things" such as architecture, technologies, bodies, and economies. As such, it is imperative to also acknowledge the role of the material in influencing leave policies and to realize how the discursive, ideational, or symbolic intertwine with material constraints to reflect organizational life (Ashcraft et al., 2009; Burrell & Dale, 2003). The interplay of these realms is only understood in relation to each other (Ashcraft, Kuhn, & Cooren, 2009).

Most of the men in this study faced real or perceived economic constraints that prevented them from taking leaves of absence. The importance of maintaining a constant paycheck was a consistent theme throughout the interviewees, regardless of occupation or financial status. Men with lower income jobs did not see time off as a feasible option at all, but men at all income ranges expressed that their families depended on their paychecks. Although this is perhaps unsurprising, it is important to look closer into the ways that economics serves as a material constraint that prevents many men from taking a leave of absence from work.

Economic dependence has always played a role in the ability of workers to take time away from work, but the recent economic climate in the United States has compounded the problem. In 2008, the Great Recession, a major global economic crisis, wreaked havoc on workers and organizations across the world. The most severe economic downturn since the Great Depression in the 1920s and 1930s, the Great Recession has changed the way employees feel about job security and has established a deep-rooted fear of economic disaster for many U.S. employees. Through the recession, entire industries and occupations experienced major shifts in workforces and expectations. These significant shifts included, for example, rampant job loss, salary and hiring freezes, mandatory furloughs, suspensions of benefits, salary reductions, and overtime restrictions. Household incomes for most U.S. Americans dropped significantly, and at the peak of the crisis, unemployment reached more than 10%. The recession hit men particularly hard in the early years, when almost two thirds of jobs lost were held by men. Because men typically hold higher salaries, it made more sense for most businesses to lay off men. However, while the "Mancession" did substantially hurt the economic viability of men, it also had a serious impacted on women. As the recovery proceeds, men have regained more jobs than women have (California Budget Project, 2010), but the cultural fear of job loss remains and contributes to a perceived inability to leave work.

The economic problems have likely increased the stress on U.S. workers and made securing equitable terms for leaves of absence more difficult. As Moe and Shandy (2010) explained,

> economic turbulence leads many employers to enter into a bunker mentality of sorts, and . . . [employees] will have a more difficult time negotiating family-friendly policies, as so many people are clamoring for the jobs and are willing to do whatever it takes to keep the jobs they have. (p. 159)

Of concern here is that employees may ignore their rights to leaves of absence because they fear that leaving, even for a short time, will make them vulnerable to layoffs. Employees' use of work–life benefits is dependent, in large part, on whether they believe they will face punishment for doing so (Ashcraft, 1999; Buzzanell & Liu, 2005; Lewis, 1997; Peterson & Albrect, 1999; Tracy & Rivera, 2009). In order to keep their jobs secure, workers frequently forgo their rights to leave, a practice that solidifies the belief that taking leaves of absence is harmful to workers' careers.

There is some evidence that, during layoffs, employers eliminate "frill" benefits and target pregnant women and women on flexible work arrangements. However, many companies maintain flexible scheduling, including part-time work, as a way to save money (Galinsky & Bond, 2009). Although telecommuting and unpaid leaves of absence save companies money, employees using these policies still feel vulnerable and fear the stigma and bias of working nontraditional schedules. Thus, even when employers maintain existing work–life programs such as flexible scheduling, many employees do not take advantage of these programs in order to avoid marginalization and penalization at work, which is a tendency exacerbated in the current economic climate (Calvert, 2009).

Many men provided examples of their perception about how economics made taking a leave of absence very difficult. A driver, Tripp said simply, "Money. If nobody is covering your bills, you gotta work. Otherwise we'd be on permanent vacation." This interviewee believed it would be very difficult for him to take *any* time off *ever*. Another interviewee, Tom, described how he took one day off at the birth of his children, a common practice in his work as a ditch digger:

> I think I have heard that some men are starting to take off. In my particular field, I think the younger generation is more prone to do that. That just wasn't done when we were having kids. You brought in cigars or brought in donuts or something. I took the next day off because I was up all night. There was no written rule, but it was just—we were there for the delivery, and then we went back to work to make some money to pay for everything!

Tom believed that no time off was standard practice for family, but he saw men take extensive lengths of time off for injury under worker's compensation. Quentin also described how his financial situation dictated his leave-taking practice:

> [It was] just because of our own personal financial situation. I couldn't really afford to go unpaid at that time, especially because my wife was quitting her work. So, nope, [taking leave] never really crossed my mind . . . if I could have afforded to go without a paycheck for that time, I definitely would have.

Quentin expressed a desire to take a leave of absence but mentioned it "never really crossed" his mind because the financial ramifications were too great. Tom agreed:

> Money is huge. You're not going to take a leave of absence if it's going to throw your family into bankruptcy. Not even just bankruptcy, but if it is going to put you into a hole for a whole year if you took two months off. Even now, I couldn't do it. At a younger age, it would have been extremely difficult if I wasn't able to make the money—especially when I was the sole provider.

Tom believed that in his early career, even a couple of days off would have put serious financial constraints on his family.

In another example, Stanley, grad student, said,

> If I don't get paid there's pretty much, I'm not married, I don't have another source of income, can't really count on my parents 'cause they're pretty strapped for cash, so I wouldn't be able to pay rent, I wouldn't be able to do much of anything.

Stanley had to rely on himself to make ends meet, which was difficult with a graduate student stipend and impossible without it. Another graduate student felt a similar financial crunch when asked if he would consider taking a leave of absence. He said, "When you're a graduate student, you're living hand to mouth. Or really from paycheck to paycheck. And you know, any sort of disruption to that has the potential to be disastrous."

A third graduate student, who was expecting the birth of his first child at the time of the interview, also expressed the financial impossibility of taking time off:

> So, I'm—just from what I've been told—expected to be back and to not fall behind on any of my coursework or anything like that. And if I do so, I'll be required to take an incomplete on any coursework, and I wouldn't be getting paid for time that I've missed. So that's not really an option for me to do given the financial constraints.

This interviewee did not plan to take any time off at the birth of his child. Another interviewee, Ryder, a driver/liquor distributor, said that his wife recently had had a baby at the time of the interview. He shared his difficulty in taking time off for the birth:

> The problem with [unpaid leave] is that I'm the only paycheck right now, because [my wife] can't work, so we could not afford for me to take off an unpaid week, so that's why I had to kind of finagle and butter up my bosses to give me these two weeks of paid vacation, because there's no way that we could have—we would have sunk if I took an unpaid week.

Although Ryder was able to "finagle" two weeks of paid vacation time, any unpaid leave time was not feasible for his family's financial survival.

John, a small-business owner, also spoke about economics as an important factor in whether or not he would take an unpaid leave of absence:

> If you can't afford it you just can't afford it. I think you can plan for it and find ways to afford it, but sometimes like an injury or things like that you may not get to plan so that's a fear that's always looming probably in every small businessman's mind is something, the unpredicted happens, will I be able to afford it?

Another small-business owner expressed a similar view: "If anybody said, you know, money isn't everything, just try to live for a little while when you don't have any. It's hard."

Regge, a baseball consultant, also described the financial difficulties of taking time off unpaid:

> Right now, I've got to make sure the lights are on and the bills are paid, and being the head of an upstart, I don't have the ability to up and go for three weeks. It's not something I could afford to do. For one, potential business that could be lost, and for two, just the simple finances.

Taking too much time off would have had negative financial consequences for Regge.

As these examples illustrate, men at all income levels perceive financial constraints as reasons that prevent them from taking unpaid time off. The men with lower paying jobs, or men without partners did not believe leaves of absence were possible at all. However, many men with middle- and upper income jobs also believed that they could not afford to take time off, particularly if they were supporting their family. As lifestyles and expenses frequently grow with income, almost all of the men interviewed believed that they could not afford to take too much time off.

While the previous examples highlighted a belief that any kind of leave would be financially difficult or impossible, many of the interviewees believed they could afford to take 1 or 2 weeks off. For example, Vincent, an accountant, shared his view on how long a leave of absence could reasonably last in his profession:

> One week for a baby. That is about all I've ever seen. Whenever they do take time off, they aren't getting their paycheck. They can use vacation and sick, but other than those, generally they've got to go back to work because they've got to keep paying the bills.

One week was a common answer in response to how long a leave of absence could last for men. Another interviewee explained:

> I've seen people take a week off for their child, but never for a longer period of time, like to take care of their parents, or for terminal diseases, but I've never seen that. I've read about it, but I think it is tough for people to take too much time off because they have to put food on the table, to pay their rent. People today are not inclined to have a large cash reserve, so they can't afford to take time off . . . Primarily because they can't afford to.

In this interviewee's experience, most people could usually afford to take a week of time off, but he believed most of his clients would have a very difficult time taking more than a week off unpaid. In a final example, Ryder, a driver, simply explained, "I could go about a week, max, if I had to. Even that would still put me behind, but I could for emergency."

Greg also shared his thoughts on the material consequences of men taking leaves of absence:

> When the men are doing it, they're gonna be doing it and gonna be losing salary. With women, at least where I work, they've always been given six weeks of paid maternity leave . . . I think if anyone took it beyond that, then they would be doing it without pay. So, I would think that's the incentive not to go any further than beyond the two weeks.

Greg's perception was that at his company, women were paid for maternity leave whereas men were only entitled to their vacation time. As these examples demonstrate, some men believed that a week or two of time off from work might be economically viable, but more than that would be difficult or detrimental to their economic security.

Other men in the study thought about the long-term economic impacts of taking a leave of absence. Vincent described the following:

> It is a difficult choice to balance your responsibilities, to your family and to the unknowns you are going to have in the future. If you take leaves, you aren't making money. People need money! We don't die like we used to. People live into their 90s and 100s. It is expensive to do that. It takes a lot of money to do that . . . my parents' generation didn't have to worry about how they were going to live after 65 to death. Now we have to worry about that. You have to think about it and make sure everyone is going to be covered, and you must earn money to do that.

Throughout the interview, Vincent explained his belief that good financial practice is to continually engage in work.

In another example, Tripp explained how his long-term financial goals precluded him from taking a leave of absence:

> I guess, I don't know, in most situations the men are making more. So if a child gets sick or something and a family member needs to take care of it, it will usually be the one who makes the least amount of money. You gotta think about the long-run effects. Who will be the one that can make more? It is a long-run family decision. Who makes more? They don't leave work. That's the way it worked in my house.

For Tripp thinking about the income of his partner and their long-term family goals was important in his decision to forgo a leave of absence. In a similar way, Tom described his experience:

> [My wife] was home for 10 years. When that was happening, I didn't have a good work–life balance. I worked 60–80 hours a week sometimes. But

I made more money and it made more sense for me to work the overtime than it did for her to get a job at a clothing store or something. I could get time and a half. We made an agreement that she would stay at home and take care of the kids, and I worked my butt off. Now I'm a little less busy. I've still got plenty to do around the house. Actually, I don't think I'm less busy, but we've shifted our focus. Now we do stuff with our grandkids. It's like, if you have the time you didn't have the money, and if you have the money, you didn't have the time. A little tug of war through life.

Tom explained his leave choices simply. He made more money so he worked more hours. His family could not afford paid time off at all, so he rarely took time off throughout his career.

Many men thought about leaves of absence in terms of their overall familial earnings. Rhett explained:

The assumption that the males are the primary wage earner, you know, if both are working, obviously whoever's job can pay the bills. If you can pay the bills and take more time off, that is great, but I don't know what kind of jobs let you take a lot of time off and still earn a lot.

Rhett took 2 weeks of paid vacation time at the births of his children but worked virtually during the time off. He did not believe he could take unpaid time off because his wife was simultaneously taking unpaid leave. Liam also described his partner's unpaid leave as a factor in his leave choices:

When you talk about people not getting paid, it can be very difficult . . . I actually intend to take my leave off when her leave ends, so that we have one of us working at any time. If that makes sense; it does for us.

For Liam, his family economics would be stable with some paid time off, as long as he could alternate with his partner.

Rocket, a marketing director, explained that he and his wife worked together to plan who and how to make money as a family:

My wife, she does bring in a portion of our income, but it's a fraction of what I bring in so being the chief kind of moneymaker for the family, taking unpaid leave, really, for that amount of time it could be done, but it's very difficult, and even if we were unpaid for even say four weeks, that actually kind of affects us for many months to come as we have to rebuild up the savings or whatever it is. So, unless she could make up the difference financially, it would be very difficult for me to leave at this time.

Earlier in the interview, Rocket explained that he did take some time off around the births of his children, during a time when his wife made more money. However, the couple's jobs changed over time, which put Rocket in a position that would be difficult to leave.

As some of these examples suggest, money was a major factor in these men's inability to take a leave of absence. These data suggest that if leaves were paid, a number of these men might take the time they need away from work. As discussed previously, the unpaid aspect of U.S. leave policies is incredibly problematic. Alexis M. Herman, secretary of labor, addressed this issue:

> We know that many working families did not get enough help as they tried to balance work and family needs. While worrying about their own health or that of a family member, or caring for their newborn child, millions of these workers were also worrying about their pay-check. In fact the number one worry, cited by more than half of leave takers, was about having enough money to pay bills . . . [in 2000] more than one-third of employees received no pay during their longest leave and . . . nearly two out of every five leave takers had to cut their leave short due to lost pay . . . Pay was not just a worry to those on leave but was a barrier to those who needed to take leave . . . lack of pay was the number one reason workers who needed leave did not take it . . . The importance of pay cannot be overstated—almost 88% of those who needed leave said they would have taken leave if they had received some or additional pay . . . There are still over three and one-half million workers who needed to take time off from work but did not do so . . . almost half of these workers needed leave for their own serious health condition and nearly one in four needed to care for an ill parent . . . many employees still worry that their job might be lost if they take time off from work. Almost one-third of all workers who needed leave but did not take it cited worries about losing their job as a reason for not taking leave. (U.S. Department of Labor, 2001)

Taken together, these statistics and the data collected from the men in this study suggest a serious problem with the issue of pay that precludes many employees from the ability to take extended time away from work for family or self-care. Because gender is so closely tied with compensation, the cultural and economic impacts of gender ideologies cannot be overlooked when unpacking the causes of the glass handcuffs phenomenon.

REFERENCES

Adler, P. S., & Borys, B. (1993). Materialism and idealism in organizational research. *Organization Studies, 14*(5), 657–679. doi:10.1177/017084069301400503

Ashcraft, K. L. (1999). Managing maternity leave: A qualitative analysis of temporary executive succession. *Administrative Science Quarterly, 44*(2), 240–280. doi:10.2307/2666996

Ashcraft, K. L., Kuhn, T., & Cooren, F. (2009). Constitutional amendments: "Materializing" organizational communication. *The Academy of Management Annals, 3*(1), 1–64. doi:10.1080/19416520903047186

Boydston, J. (1994). *Home and work: Housework, wages, and the ideology of labor in the early republic.* New York, NY: Oxford University Press.

Burrell, G., & Dale, K. (2003). Building better worlds? Architecture and critical management studies. In M. Alvesson & H. Willmott (Eds.), *Studying management critically* (pp. 177–196). Thousand Oaks, CA: Sage.

Buzzanell, P., & Liu, M. (2005). Struggling with maternity leave policies and practices: A poststructuralist feminist analysis of gendered organizing. *Journal of Applied Communication Research, 33*(1), 1–25. doi:10.1080/ 00909880420003184 95

California Budget Project. (2010, May). How the other half fared: The impact of the Great Recession on women. *Policy Points,* pp. 1–9.

Calvert, C. (2009). Work life law: Testimony before the joint economic committee hearing on balancing work and family in the recession. The Center for WorkLife Law. Retrieved from: http://www.worklifelaw.org/pubs/WLL_Testimony_to_ Senate_JEC_7_23_09.pdf

Cobble, D. S. (2004). *The other women's movement: Workplace justice and social rights in modern America.* Princeton, NJ: Princeton University Press.

Dale, K., & Burrell, G. (2008). *The spaces of organisation and the organisation of space: Power, identity and materiality at work.* Basingstoke, England: Palgrave Macmillan.

Galinsky, E., & Bond, J. T. (2009). *The impact of the recession on employers: Families and Work Institute report.* Retrieved from http://familiesandwork.org/site/ research/reports/Recession2009.pdf

Kessler-Harris, A. (2003). *Out to work: A history of wage-earning women in the United States* (20th ed.). New York, NY: Oxford University Press.

Lewis, S. (1997). "Family friendly" employment policies: A route to changing organizational culture or playing about at the margins? *Gender, Work, & Organization, 4*(1), 13–23. doi:10.1111/1468-0432.00020

McCarver, V., & Blithe, S. J. (2014, May) *This is not where we thought we would be: Still striving for the good life through feminism.* Paper presented at the annual meeting of the International Communication Association, Seattle, WA.

Moe, K., & Shandy, D. (2010). *Glass ceilings & 100-hour couples: What the opt-out phenomenon can teach us about work and family.* Athens: The University of Georgia Press.

Okin, S. M. (1999). *Is multiculturalism bad for women?* Princeton, NJ: Princeton University Press.

Peterson, L. W., & Albrecht, T. L. (1999). Where gender/power/politics collide: Deconstructing maternity leave policy. *Journal of Management Inquiry, 8*(2), 168–181. doi:10.1177/105649269982011

Smuts, R. W. (1971). *Women and work in America.* New York, NY: Schocken Books.

Tracy, S. J., & Rivera, K. D. (2009). Endorsing equity and applauding stay-at-home moms: How male voices on work-life reveal adverse sexism and flickers of transformation. *Management Communication Quarterly, 24,* 3–43. doi:10.1177/0893318909352248

U.S. Department of Labor. (2001). *Balancing the needs of families and employers: Family and medical leave surveys, 2000 update.* Retrieved from http://www.dol. gov/whd/fmla/cover-statement.pdf

The Women's Studies Work Group. (1975). Loom, broom, and womb: Producers, maintainers, and reproducers. *Frontiers: A Journal of Women's Studies, 1*(1), 1–41.

9 "Who Needs Time Off?"
Reframing Leaves of Absence as Unnecessary

A final cause of the glass handcuffs is resistance to the concept of time away from work. Many of the men in this study rejected the notion that leaves of absence were necessary or desirable. They primarily resisted leaves in four ways: First, many men described their ability to work virtually as mitigating any need for time off. Second, most of the men in this study used vacation time in lieu of leave, and almost all the men in this study conflated vacation time with leave time. Third, a surprising number of men described quitting to get time off at crucial moments in their lives as preferable to taking a leave of absence. Fourth, some men described the distinction between work and life as completely irrelevant or nondescriptive of their lives. Instead, they cast work *as* life and, in some cases, life *as* work. These explanations were clearly depicted as practices that were *not* leaves of absence, which were preferable to leaves of absence, and which determined why many men did not and would not take a leave of absence.

VIRTUAL WORK

Throughout the study, many men talked about working virtually as their preferred work–life balance strategy. Flexible schedules, telecommuting, and completely virtual organizations are increasingly available for many employees.[1] Roughly 63 million individuals work virtually in some capacity, up from 34 million in 2010 (Meyer, 2012), and virtual and flexible schedules are often credited with increasing work–life balance. Although most virtual work implies working from an office at home, virtual employees are not bound by location—work can occur "anywhere, anytime, and with anyone" (Igbaria & Tan, 1997, p. i). This could mean that employees can work while on the sideline of a soccer game, at a gym, or at a Starbucks. If employees can work from anywhere, they can theoretically live and work at the same time, unbound by physical workspace or traditional conceptualizations of time (Crandall & Wallace, 1998). Virtual work, thus, erases traditional workplace boundaries and can facilitate work–life balance for some workers.[2] However, scholarship on virtual work suggests that balance is also compromised in this kind of work, as technologies invade the home, work hours increase, and many employees working from home experience a sense that work never ends (Parlapiano & Cobe, 1996). Still, many workers believe that working from home improves their work–life balance, and the men in this study overwhelmingly believed that their time spent virtually working enabled them to avoid taking a leave of absence. For example, A.J., who took some time away from his office for a broken leg, explained how working virtually enabled him to avoid a leave of absence:

> At first, I just couldn't even work, but I still got paid. I don't even think they deducted my vacation. But then the rest of my time that I was in the cast, I worked from home, and they allowed me to do that.

Although A.J. could not work because he was heavily sedated in the first few days, he was relieved that his company allowed him to work virtually for the duration of his time in the hospital and while he recovered at home.

Another interviewee, Owen, also described how working virtually enabled him to avoid taking a leave of absence while he was undergoing treatment for cancer:

> When I was in the hospital having chemo, I was still feeling okay so I could still do work with my laptop. When you do a leave of absence, be it for health or even the guys or the ladies that take FML for paternity, they could still do work at home because they're mobile . . . There's a lot of times you can do the work, and, given the ability from the company to take your laptops home, [this] can really help out a lot to be able to do your work.

Work was a welcome relief from treatment for Owen, who was grateful for the opportunity to keep working through his treatment because it made him feel like himself and took his mind off his health problems. The ability to work virtually eliminated the need for him to take a full leave of absence. Owen was approved to take an extended leave through FMLA but found he preferred to work. Thus, he took a few days off and then worked some from home. He explained that virtual work enabled him to balance time to take care of himself with time for work.

In another example, Nick also described how his full-time work-from-home schedule alleviated work–life conflict:

> I think I have a pretty good work–life balance. I can fix my hours pretty easily. I can go up and have lunch with my family [and I am] able to go work out at lunch if I wanted to. I mean, I have a twenty second, if that, commute from bedroom to basement to office. It's not like I need to go get in the car and drive 45 minutes each way, which cuts into either my family time or work time, you know, as far as the work–life balance. So,

I feel like I have it pretty good working out of the house because I can get up earlier, or stay later, and flex my time during the day so that I can have some balance. From that perspective, I don't have an issue with it [and] I don't feel overworked [and] I don't feel underworked.

Just to give you an example, today I got up and started work at 6:00 A.M. so that I could run up at 7:30-ish to help my wife get the kids dressed and fed. Then at 8:30 A.M. she took off with two of the kids, leaving one kid here in the swing, the four month old, so she could go get groceries. So, you know, I'm trying to work and manage watching the baby, and our days are blending together. I guess there's a saying [that] the days are long, but the years fly by, which so far has been the case. So, yeah, right now it's managing and it's supporting the family and at lunch or if I try to get out in the morning to work out, I do.

Blending parenting and work facilitated work–life balance for Nick, and alleviated his need for leaves of absence.

Another interviewee, Jesse, also noted that the ability to work virtually saved him the hassle of taking a leave of absence when his child was born:

I basically juggled working over the phone and on the computer with customers with [my child] being here. He just barely started going to preschool three days a week. But my boss knows all about this . . . and so, I didn't really need to [take leave] because I was at home already.

Jesse moved to a virtual office when his first child was born, and continued to work in that capacity so he could parent full-time while his wife worked. Jesse also described experiencing work–life conflict from his arrangement but felt strongly that working from home enabled him to successfully balance his life and family responsibilities in a way that worked for him.

In a similar example, Doug explained how virtual policies enabled him to avoid taking a leave of absence:

The newer trends are things like flex time [and] working from home, but taking long leaves is definitely frowned upon. I think having the freedom to take a day whenever you need or [to] take a half-day, or just leave for a few hours actually accomplished balance in a better way than long periods of time away . . . Not being confined to rigid hours or a rigid work-type structure leads to better work–life balance, because you can deal with things that could be stressful to you, like if you couldn't just deal with them right away then they would lead to stress.

And I think removing that stress is what maintains work–life balance. I don't think it necessarily has to be a certain number of hours away, or even necessarily a rigid separation between the two. Taking the kids to the park and working on your laptop, that's a very blurry thing. But that contributes to work–life balance. I don't think it's necessarily a dividing line between "this is work" and "this is life." Taking a leave doesn't accomplish this[; rather,] it creates more stress because you aren't getting stuff done at work.

For Doug, taking longer leaves of absence created stress because work would build up. In this way, it paradoxically hurts the balance of work and nonwork pursuits. Thus, Doug found flextime to be more beneficial for finding work–life balance than leaves of absence. Darrell, a music producer, explained a similar experience:

> The job is pretty flexible so, assuming that I can stay on top of things, there's rarely anything that has to be done at any specific time. So I am able to, you know, I'm able to work from anywhere. So I can go home for a week and work more or less depending on what's going on around the house. So when my kids were born I didn't really take a leave, I stopped touring five months before our first kid was born and used that time to sort set up some systems and get settled into a routine that would give me some flexibility.

Like many of the examples presented, Darrell found that technology and flextime enabled him to mold his work tasks around the rest of his life, which made leaves of absence unnecessary.

One network salesman explained that leaves of absence were unnecessary for him because of his ability to work remotely:

> So my wife and I, before we had kids, every February we would take a road trip to California, and we would rent a house there and I would pack—we would pack—all of our stuff up, because she works from home, too, and we would just stay there for a month. It was a vacation that we took, because we didn't really take time off, but we would work while we were there. So I didn't have to go and take time off at my vacation, but sure as heck, I was wearing shorts and a tee shirt in February.

Mobile work enabled this worker and his spouse to take a very long time away from their usual offices without needing a formal leave of absence or even vacation time.

As a final example, Greg also worked virtually when he had his first child. He explained:

> The details that needed to be dealt with I just, I dealt with from home. I'd log in for an hour here or there and help out. So, in terms of planning for it, you know, it really wasn't too big of a deal.

Greg found that leaving work was fairly easy because he could continue to handle details and other work expectations virtually. The merits of virtual work were mentioned in a variety of contexts in this study, but particularly in explaining why the men interviewed here did not take formal or official leaves of absence.

Although the men drawing on virtual work as a strategy to avoid leaves of absence were certain about their ability to achieve balance, virtual work is only available for certain occupations. For many trade or manual workers, and for some executive-level men interviewed, virtual work was not an option discussed. So although virtual work may indeed help avoid stigmatized leaves of absence, this strategy in particular is only available for a specific group of men—mid-range-knowledge workers who had some control over the portability of their work. Some executive-knowledge workers spoke about virtual work as well but generally expressed stronger concerns about face time in their leadership roles and suggested virtual work would only be an option during an emergency or a special situation.

VACATION TIME

Some men in this study claimed they *did* take leaves of absence at various points in their lives. However, these "leaves of absence" for the men in this study were almost unanimously accomplished through saved vacation time. One interviewee, working in academia, described how he structured his ability to take 6 months off from work for the upcoming birth of his child:

> We get FMLA, [so] you have to take, or you can take, up to six months of accrued sick or vacation leave during the first year that your child is born. It's very generous enough, especially when compared with industry or anything else. It has to be accrued leave—it's not a gift. They sort of encourage you to manage your sick and vacation leave in with your family planning. So, if you've been here 12 years [and] you have 6 months accrued, then you can have one kid and take six months, or you can have three kids and take two months, or you can have six kids and take one month. It's really up to you—you get to manage how you get paid during that time.

Even in this extreme case (the only leave in this study to last longer than 3 weeks), the employee still drew almost exclusively on vacation time.

Another interviewee, Christopher, took 3 weeks off work. He explained:

> We actually have a very generous leave plan. I think I have like four weeks of vacation [and] I can carry it over from year to year, up to [a total of] six weeks. So, I have a very generous leave with pay, vacation, and I also accrue four hours of vacation or of sick leave per pay period,

which carries over. I can [also] carry over unlimited amount of sick leave. So I took a month off at the birth of my daughter. I used, sick time, but I actually came back after three weeks.

Although he was able to take what he called a leave of absence, Christopher's time off was his earned vacation time. Adam cited a similar strategy to take time off and explained, "I had vacation time saved up, and I just went to my boss and asked if I could take a month off or six weeks off, and they said it was okay." Using vacation time, even in block amounts, was an acceptable alternative to leave for some of the men in this study.

As another example, Quentin claimed, "I haven't taken a leave of absence. The most I did was two weeks when my son was born, but that was more just time off. It wasn't extended leave. I used my vacation time." Quentin's company required him to use vacation time before he could access the FMLA benefits, and he decided not to take additional time off. In a similar way, after saying that he took a leave of absence on the birth of his daughter (just 3 weeks before his interview), Ryder, a driver/liquor distributor explained:

> I get three weeks. I've been with the company for eight years, so I have three weeks paid vacation a year, and I just so happen to have two more weeks left this late in the year, and I took the week that she was born. And then I went back to work for a week, and then I took this week off.

As a final example, Jeff explained:

> When I had each one of my sons, I took one week of vacation time each time. And that wasn't paid time off, I mean it wasn't above and beyond my vacation time, or those three weeks that I have.

These employees' substitution of vacation time for leaves of absence was nearly an invisible marker and one that complicated this study. When asked if they had ever taken a leave of absence, a few men answered yes and then later explained that they used sick or vacation time to address non-work issues. Other men asked questions about the definition of "leave" and were quite unsure about what would or would not constitute a "leave." In general, they seemed to equate "leaves of absence" with time off spent with their children, which was not described as culturally supported except through earned vacation time, or with personal health, which was perceived as unavoidable. For the men in this study, however, when talking about their own personal experiences with leave, it was always (with only one exception) discussed as vacation time, and positioned such that using time already earned was preferable to "taking time from your company," as one interviewee described. When questioned about the correlation between leave and vacation time, some men explicated that formal organizational policy dictated that they take vacation or sick time first, before they could take unpaid "leave," while others did not challenge the trend to use vacation time completely in lieu of a formal leave of absence.

QUITTING

Another prevalent way that men avoided taking official leaves of absence was to quit their jobs. In perhaps the most interesting finding of this study, a number of men cited a trend to quit their jobs in order to generate a lengthy time away from work. For example, Max, a courier said,

> Work–life balance means family first and then money. Whatever family needs, that always comes first. I would quit my job in a heartbeat and go out to be with my dad if he needed me. I'm a hard worker, but I'll quit a job in a heartbeat, if it is something that needs to be done.

Max emphasized this attitude throughout his interview, consistently suggesting that no job was more important than his family, that he had quit previous jobs to address the needs of his family, and that he would easily quit again if he felt it would benefit his life.

In another example, A.J. explained that many men who need balance "just went and found another job to get peace of mind. It's kind of like therapy: take a couple months in between." In a similar vein, Oliver explained:

> I've had a little bit of a pattern where every time we had a child, I just quit my job and didn't take a leave. It just happened to always be at a time where I was sort of done with that job and I would, you know, take that as a reason [to quit]. So when our first was born, I worked from home and as a consultant, independently, for about a year and a half. And when the second was born, well, [I had] about the same—not quite as long, but probably ten months—where I took off and was at home and worked out of the basement.

Oliver's "coincidental" scheduling of hiatuses around the births of his children enabled him to achieve long stretches of time away from work. However, quitting a job seems precariously risky, particularly in an unfriendly labor market.

Despite the risks, another interviewee reflected,

> I've seen a decent amount of men leaving when they have kids, kind of using it as a stepping stone to leave the company and then do something else, like a take a break and then do something else. I know at least three or four people that have done that.

Thus, quitting to secure time off was presented as an ordinary practice that could facilitate work–life balance. In another example, when asked if he would ever take a leave of absence, Adam said,

> I think the policy is that they would terminate you. There's no sabbatical, but I know that for a fact because I actually talked to people and they want to go on like a one-year leave, and the only way is to get fired or to resign and come back later, to get rehired. I think we're pretty good about hiring people back though.

Adam went on to explain that it was common practice to rehire workers who quit or were laid off, particularly because laying workers off between projects when the workflow slowed was a regular experience.

Shawn, an engineer, also explained that quitting was a common practice:

> I know a guy who quit his job so that he could spend more time with his child. He got a new job, but that's standard. It's like if you want to be spending time with your kid, you leave your job, find something else that's more accommodating.

Shawn's example demonstrates a prevailing assumption that occupational roles or organizations do not need to change to accommodate work–life concerns but, rather, that individual workers should claim responsibility for managing balance.

Gabriel, a nonprofit worker, also viewed quitting as a viable option to help facilitate better work–life balance:

> If somebody did have a baby or somebody had something and they thought well, you know, [getting leave approved] isn't going to happen, rather than even attempting to do it, [they] might just go ahead and either just quit or find a new job.

Gabriel believed quitting would be easier than getting a leave of absence approved for many workers. Another nonprofit worker, Pat, described his own experience quitting to gain extended time away from work:

> I've taken a couple of months off many years ago from a different employer. Um with the understanding that my job would be waiting when I came back if I wanted it, but that leave of absence, it was more of a separation with the understanding that I would be re-hired. It wasn't a, uh, truly a leave.

That quitting is an easier option than taking a leave of absence is speaks to the cultural bias against formal leaves of absence. It also suggests that work and nonwork pursuits are not compatible, and instead, one must completely separate the two realms rather than combine them with the use of periodic stretches away from work.

THE WORK–LIFE DISTINCTION IS IRRELEVANT

> If you truly are passionate and you love what you do, you won't work another day of your life.
>
> —Regge, baseball consultant

Many interviewees claimed that any distinction between work and life was irrelevant. These men claimed that, for people with a true passion for their work, work is life and life is work; thus, any distinction between the two is not useful. The preceding quote was repeated, with slight modifications, in quite a few interviews. For example, a security guard said, "If your work is something you absolutely love, it's a part of your life whether you're at the office or not." These men strongly resisted work–life as separate spheres, and claimed that they personally experienced work as life and their lives as their work.

Nathan, a graduate teaching assistant, explained how his work is entrenched in his life passions:

> Because so much of who I am and what I do is also tied up in the kind of scholarship that I do. So you know, the homeless shelter where I was doing my research—I still go and volunteer there. And I'm not doing active observations or anything like that anymore, but that's still very much a part of my life in the work that I do. There's not a good clear boundary.

Nathan experienced his research, teaching, and life passions as completely enmeshed together and could not make sense of separating them. In a similar way, Darrell, a music producer, shared the following:

> I wonder how much of what I'm doing now is driven by sort of the financial benefits and the comfort that it provides to our life and how much of it is because it's what I would like to be doing. I don't imagine like I said not having the work would kill me. You know I would go bonkers if I didn't have it. So it may be in that way is sort of a life thing . . . It's a little bit of life melding into work.

Because Darrell found a career in his dream industry, work did not always feel like work, but rather felt fun. Regge, a baseball consultant, also described his career as in his dream industry. He claimed, "When your work becomes something that you love to do, it's hard to get burned out on doing something you love. I'm lucky to be in the field I've always wanted to be in." Regge's passionate commitment to his work stemmed from his love of baseball and the efforts he put into building a career in the industry.

Michael also believed that his work was wrapped in his life passions and could not be easily separated:

> The great majority of people I've known in this business [believe that] work is life. Doing hardware [and] software development is a very, very large part of their li[ves]. I don't know that they're thinking of balance in many other respects. I hesitate to say it's even work. I mean, that's obviously what they're doing for a living and making money, but they are just so interested in this stuff that that's pretty much most of their life. [Work], to them, is balance. They aren't thinking a whole lot about other things; when they get home and sleep, they're dreaming about solving their work puzzles.
>
> I'm really that way. I really like my work. It's problems that I'm thinking about [that] stay in my head. I'll wake up in the middle of the night and have an idea for something, [and] I'll run downstairs and write a note on it or something. I don't really, in that sense, draw a firm line between my work and the rest of my life. I just enjoy both . . . I think, in a perfect world, you don't have the distinction, [and] that work is just another part of life like everything else and that it's all just life. It's just that some of it is a life you get paid for, and some of it is not. That all of it is things that matter to you. I think [there is a] strong defense against thinking that your life is futile and fractured.

Michael felt that his life was not split into work and nonwork pursuits because he so passionately loved his work. Solving work problems gave him significant satisfaction during nonwork hours. He mentioned that he felt uneasy if he left a problem unresolved and that he was better able to manage his stress if he continued to work on work problems at home after work hours.

Arie, a graduate student, also believed that any distinction between work and life was irrelevant for his life experience:

> My work and my life are very much intertwined, but at the same time I think that there should be space in that life for my family, and not having to work all the time. Being able to do things I enjoy . . . But I am a teacher, and I will teach my children anyway, sort of in the same role as professor to some extent. That kind of bleeds over within that parental role. So I think that for me, [work and life] are highly connected. I don't think that there's a way that I can create a big divide between my work and my life.

Nathan described similar feelings and explained:

> When I get to a weekend, if there's an interesting problem that I've been working on, if I get some time during the weekend, I'll go up into

my home office and work on it, not just because it's my job, but because I just love it. So, I've thought to myself on any number of occasions that I probably don't have enough hobbies. And I probably don't have enough male friends that I can just call up and say, "Hey, you want to hang out?" I guess in my more wistful moments, I sort of wish I did. Maybe that would be my idea of balance, but it's my choice, [and] I choose to be that way. Like this weekend, I sort of forced myself to go up and ski a little bit. But what was keeping me from doing [work] was that there was an interesting computer problem that I wanted to looked at, and I realized in my head that I'd spent too much time looking at it, and I'd be better off just going off and giving it a rest and come back to it. But I had to force myself to do that. So, I might not be very balanced, so I might not be the best person to talk about it. But, I'm imbalanced because it's the way I want to be, if that makes any sense.

For both Michael and Peter, their passion for their work did not stop when working hours stopped. They brought their work problems home and framed this practice as a positive way that they constructed their lives outside of their workplaces.

Other interviewees also resisted the notion of work–life balance. For example, Shawn resisted the idea that work and life were separate entities at all. He argued,

I don't think it's separated by time slot necessarily because there are times when I'm at [work] and I'm in the office, and being in the office, I think you have to live life where you're working. [You need to] take time to see how the people around you are doing and build those relationships. That's life, too, and, so, a work–life balance is being a human in that situation, instead of just being a robot trying to get my stuff done. It's not like I'm a machine performing only one thing at one time.

For Shawn, the overlap of work and life was necessary, inevitable, and beneficial for his conception of a balanced life.

Phillip also asserted that distinctions between work and nonwork were impractical:

I could technically work from nine to five, 40 hours a week, but it's just not realistic. It's just not something that exists. What if during those hours there's no work to be done, or there's nothing interesting happening, or I'm bored? I find I get a lot of work done when I want to get work done. You know, I need to think about problems. Anything can be done, I just need to think about how to do it. So, I find I work often at night [and so] there's no relevance to sort of that status quo [of] nine-to-five in this industry [and particularly] in web development, in programming, in engineering, and stuff.

In Phillip's example, dividing work and nonwork by time was useless.

Desmond also noted that the distinction between work and life was not particularly useful. He described the practice of socializing with work acquaintances as a gray area that complicated a neat work–life binary:

> Some companies attempt to promote the idea of work–life balance, and they introduce different social aspects of company picnics and they provide facilities where employees can take part in some other social aspects. It may be a social club or maybe a get-together to do something [where] the people you see are all people from your own company. These are the coworkers. And people, invariably, would talk about work or work-related issues. So, in my mind, I don't get involved with those types of activities and I think those types of activities are kind of a gray area. [They] could be considered a life outside of work, [but] on the other hand, [they are] so closely related or closely organized by the company itself [that] a lot of people consider it kind of work.
>
> For example, think about a company picnic. People will say, "But I don't wanna go to a picnic!" I see my workers all day and I don't want to go to my company picnic. And people will say, "Oh you better go, otherwise you're not a team member," or something like that. So they feel obliged to go, and even though they may go and they play a game of baseball, there is still, for many people, the perception that it's kinda work.

Casting work and nonwork pursuits as work–life by activity is problematized in Desmond's example, and the people involved or present during these activities are implicated in whether or not the activity is considered work or nonwork.

Jerick, a life coach, explained why he thought a work–life distinction was not relevant:

> In my opinion, balance is an overused word. It is impossible to have balance if you have deadlines and activities, and all of that. I would say harmony. Harmony is about being harmonious, which is about pushing yourself and time. I'm not looking for balance . . . People think they have to have balance. But if they are training for a competition, it is kind of healthy to push yourself to grow and stretch yourself out of the comfort zone. It isn't healthy if you push yourself over and over. Run 100 meters and then recover. Many people don't do that. We don't have culture of recovery. But it is never training only for work or only recovering. People should harmonize between both.

Jerick found the distinction between work and life as unproductive and preferred to see work–life as constantly integrated.

CONCLUSION

These excerpts reveal that many men resist leaves of absence in four primary ways: (a) They believe virtual work mitigates the need to take time off because they can work from home to manage their work–life balance; (b) they can use generous vacation time in lieu of a formal leave of absence; (c) they can quit and take time off between jobs at critical points of their lives, such as around times which require extended care work; and (d) they believe that a work–life distinction is irrelevant because work is life and life is work. Most of the workers interviewed in this study were personally supportive of other people—men and women—taking leave, and most viewed themselves as personally balanced. These findings create a difficult double standard. If leaves are supported for others, yet not a practice in which men would participate themselves, there remains an invisible judgment about taking a leave, which has quite visible material and immaterial consequences. This finding might suggest that some men are viewing leave in more favorable terms while others continue to believe that it is a policy primarily for women.

NOTES

1. Traditionally, "telework" or "telecommuting" referred to home-based work conducted by employees that replaced face-to-face work conducted in the office. Most often, telework transpired only 1 or 2 days a week or when the employee was traveling for work, "telecommuting" from out of town. Virtual work and virtual teams are now so common they are rarely referred to as such, and many knowledge workers have the option to work from home.
2. Olson and Primps (1984) studied telecommuters and found employees' relationships with their children improved by working at home.

REFERENCES

Crandall, N. F., & Wallace, M. J. (1998). *Work and rewards in the virtual workplace: A new deal for employers and employees.* New York, NY: American Management Association.

Igbaria, M., & Tan, M. (Eds.). (1997). *The virtual workplace.* Hershey, PA: Idea Group Publishing.

Meyer, J. (2012). The new world of work: Time to think virtually. *Forbes.* Retrieved from http://www.forbes.com/sites/ciocentral/2012/08/23/the-new-world-of-work-time-to-think-virtually/

Olson, M. H., & Primps, S. B. (1984). Working at home with computers: Work and nonwork issues. *Journal of Social Issues, 40*(3), 97–112. doi:10.1111/j.1540–4560.1984.tb00194.x

Parlapiano, E. H., & Cobe, P. (1996). *Mompreneurs: A mother's practical step-by-step guide to work-at-home success.* New York, NY: Berkley Publishing.

Part III

Finding the Key
Why Understanding the Glass Handcuffs Matters

10 Conclusions and Implications of the Glass Handcuffs

The data presented in this project suggest that men are bound to work through an invisible apparatus discussed here as the glass handcuffs phenomenon. As shown in the previous chapters, this binding materializes in a few ways: They do not *want* to leave because they are passionate about their work, enjoy their roles as workers, or foreground their occupational identities above other identities in their lives; they don't *need* to leave because they have a partner to manage their non-work responsibilities, because they can use technology to work virtually or because they do not believe they need to take significant time away from work; they *cannot* leave because they fear they can get fired or be overlooked for promotion or because their paycheck is vital to their survival; or they *reframe* leave and are satisfied with taking smaller increments of time off and feel balanced without leaves of absence. In unpacking these claims and explanations about leaves of absence by the men in this study, a few conclusions emerge.

First, the FMLA and other leave policies are not connecting with men. Second, support for men to take a leave of absence at work remains minimal, despite progress and colloquial support for men to engage more regularly in self and family care. Third, leave is only an option for very few men. Men working part-time, sole breadwinners, and low-income men did not believe leaves of absence were a viable option in their lives. Fourth, parental status and parental identities are devalued for men, even when they are individually committed to family engagement and/or care work. Finally, the times when leaves are deemed acceptable by men and their managers are for burnout or for serious personal medical crisis, such as worker injury or life-threatening illness, which suggests men are literally expected to work themselves to death, unable to leave unless their lives are in danger.

Many men knew about FMLA policies, particularly knowledge workers or union workers. However, most men believed that the FMLA was not something they personally would ever use, except in the case of a personal medical emergency. Only one man interviewed in this study took a leave through the FMLA for the birth of a child, and took a full 12-week paternity leave. Other men accessed the FMLA benefits for medical reasons but claimed that they worked from home or part-time during their leave, and none of these lasted for 12 weeks. Instead, most of the men interviewed in this book claimed that they could manage their family responsibilities, personal health, and other life commitments through virtual work, vacation time, quitting, and so on. However, they individually chose to manage the sometimes conflicting responsibilities of work and nonwork without the use of FMLA.

Other men believed that FMLA policies are simply for show and that workers using FMLA would likely be punished at work by losing priority shifts or routes, being overlooked for promotion, getting fired, or other work-related consequences. Men explaining FMLA in this way believed their employers would not support leaves of absence under any circumstance, and would take action against men leaving. Other men thought that taking FMLA might be possible, but imagined they would be ridiculed at work or not taken seriously by their peers and managers. Of the wide variety of individual perspectives about the FMLA, the major theme was a general disconnect. Many men knew of the policy and could imagine a circumstance in which the FMLA might be used but usually did not personally use or imagine they would ever use the FMLA. This is important to consider: If the FMLA is supposed to cover all employees but is not accessible (figuratively and sometimes literally) to half of the population, the policy might need more than a simple revamping. Instead, a complete overhaul of how the policy works is required.

The second conclusion drawn from the data is that managerial and executive support for FMLA remains minimal. Although almost all the men in this study believed their individual manager would be supportive, they also explained that in general, management does not support leaves at all. This seemingly contradictory position might be explained by the men having close personal relationships with their managers, while also understanding that leaves have consequences for other managers. Many men explained that they heard light teasing if they took time away to care for their children but believed it was usually in jest. However, they simultaneously believed that their occupations and managers, in general, would not support leave—that they were somehow lucky to have a positive relationship with their manager. Thus, while managerial support was cited as vitally important, and while most men believed their individual managers supported them, they did not believe most managers in the industries would support leaves of absence, and they did not believe organizational leaders supported them at all.

Many of the men explained the human contract when talking about managerial and executive support. They thought that they were paid to be present and did not blame managers for not allowing them to take extended time away from work. They claimed to understand the business need for keeping men at work, and most of the men interviewed seemed to believe it was management's "right" to forbid or discourage leave for the sake of the business. Importantly, the men in this study also could not identify times when their managers or executive leaders took time away from work unless it was for serious medical crisis. The lack of modeling from organizational leaders speaks louder than the assumption that individual managers might be supportive.

A third conclusion drawn from the data is that leaves of absence are only an option for very select, privileged men. Part-time workers and low-income workers described virtually no access to leave of absence policies. They explained simply that, if they requested time of, they would be let go or their shifts given away to another employee. Unionized laborers had more access to leaves of absence, particularly for onsite workplace injuries. Workman's compensation was frequently referenced as one way to use the FMLA, but the men in these groups did not believe they could take leaves of absence for family or other nonmedical reason. Small-business owners and high-level executives also believed leaves were impossible for them because the company needed their expertise to continue. They thought it was completely impractical to take more than a week or two away, and believed it might be detrimental to their organization. At the same time, many middle-class men did not think they could leave because they were the primary breadwinner and would not be able to afford to take unpaid time off. Essentially, the only men who believed they could take a formal leave of absence were those who had successful, well-paid partners or who held well-paid positions themselves that would remain secure in their absence. Men in this group were almost non-existent.

It is surprising that men in all occupations and across the occupational hierarchy experience the feeling that leaves of absence would be impossible. Economic security (either through self or partner) was the best indicator of which men could take leaves, but having a high-paying job did not necessarily equate to the ability to take a leave. Rather, men with high-paying jobs and who had a partner with a highly paid job were the group more likely able to take extended time off. The ability to step out of work for extended time is a privilege few men believed they could exercise.

A fourth conclusion from this study is that parental identities are devalued for men. Many men in this study were personally committed to spending a large quantity of time with their families. However, they did not feel supported in their desire to spend more time at home. In general, many fathers interviewed in this study believed their identities as workers were more important than their identities as fathers. The men who prioritized their roles as fathers explained that their parental status was usually devalued (relegated below work responsibilities) and that they still felt a strong connection to work. This complicates life for engaged, employed dads. In a time when men are expected to contribute more quality and quantity time with their children, their parental statuses remain devalued compared to work. This can create stress and strain as men begin to "do it all," a phenomenon employed women have grappled with for decades.

A final conclusion from this study is the expectation that men will literally work themselves to death. When asked about times that leaves of absence are appropriate for men, they overwhelmingly explained that life-threatening medical emergencies, such as broken necks or cancer, would be an appropriate time to take a few weeks off from work. They also described taking a leave of absence to avoid "burnout," which they described as a serious mental breakdown (which might include suicide risk), heart attacks, alcohol or drug addictions, or depression from divorce. The ways these were explained, in conjunction with the conclusions presented previously, suggest that men are expected to keep working unless and until a life-threatening issue arises. Other reasons they might leave work for extended periods were not as excusable.

IMPLICATIONS OF THE GLASS HANDCUFFS PHENOMENON

There are four evident implications of the glass handcuffs phenomenon. First, when men do not take time away from work, workers who do take leaves of absence look less committed to work. In other words, leaves of absence are situated as incompatible with work and with career success. This phenomenon has serious implications for parent workers, workers with disabilities, and women, who, as discussed previously, are overwhelmingly responsible for caring for children, housework, and aging parents. Thus, when these workers take leaves of absence, they suffer career consequences including fewer bonuses, less pay, loss of job, harassment at work, and lower performance evaluations.

A second implication of the glass handcuffs phenomenon is that it explains the increasing difficulty that men experience in getting more involved in their family lives. A multitude of campaigns suggest that men's presence as fathers in the home might produce better adjusted children, decrease stress for mothers, and contribute to less crime. However, if men do not give up a portion of their time at work, they cannot possibly contribute as fully as they might in the home. The *superwoman phenomenon* suggests that "doing it all" is not sustainable for long periods and that there must be given in either women's life or work in order for them to participate successfully in both. Thus, it goes to say that if men desire to participate more fully in their home spheres, they must be able to relinquish some of their time at work.

A third implication of the glass handcuffs phenomenon is that it can create serious health problems for men. As discussed, employees who work nonstop can incur serious health effects, even for white- or gold-collar workers. For example, severe stress, sleeplessness, back problems, obesity, and chronic eye or joint pain are just a few problems that emerge from uninterrupted deskwork. Steve Jobs famously attributed his cancer to his extreme overworking habits, and other executives have described working themselves—quite literally—to death. Other men in this study described delaying health treatments or checkups in order to work. Putting off checkups or treatments can create health problems and contribute to the shorter life expectancy for men.

A fourth and final implication of the glass handcuffs metaphor is that it allows for the perpetuation of the ideal worker norm. By continually working, men are striving to be the ideal worker. This worker is unattached, has no responsibilities, and is healthy, independent, young, and completely committed to his or her organization. The pursuit of this ideal suggests that it is both possible to attain and desirable, despite practical implications that make it nearly impossible for workers to either achieve and sustain. Allowing the ideal worker to guide work policies is to ignore the structural inequalities that make the ideal even more difficult for some workers to achieve than for others.

RECOMMENDATIONS FOR EQUITY ACTION

The analysis of the glass handcuffs and the conclusions that emerge allows for some actionable recommendations for equity action. The remainder of this chapter will outline why these suggestions are important and how managers, executive leaders, scholars, activist policy reformers, and individual workers might take them up. Following is a list of some recommendations for gender equality reform for work–life issues:

- Reform the FMLA
- Implement national paid sick days
- Revalue care work
- Support other work–life policies and technologies
- Broaden the "life" part of work–life
- Recognize the importance of occupational identity
- Encourage managerial support and executive modeling
- Shift gendered expectations at home
- Get men involved in the gender equity movement
- Connect work–life with corporate social responsibility

Reforming the FMLA

The FMLA must be reformed. In its present iteration, the FMLA is raced, classed, ableist, and heteronormative. It is inaccessible to a majority of workers, and does not meet the work–life needs described for the men in this study. Currently, rights to paid maternity and parental leaves are given in every country in the Organisation for Economic Co-operation and Development except for the United States (Kamerman & Moss, 2011). Because the FMLA provides for unpaid leave, it privileges people who can financially support themselves for 12 weeks without pay. For low-income families or families with only one income, taking leave, thus, becomes exponentially more difficult. Additionally, in heterosexually coupled families in which men earn more money, it is likely that men, in particular, cannot afford to take unpaid leave.

Furthermore, because managers determine whether health events qualify for the FMLA, the policy is quite ableist in that it favors types of leaves that can be planned for ahead of time and that might only occur once or twice in an employee's life (e.g., weddings, planned surgeries, planned pregnancies).

In light of these concerns, scholars studying leave policies have come to some general consensus about what must be done in order to improve FMLA. A great majority of available work suggests that FMLA parameters must be restructured, and some work suggests that FMLA interventions must occur at the organizational or managerial levels. As mentioned in Chapter 3, FMLA reform must include a paid leave program. Simply put, if leaves of absence remain unpaid, FMLA will never be equitable. Paid state-leave policies in the United States have had tremendous success. The paid family-leave insurance programs in California and New Jersey have created positive results for workers and organizations at minimal cost (Wu, 2011).

Successful reform of the FMLA must also expand the parameters of who is covered. By lowering the minimum required hours and by lowering the company size requirements even just slightly, many more U.S. Americans will have legal access to take a leave of absence. Other important developments might be to increase the length of time that leaves can last[1] and broadening the concept of family to include in-laws, grandparents, and so on.

Another basic reform suggestion would be to educate managers and executive leaders on a widespread scale about the benefits of work–life policies. Kirby and Krone (2002) extolled the benefits of circulating success stories of leave taking in organizations and promoting programs as companywide benefits rather than women's or parents' benefits. They also claimed that all employees should know the reasoning behind polices, including expectations and organizational benefits. Similarly, Wayne and Cordeiro (2003) claimed that training programs as part of managing diversity efforts should inform managers of how gender stereotypes may influence how men are perceived when using family policies, particularly by male managers.

Finally, Schultz (2007) discovered that information about family-leave policy was difficult to locate, which prevented employees from knowing their rights to take leaves of absence. These suggestions seem to be the first steps in reforming FMLA as it is currently drafted. However, when analyzing successful leave policies around the world, other models present a more comprehensive approach to time away from work. For example, Kamerman and Moss (2011) suggested that we might build leave policies around a life. For example, each citizen might have an allocated paid leave time to use throughout his or her working life and could use this leave for a range of reasons. Belgium has such an approach and has realized several advantages, including eliminating potential hostility from nonparents.

Implementing Paid Sick Days

As discussed, many men in this study equated leaves of absence with sick time. Sick time is used more often than leave time by men and causes fewer repercussions for employees. As such, the next work–life policy action should be to mandate sick time for all employees. Currently, more than 40 million employed individuals in the United States do not have access to any sick time to use when they get sick, and millions more do not have and cannot earn any time designated to care for sick family members (National Partnership for Women & Families, 2014; Williams & Gault, 2014). One fifth of employed women reported that they did or feared they would lose their jobs for taking sick time. If employees do not have access to paid sick time, and/or if they fear losing their jobs, sick time cannot take the place of leave.

However, the men in this study overwhelmingly relied on paid sick time in lieu of leaves of absence. The discrepancy here has catastrophic results for many families. Taking 3.5 unpaid days off from work can cost a family, on average, an entire monthly grocery budget (Gould, Filion, & Green, 2011). Furthermore, paid sick day access differs by race/ethnicity, occupation, and earnings such that the lack of a national policy for sick time further exacerbates the inequality inherent within FMLA and other work–life policies. Only 47% of Latino/a workers have access to paid sick days, while 66% of Asian American workers do have access to paid sick time (Williams & Gault, 2014). Workers earning less than $20,000 per year are much less likely to have access to paid sick time, while workers making more than $65,000 are the most likely to have paid sick days (Williams & Gault, 2014). Supporting legislation to create a national policy for paid sick days is a critical next step in making workplaces more equitable in terms of the ability to leave work.

Revalue Care Work

Bornstein (2000) asserted that "men need to take leave in order both to alleviate the unequal burden of child care on their female partners and [also] to transform workplace norms about the traditional worker" (p. 122). Leave-taking to assist their partners with child care makes financial sense for men because other child care options are incredibly expensive, ranging, on average, from $4,000 to $15,000 a year per child. In most states, it is more expensive than in-state college tuition (The White House, Office of the Press Secretary, 2014). Furthermore, high-quality child care is not readily available—there is a significant shortage of available care spaces for children compared to the number of children with working parents (Douglas & Michaels, 2004). Thus, work policies and schedules that do not allow men to contribute to care work are problematic.

It is time to revalue care work, (Douglas & Michaels, 2004; Tracy, 2008) and imperative we recognize that time spent caring for others (e.g., children, ailing relatives, aging parents) or volunteering is valuable time. Organizations can and should begin valuing care work, because care work benefits everyone. Raising future generations comprised of individuals who are well cared for results in better future employees, better individual and community health, and likely less crime (Tracy, 2008). Care work should fall under the purview of corporate social and ethical responsibility (e.g., in the same framing as protecting the environment), and organizations should provide paid time off to support care work (Tracy, 2008).

Other Work–Life Policies and Technology

The men in this study clearly found both virtual work and flextime to be highly supportive in their endeavors for work–life balance. Virtual work and flextime were used to describe why leaves of absence were unnecessary because they allowed the men to conduct nonwork pursuits with minimal interruption to their careers. This, then, is a contradictory recommendation in that while virtual work and flexibility were cited as increasing work–life balance, they also functioned to eliminate the opportunity for men to take time off completely from work, which could hurt or diminish their work–life balance (Edley, 2001). Still, the workers in this study overwhelmingly credited these two work–life policies as providing a means to a balanced life and claimed they were lucky to have access to such policies. More analysis of these particular practices is needed and could potentially illuminate some of the complexities of balance.

As technology increasingly makes work portable, its facilitation toward and intrusion on work–life balance is important to monitor. Because they can work from anywhere, men did not believe they had to completely leave work but could "check in" from home or the hospital. Some of the men in this study welcomed technologies as assistive of their work–life management, while others resented work's intrusion on "family time." Of course, mobile technologies accomplish both at any given time, but their use in replacing work–life policies, or as integrated into work–life policies, should be carefully considered. How frequently companies decide to allow workers to work in a mobile capacity, or how much workers allow work to continue at home, are important aspects to consider in the very new policy development in this area.

Broaden "Life"

The findings in this study are clear: "Work–life balance" does not always have the same meaning for men as it does in the colloquial use of the term. When asked about work–life balance, many men believed it was not a concept that necessarily fit into their lives primarily because they perceived it as a women's issue or as only for men with families. Workers without children regularly explained that they do not feel included in conversations about balance because they do not have children. Balance is not always equivalent to family, despite the frequent conflation of the two. Current framings of work–life policies sometimes favor family time as the only "life" option. As work–life policies develop, an important step is to broaden the conception of the "life" bucket. Men have a variety of life commitments that are not family. Allowing work–life to include other aspects of life, such as education, fitness, preventative checkups, travel, pets, friends, and hobbies will reduce the backlash that has occurred when leaves of absence and other work–life policies are cast as exclusively work–family. Certainly, family and care work commitments take up a large portion of "life" for many workers, but stigma about care work and family commitments can be reduced when work–life policies address the lives of all workers. Broadening what counts as "life" can make these kinds of policies more equitable, and perhaps can reduce gender discrimination at work when employees lose the ability to claim that work–life policies privilege women. Casting work–life only as work–family can cause incongruity with workers who do not have children and can make workers who actively raise children appear as if they decided to sacrifice their careers. Thus, disconnecting balance and family can open up the currently narrow scope of what "life" can mean for men and might be useful for reconstructing leave policies.

Managerial/Executive Support and Modeling

The data also suggest that if work–life policies are to be successful and adopted in practice, leaders in organizations must fully embrace them. Bornstein (2000) claimed,

> Because male senior executives do not take leave, a cycle is perpetuated in which male employees identify success and achievement with minimal disruptions in work life. As long as these highest ranking employees do not take leave, there is an unspoken message that the top officials neither sanction or embrace such behavior. (pp. 118–119)

Bornstein (2000) further contended that executives should proclaim family leave as a valued practice, and refrain from punishing employees who use leave policies. How high-ranking men do or do not mention leave is important for understanding prevailing discourses about work leave.

The personal opinions of executive leaders hold significant influence over workplace policies and cultures, particularly including work–life benefits such as family leave (Tracy & Rivera, 2009). How and whether leaders model workplace behavior greatly impact how employees interpret organizational policies and cultures. Executives' everyday talk is equally influential, and the actual utilization of work–life benefits requires the endorsement of executives and employees' perception that they will not be punished or viewed as uncommitted if they exercise leave rights. Thus, if leaders claim to endorse work–life policies while simultaneously forgoing the use of such policies, employees will not assume that using policies is possible (Tracy & Rivera, 2009).

In line with this conceptualization, the men interviewed in this study clearly articulated that the support or lack of support from their managers, peers, and organizations played a large role in their personal leave taking practices. Whether the interviewees took a leave of absence was determined, in large part, by their perception of a supportive work environment. Although most interviewed men felt supported by their companies enough to take a leave if they needed to, they also presented some data that suggest that some work environments did not always provide support for taking a leave of absence. For example, one interviewee who took paternity leave explained that his company was completely supportive but also shared that his coworkers and his boss engaged him in "lighthearted joking" about his decision to take time off work:

> No, my boss is absolutely supportive. Of course, he gave me the ball busting too, but it was never a question, because, I mean, I told him, you know, I knew how when the baby was going to be born, I told him—like, first of all, because I had horror stories—but it was never questioned, never a chance I was going to be denied a request.

In this instance, the employee's leave-taking was supported but also came with jokes and "ball busting" that signaled that taking a paternity leave was uncommon. This interviewee did not experience any formal or informal punishments for his time away from work, which he classified as a leave, despite the fact that it was paid for with his vacation time and lasted only three weeks.

Although most men felt leaves of absence were supported, some men experienced quite the opposite impression of their own work environments. As one interviewee explained,

> You'd worry about what your peers [would say]. There was certainly a stigma in the rumor mill around that. I couldn't imagine any of these old, 20-year, 25-year corporate guys taking a leave of absence. I just don't believe that it would happen. It's really a big stigma attached with these absences and the rumor mill just starts churning, so it's difficult when they come back to, you know, be accepted.

In this case, the unsupportive work environment convinced this employee that it would not be a good idea to take a leave of absence for any reason.

Shifting Gendered Expectations at Home

As the dual-earner family has become the most representative model of U.S. families, both breadwinner and caregiver roles require revision. The position of women and men, in the home and at work, are linked. Researchers cannot consider women's employment in isolation; rather, women's employment must be considered in relation to men's participation at home

(Kamerman & Moss, 2011). As Callister and Galtry (2006) claimed, in order for gender equity to occur both in the labor market and the home, one, or preferably both, of the following needs to take place:

1. Women need to increase their employment tenure and their lifetime hours of paid work and, related to both of these, their yearly and lifetime earnings from paid work.
2. Men need to undertake an equal share of child care and household work. This will generally require a reduction in their paid work hours. (p. 44)

Gender equality at work and home requires changes in the ways men participate in the home, including increasing responsibilities in child care and domestic work. Gender equality is only possible if workplace expectations, particularly expectations of organizational face time based on an outdated ideal type of worker, change.

However helpful men's participation in leave-taking would be, most men feel they cannot, should not, or would not take leave (Judiesch & Lyness, 1999). Wayne and Cordeiro (2003) pointed out that men do not use family-leave benefits because they often fear that by doing so they will be viewed by employers as uncommitted and, as a result, might suffer career penalties. Indeed, gendered organizational culture theory (Acker, 1990) suggests that all leave-takers will be penalized, regardless of their gender, and that people are penalized whenever their actions violate expected gender roles. Wayne and Cordeiro (2003) studied perceptions about good organizational citizenship and found that men who took leave for birth or elder care were, in fact, perceived as more selfish than men who did not take any leave or women who took leave for the same reasons. Furthermore, Albiston (2010) described how "men who took parental leave are perceived to be less likely to help their coworkers, be punctual, work overtime, or have good attendance than men who did not take parental leave, even when performance was held constant" (p. xi). Researchers should take these findings seriously, especially because organizational citizenship behaviors and perceptions of these behaviors are often tied to workers' salary increases.

Apparently, men are well aware of the penalties they might face for taking leave. For example, in 1993, the Bureau of National Affairs found that only 7% of men would take twelve weeks of parental leave on the birth or adoption of a child (Grill, 1996). As another example, current data suggest that 23% men do take time off to care for new children but that these men take significantly less than the possible 12 weeks (American Association of University Women, 2012).

These statistics are a particularly discouraging in light of the recent push for fathers to be more involved in their children's lives. Sheridan (2004) asserted that professional men face a dilemma due to the increasing discourse about changing roles for fathers without concomitant changes in the workplace to allow these men to take up their new roles. As Moe and Shandy (2010) described,

> men, too, can face a so-called maternal wall with regard to their parental responsibilities. Likewise, even those who don't have children may have living parents, and the care needs of that generation are growing rapidly. These issues are not only women's issues. Rather, anyone with care giving responsibilities, whether for an aging parent, an ailing family member, or a child, can face many of the same obstacles. Indeed the "maternal wall" can be construed more broadly as a "caregiver wall." (p. 60)

Modern dads are more involved in parenting than previous generations. For example, the total hours married fathers spend with their children has increased to 33 hours per week, the highest amount since the Industrial Revolution. Furthermore, many dads are starting to articulate their need for more time at home in the workplace (Chethik, 2006; Moe & Shandy, 2010). This increased parental presence has positive outcomes for men, including better marriages and improved relationships with their children (Golden, 2007). As another example, fathers provide care for approximately 20% of preschool children while their mothers are at work. These families typically coordinate their work schedules so that they do not work the same hours and, thus, reduce the amount of time their children are in the care of others (Moe & Shandy, 2010). However, despite fathers' increased participation in child care, men have only realized minimal structural and/or cultural changes in the workplace. If men are increasing the amount of time spent on care work, they too will likely face higher levels of work–life conflict.

Men Must Play an Integral Role in Gender Reform

Men must play an integral role in gender reform (Kimmel, 1996). In much work–life research, and particularly in feminist work, the studies and the resulting discussions about equity focus largely on women's experiences. Moreover, equity itself is frequently characterized as a "women's" movement. However, organizational reform necessarily involves men, and achieving gender equity would include an improvement in the lives of both women *and* men (Tracy & Rivera, 2009). Thus, gender equality in organizations will not be realized until men shift their organizational practices and values.

Beyond their roles as gatekeepers and mentors, men are also as workers who would benefit from culturally accepted leave policies. A recent study by Galinsky, Aumann, and Bond (2009), for example, revealed that men are reporting increased levels of work–life conflict. Understanding why men do or do not take leaves of absences, thus, is critical on two levels: first, as a means for men to achieve equity in their own right as workers constrained by gendered discourses and, second, because women can never safely take leaves of absences in their organizations if men do not also take leaves of absences.

Gender functions as a dialectic and understanding masculine practices are essential for broad-scale emancipation. Alvesson and Willmott (1992) defined emancipation as "the process through which individuals and groups become freed from repressive social and ideological conditions, in particular those that place socially unnecessary restrictions upon the development and articulation of human consciousness" (p. 432). Although the concept of emancipation has been critiqued as unrealistic, utopian, and essentialist, individuals can begin to undermine power imbalances by reconceptualizing emancipation as *microemancipation*, or the everyday activities and techniques that facilitate resistance (Alvesson & Willmott, 1992). Emancipation, thus, is an important process by which workers can begin to move beyond organizational colonization of the personal and achieve equitable organizational status.

Connect Work–Life Issues with Corporate Social Responsibility

Corporate social responsibility (CSR) has gained significant traction in most large organizations. Peter Drucker, management guru, related that currently, large corporations cannot ignore their multiple societal responsibilities (Murray, 2010). Indeed, these organizations have a responsibility to take care of the communities in which they operate. The concept of CSR was widely represented in books written by powerful businessmen. From Coca-Cola's support of polar bear conservation to Dow Chemical's support of green initiatives, organizations seem to be acknowledging the their responsibility to give back to the larger community. Although there is sometimes a cost associated with CSR campaigns, organizations often depend on the goodwill of communities to operate and can see tax benefits for their support.

Extending the parameters of CSR to work–life issues for employees is one way to engage organizations in unlocking the glass handcuffs. If work–life management remains an individual responsibility, as the data from this book demonstrated, it will be difficult for employees to actually achieve the balance they seek. If, however, some of the burden for managing work–life shifts from the individual to the organization, policies and programs to support employees could make improvements possible. Because the rhetoric of CSR is successful with powerful decision makers and organizational leaders, couching work–life as a corporate social responsibility is a good idea.

CONCLUSION

As organizations, employees, and families continue to grapple with increased demands at work and at home, fleshing out the ways in which leaves of absence policies and other work–life policies are enacted in everyday life is important. Like other forms of gendered organizational discrimination, the glass handcuffs present particular problems that must be resolved before workplace equity is possible.

In his speech for the 2014 White House Summit on Working Families, President Barack Obama said,

> Every day, I hear from parents all across the country. They are doing everything right—they are working hard, they are living responsibly, they are taking care of their children, they're participating in their community—and these letters can be heartbreaking, because at the end of the day it doesn't feel like they're getting ahead. And all too often, it feels like they're slipping behind. And a lot of the time, they end up blaming themselves thinking, if I just work a little harder—if I plan a little better, if I sleep a little bit less, if I stretch every dollar a little bit farther—maybe I can do it . . .
>
> These problems are not typically the result of poor planning or too little diligence on the parts of moms or dads, and they cannot just be fixed by working harder or being an even better parent. (Applause.) All too often, they are the results of outdated policies and old ways of thinking. Family leave, child care, workplace flexibility, a decent wage—these are not frills, they are basic needs. They shouldn't be bonuses. They should be part of our bottom line as a society. That's what we're striving for. (Applause.) . . .
>
> All too often, these issues are thought of as women's issues, which I guess means you can kind of scoot them aside a little bit. At a time when women are nearly half of our workforce, among our most skilled workers, are the primary breadwinners in more families than ever before, anything that makes life harder for women makes life harder for families and makes life harder for children. (Applause.) When women succeed, America succeeds, so there's no such thing as a women's issue. (Applause.) There's no such thing as a women's issue. This is a family issue and an American issue—these are commonsense issues. (Applause.) This is about you too, men.

Clearly, it is time for some of these revolutions to occur. Individual employees and families are struggling, in desperate need of national and organizational policies to support them in finding a way to engage in care work and employment. As momentum grows to improve workplace equity, considering the ways in which men, as workers and gatekeepers, are implicated in the national dialogue about work–life policies and practices is imperative. If glass ceilings are to shatter, so, too, must the glass handcuffs.

NOTE

1. Galtry (2002) argued that a comprehensive leave plan should have at least 6 months of leave to accommodate breastfeeding.

REFERENCES

Acker, J. (1990). Hierarchies, jobs, bodies: A theory of gendered organizations. *Gender & Society, 4*(2), 139–158. doi:10.1177/089124390004002002

Albiston, C. (2010). *Institutional inequality and the mobilization of the family and medical leave act: Rights on leave.* Cambridge, England: Cambridge University Press.

Alvesson, M., & Willmott, H. (1992). On the idea of emancipation in management and organization studies. *The Academy of Management Review, 17*(3), 432–464.

American Association of University Women. (2012). FMLA facts and statistics [Fact sheet]. Retrieved from http://www.aauw.org/act/laf/library/fmlastatistics.cfm

Bornstein, L. (2000). Inclusions and exclusions in work–family policy: The public values and moral code embedded in the Family and Medical Leave Act. *Columbia Journal of Gender and Law, 10*(1), 77–85.

Callister, P., & Galtry, J. (2006). Paid parental leave in New Zealand: A short history and future policy options. *IPS Policy Quarterly, 2*(1), 38–46.

Chethik, N. (2006). *VoiceMale: What husbands really think about their marriages, their wives, sex, housework and commitment.* New York, NY: Simon & Schuster.

Douglas, S., & Michaels, M.W. (2004). *The mommy myth: The idealization of motherhood and how it has undermined women.* New York, NY: Free Press.

Edley, P.P. (2001). Technology, employed mothers, and corporate colonization of the lifeworld: A gendered paradox of work and family balance. *Women and Language, 24*(2), 28–35.

Galinsky, E., Aumann, K., & Bond, J. (2009). Times are changing: Gender and generation at work and at home. Family and Work Institute. Retrieved from www.familiesandwork.org

Galtry, J. (2002). Child health: An underplayed variable in parental leave policy debates? *Community, Work & Family, 5*(3), 257–278. doi:10.1080/1366880022000041775

Golden, A.G. (2007). Fathers' frames for childrearing: Evidence toward a "masculine concept of caregiving." *Journal of Family Communication, 7*(4), 265–285. doi:10.1080/15267430701392164

Gould, E., Filion, K., & Green, A. (2011). *The need for paid sick days: The lack of a federal policy further erodes family economic security* (Briefing Paper 319). Retrieved from http://www.epi.org/publication/the_need_for_paid_sick_days/

Grill, A. (1996). The myth of unpaid family leave: Can the United States implement a paid leave policy based on the Swedish model? *Comparative Labor Law Journal, 17,* 373–397.

Judiesch, M., & Lyness, K. (1999). Left behind? The impact of leaves of absence on managers' career success. *The Academy of Management Journal, 42*(6), 641–651. doi:10.2307/256985

Kamerman, S., & Moss, P. (Eds.). (2011). *The politics of parental leave policies: Children, parenting, gender and the labour market.* Bristol, England: The Policy Press.

Kimmel, M. (1996). *Manhood in America.* New York, NY: The Free Press.

Kirby, E., & Krone, K. (2002). The policy exists but you can't really use it: Communication and the structuration of work-family policies. *Journal of Applied Communication Research, 30*(1), 50–77. doi:10.1080/00909880216577

Moe, K., & Shandy, D. (2010). *Glass ceilings & 100-hour couples: What the opt-out phenomenon can teach us about work and family.* Athens: The University of Georgia Press.

Murray, A. (2010). *The Wall Street Journal essential guide to management: Lasting lessons from the best leadership minds of our time.* New York, NY: Harper Collins.

National Partnership for Women & Families (2014, September). Not enough family friendly policies: High stakes for women and families [Fact sheet]. Retrieved from http://www.nationalpartnership.org/research-library/work-family/not-enough-family-friendly-policies.pdf

Schultz, N. (2007, November). *The challenge of negotiating family leave in higher education for women faculty: An issue of policy, practice, and access.* Paper presented at the meeting of the National Communication Association, Chicago, IL.

Sheridan, A. (2004). Chronic presenteeism: The multiple dimensions to men's absence from part-time work. *Gender, Work & Organization, 11*(2), 207–225. doi:10.1111/j.1468–0432.2004.00229.x

Tracy, S. J. (2008). Care as a common good. *Women's Studies in Communication, 31*(2), 166–174. doi:10.1080/07491409.2008.10162529

Tracy, S. J., & Rivera, K. D. (2009). Endorsing equity and applauding stay-at-home moms: How male voices on work-life reveal adverse sexism and flickers of transformation. *Management Communication Quarterly, 24,* 3–43. doi:10.1177/0893318909352248

Wayne, J., & Cordeiro, B. (2003). Who is a good organizational citizen? Social perception of male and female employees who use family leave. *Sex Roles, 49*(5/6), 233–246.

The White House, Office of the Press Secretary. (2014, June 23). Remarks by President Obama at the White House Summit on Working Families. Retrieved from http://www.whitehouse.gov/the-press-office/2014/06/23/remarks-president-obama-white-house-summit-working-families-june-23-2014

Williams, C., & Gault, B. (2014, March). Fact sheet: Paid sick days access in the U.S.: Differences by race/ethnicity, occupation, earnings, and work schedule [Fact sheet]. Retrieved from http://www.iwpr.org/publications/pubs/paid-sick-days-access-in-the-united-states-differences-by-race-ethnicity-occupation-earnings-and-work-schedule

Wu, P. (2011, February 5). On the FMLA anniversary, let's focus on the unmet needs of working Families [Blog comment]. Retrieved from http://www.nationalpartnership.org/blog/general/on-the-fmla-anniversary.html

Appendix A
Feminist Standpoint Theory and Researcher Positionality

Feminist standpoint theory assumes that social location produces particular worldviews or narratives and that, historically, some social locations have been systematically othered and excluded from the matrix of knowledge construction (see, e.g., Bullis, 1993; Harding, 1998; Lugones & Spelman, 1983; Sprague & Hayes, 2000). Whereas feminism is a response to the problem of women's historical and constant oppression and exclusion, feminist standpoint theory rejects the essential category of "woman" and instead seeks to understand how the intersection of multiple social identities produces different worldviews. Standpoints are not simple categories; rather, standpoints are composed through a combination of influences, resources, material and symbolic realities, and contexts that construct understanding through experience (Allen, 1998; Sprague & Hayes, 2000). It is problematic to assume the standpoint of a "woman" as an essential category. Instead, it is important to consider how other aspects of social influence create a variety of gender identities over time.

Feminist standpoint theory gives credence to intersectionality, or the way that gender and other factors (e.g., race, sexuality, class, [dis]ability, and nationality) interact to create different subjectivities. All too frequently, differences—especially among women—are silenced by essentialism. However, different social locations produce worldviews that are strikingly different and that bring forth different responses. For example, Friedan's (1962) "problem that has no name," which refers to middle- to upper class white women's boredom and even imprisonment as housewives, was a problem only for wealthy white women. Women of color and working-class women typically do not experience the same kind of "problem," because working class women have always worked. Thus, standpoint theory encourages feminisms so that women's different identities can be accounted for in talk about "women's" issues. This "interlocking nature of oppression" (Collins, 1986, p. S19) accounts for the way that oppression works through intersections of social identity—particularly through race, gender, and class—to strike some women (e.g., women of color and low-income women) so that these women experience simultaneous oppression as women, as individuals of color, and as individuals of the working class. First, recognizing these simultaneous instances of oppression and, then, unlocking the occurrence of such simultaneous oppression requires constant critical examination of knowledge, policies, institutions, and organizations that were designed for and by individuals with the dominant standpoint and social location (i.e., white, heterosexual, abled, wealthy men).

From a feminist standpoint perspective, reform suggestions for the FMLA, for example, must consider not only women's needs for a supportive policy but, more specifically, must consider what diverse women need. For instance, women with disabilities might need more time, whereas single mothers might need more financial support and lesbian mothers might need reformed definitions of family. Any kind of discussion or effort to improve policies must account for a variety of social locations, lest it risk the continual submission to dominant groups and assumptions that have marginalized particular people throughout history. As Sprague and Hayes (2000) argued,

> a first step in the evaluation of community and institutional policies should be to turn the tables on the old implementation of the normal/other distinction. Let us decenter our idea of normal and evaluate policy and practices also from the standpoint of people who do not drive, are not comfortable with counting money, learn at radically different paces in a wide variety of styles, do not read, do use a wheel chair, do push a stroller, and/or are personally responsible for the care of others. (pp. 690–691)

Equality is only possible when multiple standpoints and social locations are included in the way knowledge and policies are determined.

Feminist standpoint theory makes space for silenced voices, which allows not only for understanding and changing existing dominant practice but also for producing socially responsible discourse (Bullis, 1993). This project embraces the assumptions of feminist standpoint theory, particularly as a lens through which to analyze dominant discourses. In doing so, I assume that it is through discourse that society's institutions, including gender itself, are constituted. Specifically, I seek a deeper understanding of men's leave-taking practices through this discursive lens, with the express purpose to effect social change.

A discursive lens is important to both the theoretical foundation and methodological practice for this project. Theoretically, standpoint theory requires the identification of unchallenged dominant discourses by continually asking *when, how,* and *whose* standpoints are represented in discursive practices, formations, policies, and organizations. Discourses both shape and are shaped by everyday behaviors in that they are overarching understandings of reality that produce rules that guide action. Discourses, however, are always political and must be analyzed to uncover how they work as powerful distributors of inequality. Thus, methodologically, studying discourses requires attention to discursive practices as the ways in which humans engage with discourses in their everyday lives to shape reality. Jorgenson (2002) noted that for feminists working with discourse, "of particular interest is how, in the learning and use of discursive practices, women and members of other marginalized groups take up and are placed in locations from which they interpret their lives" (p. 358). Thus, all knowledge and all identities are the political productions of discourse.

Taking a standpoint feminist epistemology, then, suggests that my perspective as a researcher is necessarily guided by my own social location. In essence, this means that from a standpoint perspective, this study and all studies are always political and shaped by the researcher's positionality, which is shaped by social location and experience, to produce a subjective view on all phases of this research. The intersections I have selected and the conceptual framework from which I operate undoubtedly work to create the outcomes of this study. Social location cannot be overlooked. This project has developed from my own experiences in a particular body at a particular point in time and, thus, reflects my personal standpoint.

In this study, standpoint feminism is employed to interrogate the implied neutrality of leave policies and practices as organized processes, and suggests that, instead, preexisting social and cultural practices are (re)produced in the gendered power relations around leave policy. As discursively constructed phenomena, leave-taking policies are thus open for renegotiation and transformation, despite the seemingly hardened or naturalness of such policies (Buzzanell & Liu, 2005). Despite this transformative potential, studies about leaves of absence are relatively sparse.

To apply standpoint feminism to men's experiences requires care. Because men have experienced extensive privilege in organizations and elsewhere, to position them as individuals with marginalized standpoints requires careful consideration. It is not my purpose here to suggest that men are oppressed in organizations. Rather, it is that in the context of using leave of absence and other work–life policies, men are frequently marginalized. As such, applying standpoint theory to men's experiences is a useful way to shed light on leave policy inequality. As hooks (1995) explained, lived experience in a marginalized social location is central for completely understanding existing power structures. She argued that such perspectives provided unique and valuable contributions that are not possible for others to explicate. Clearly, hooks was not talking about men—particularly privileged white men—however, the notion that power structures are illuminated from the margins is a valuable tool that can help illuminate the (hidden) power structures of leaves of absence and other work–life policies. Thus, I apply standpoint theory here with caution and care, as a means to understand a particular facet of organizational life in which men are frequently marginalized.

In conclusion, feminist standpoint theory functions as a theoretical framework to study leave policies and practices. Such an approach allows for insightful analysis of discourse and a reimagining of structures and policies in more equitable terms. However, in order to fully comprehend the difficulties of such a reimagination, it is necessary to understand how discourses provide a context for which a reimagining would occur.

RESEARCHER POSITIONALITY

As required for sound feminist qualitative research, my own standpoint in relation to my research is important. I have already discussed in detail my ontological and epistemological commitments that guide this work; however, my relationship to the particular constructs is also important to what I have chosen to study and to how I interpreted the data. In particular, I became interested in leave policy after I was laid off from my job as a consultant 2 days after I announced my first pregnancy. I heard from colleagues that the company felt it could not afford my absence. Later, when a client who did not know of my pregnancy hired me, she expressed anger and felt "tricked" when she found out about my "condition." My new boss *allowed* me to take 12 weeks of unpaid leave, despite the fact that I was not covered under the FMLA. However, complications arose in projects at the workplace, and my employer soon asked me to work a few days during my leave, which I did.

My relationship with leaves of absence intensified just before the arrival of my second child. During this pregnancy, I was working for a university as a teaching assistant. There were no university policies or provisions at that university for students who needed leaves of absence. Because there were no provisions for students to take a semester off, I had to enroll in one class to be considered a continuing graduate student. One university employee suggested that I apply for a study abroad in order to obtain the necessary permission to leave the university for a semester; however, this process seemed like more trouble than taking and paying for a single class. In order to allow for time to give birth and to care for my new infant, I had to take an entire semester off from teaching, which not only meant lost wages but also meant I had to pay for my course work that semester, which would have been covered through my teaching contract. These personal experiences with leave undoubtedly shaped my assumptions that leave policy and practice is problematic for women and that it requires reform.

Another experience that has shaped my perception of leaves of absence is my view of my partner's experience with leave. At the birth of our first child, my partner took all of his vacation time and sick time (a total of less than 3 weeks) to help me recover, to adjust to the new familial addition, and to bond with our daughter. He did not see any other option for his time away from work. At the birth of our second child, who happened to be born in late December, he enjoyed time away from work while his office was closed for the holidays. He then worked 3 half-weeks, so that the impact of his absence at work was not as great. The differences between the two experiences were, in large part, due to the economic pressures we felt as a family. His company had gone through massive layoffs and the threat of losing his job for any reason was real. He knew a few people who had openly taken advantage of family friendly policies and were asked to revert to "normal" 40- to 60-hour weeks or to leave the company; others were simply let go. These explicit and implicit discourses around leaves of absence greatly influenced my partner's decision to forego using the FMLA and to simply work reduced hours for a short time so that his leave was less visible in his organization. As a result, he experienced stress over working so frequently on so little sleep with a newborn and was consistently anxious about the possibility of losing his job. This experience made me begin to see how leave reform is necessary not only for women, but also for men and that leave policy has implications for organizations and families, not simply for individual workers.

RESEARCH CONCERNS

Conducting gender research that focuses only on "men" risks reinforcing the gender binary. Although I contend that emancipation requires an understanding of both men and women, I also recognize that the concept of "both" men and women is limiting. I considered eliminating gender as a requirement for the interview sample, but because there is such a difference in the work–life practices of people who identify as men and people who identify as women, I wanted to investigate this further. Studying gender is quite often a slippery slope, in that it is easy to rely on simple categories that do not capture the complexity of gender. Gender is so complex, in fact, that I was not able to capture it all here. Thus, my reliance on categories was not merely one of convenience, but rather a strategic tactic used to highlight the way work–life policies are gendered with the ultimate goal of emancipation. Future work should certainly take the findings from this study and move beyond this categorical frame.

In addition, studying only men risks eclipsing the important goals of emancipation for everyone in organizations. Conducting a study that might further privilege white men at the expense of other workers is a serious and upsetting risk of this work. I have proposed that the men in this study should be emancipated from the constraints not only that keep them at work for their own sake but also so that women can enter and exit their organizations with less stigma and material consequences. This driving goal might be overlooked because of the relative novelty of studying men in relation to work–life. The emphasis that men and masculinity and women and femininity are always constructed in light of the other is critical for the dual goals of emancipating men from work and creating more equal opportunities for women at work to be realized.

REFERENCES

Allen, B. (1998). Black womanhood and feminist standpoints. *Management Communication Quarterly, 11,* 575–586. doi:10.1177/0893318998114004

Bullis, C. (1993). Organizational socialization research: Enabling, constraining, and shifting perspectives. *Communication Monographs, 60,* 10–17. doi:10.1080/03637 759309376289

Buzzanell, P., & Liu, M. (2005). Struggling with maternity leave policies and practices: A poststructuralist feminist analysis of gendered organizing. *Journal of Applied Communication Research, 33*, 1–25. doi:10.1080/ 0090988042000318495

Collins, P. H. (1986). Learning from the outsider within: The sociological significance of black feminist thought. *Social Problems, 33*, S14–S32. doi:10.1525/ sp.1986.33.6.03a00020

Friedan, B. (1962). *The feminine mystique*. New York, NY: W. W. Norton.

Harding, S. (1998). *Is science multicultural? Postcolonialisms, feminisms, and epistemologies*. Bloomington: Indiana University Press.

hooks, b. (1995). Black women: Shaping feminist theory. In B. Guy-Sheftall (Ed.), *Words of fire: An anthology of African-American feminist thought* (pp. 270–282). New York, NY: The New York Press.

Jorgenson, J. (2002). Engineering selves: Negotiating gender and identity in technical work. *Management Communication Quarterly, 15*, 350–380. doi:10.1177/089 3318902153002

Lugones, M., & Spelman, E. (1983). Have we got a theory for you! Feminist theory, cultural imperialism and the demand for "the woman's voice." *Women's Studies International Forum, 6*, 573–581. doi:10.1016/0277–5395(83)900195

Sprague, J., & Hayes, J. (2000). Self-determination and empowerment: A feminist standpoint analysis of talk about disability. *American Journal of Community Psychology, 28*, 671–695.

Appendix B
Data Collection and Analysis

Data Collection

I gathered data for this book in two primary ways: (a) through a textual analysis of popular biographies about, and autobiographies and books by, founders and CEOs of *Fortune* 500 companies and (b) through interviews with men in a variety of occupations. Interviews are the most popular approach to answer questions about identity and everyday practices (Alvesson, Ashcraft, & Thomas, 2008). However, interviews alone are not comprehensive enough to encapsulate identity and everyday practices, because the interview itself is a socially constructed site that is political and that involves impression management. Providing multiple sources of data helped me gather a more nuanced understanding of men's relationship to work–life balance and leaves of absence practice. Using these dual methods illuminated a complex interplay of occupational discourses and everyday lived experiences. The following subsections discuss textual analysis and interviewing in the context of this project.

TEXTUAL ANALYSIS

Organizational leaders play a large role in constructing and perpetuating the culture of an organization, and often of industries. As such, I analyzed the discourses of high-ranking male executives through their popular biographies and autobiographies. As Ashcraft and Flores (2000) suggested, texts comprise cultural discourses and, as such, are part of larger cultural narratives. Accordingly, texts provide one way to understand organizations and, more specifically, how organizational and/or managerial discourses work on/with employee identities. Carl (2005) argued that organizational textual documents continually act as macro actors in the discursive construction of organizations, either with or without the original producer in place. This is particularly true of popular texts, which have such broad audiences that they often transcend organizations or occupations. Additionally, Nadesan (2001) argued that popular texts help shape managerial discourses by drawing attention to particular workplace practices, management trends, and economic relations. In this project, I argue that popular texts inform and promote specific kinds of practices and behaviors in occupations.

Popular writing, including the texts I analyzed here, is both important and different in many ways from traditional academic writing. Lewis, Schisseur, Stephens, and Weir (2006) explained that popular press books serve as a discursive framework for organizational life and affect the feelings and confidence of managers at a micro level. They claimed that "it is useful for researchers of business practices to examine [popular press books] to better enable theoretical explanation for the tendencies observed in managers' choices of communication strategies and tactics" (p. 115). Indeed, the ways in which organizational communication is influenced by popular press books is an important focus of this study.

May and Zorn (2001) claimed that studying popular writing is important for organizational communication scholars because this genre largely focuses on the same phenomena as scholarly literature in the same genre, but unlike that body of academic writing, popular writing reaches millions of readers. Furthermore, managers and other workers consume this material and subsequently enact the strategies they learn in their day-to-day activities. Whereas the publication and methodological standards of popular writing are different from those scholars may be accustomed to in academia, these texts, nonetheless, comprise a substantial and highly persuasive body of work. May and Zorn (2001) concluded that if popular "writing is important to the people we study, it should be important to us" as academics (p. 472).

Indeed, popular business texts have not lost any traction in their massive and persuasive appeal. Furusten (1999, cited in Jackson, 2001) argued that the "textual representations of managerial and organizational life that are presented in popular management books create a powerful isomorphic pressure that contributes to the increasing homogenization among organizations throughout the world" (p. 486). Because popular texts about iconic figures are produced and consumed in mass quantity, they become part of the fabric of organizational life. Ashcraft and Mumby (2004) even asserted that text is a central means through which organizational communication scholars might begin to analyze larger societal discourses. Thus, as individuals consume the occupational representations in texts, they are able to either enact or resist the offered scripts in organizational life. As such, organizational communication scholars are not only poised to, but are also responsible for, studying how these texts influence organizing and life in organizations.

To begin collecting data from popular texts, I started with the most recent *Fortune* 500 list of companies (2014) and *Forbes* magazine's list of "The World's Most Powerful People." Next, I searched Amazon.com by each name of the CEOs and founders of *Fortune* 500 companies to find CEOs and founders that had biographies or autobiographies. I searched the additional "powerful people" directly to find biographies and/or autobiographies. I found that most of the individuals on my generated list had not written books themselves and did not have books written about them, but a few iconic figureheads (e.g., Bill Gates, Steve Jobs) did have either autobiographies or biographies, and that in some cases (e.g., Bill Gates), a number of books were written about the icon. In this case, I prioritized autobiographies, then authorized biographies, and then biographies. In a couple of cases, I discovered biographies of firms, which included chapters about (with interview data from) former CEOs and books about business strategy written by the men. I included these in the analysis as well. Finally, a few of the men wrote books about management strategy, which I also included.

A total of thirty-four books were identified as appropriate and located for this study, all written by or about high profile firms and/or male executives, including CEOs, company founders, chairmen and senior partners. Refer to Table B.1 for a list of all 34 books about the men and the companies for which they worked.

Table B.1   Books Used for Textual Analysis

Paul Allen	Microsoft	Allen, P. (2011). *Idea man: A memoir by the cofounder of Microsoft*. New York, NY: Portfolio/Penguin.
Steve Ballmer	Microsoft	Maxwell, F. (2002). *Bad boy Ballmer: The man who rules Microsoft*. New York, NY: William Morrow.
Jeff Bezos	Amazon.com	Brandt, R. (2011). *One click: Jeff Bezos and the rise of Amazon.com*. New York, NY: Portfolio/Penguin.
Michael Bloomberg	Salomon Brothers, Bloomberg L.P., New York City	Bloomberg, M., & Winkler, M. (1997). *Bloomberg by Bloomberg*. New York, NY: Wiley.
Sergey Brin	Google	Lowe, J. (2009). *Google speaks: Secrets of the world's greatest billionaire entrepreneurs, Sergey Brin and Larry Page*. Hoboken, NJ: Wiley.
Warren Buffet	Berkshire Hathaway	Schroeder, A. (2008). *The snowball: Warren Buffett and the business of life*. New York, NY: Random House.
George W. Bush	The United States of America	Bush, G. W. (2010). *Decision points*. New York, NY: Random House.
John Chambers	Cisco Systems	Waters, J.K. (2002). *John Chambers and the CISCO way: Navigating through volatility*. Hoboken, NJ: Wiley.

(*Continued*)

Table B.1 (Continued)

Jon Corzine	Goldman Sachs	Cohan, W.D. (2012). *Money and power: How Goldman Sachs came to rule the world*. New York, NY: Random House.
Michael Dell	Dell Computers	Dell, M., & Fredman, C. (1999). *Direct from Dell: Strategies that revolutionized an industry*. New York, NY: Harper Business.
Jamie Dimon	JPMorgan Chase, Citigroup	Crisafulli, P. (2009). *The house of Dimon: How JPMorgan's Jamie Dimon rose to the top of the financial world*. Hoboken, NJ: Wiley.
Walt Disney	The Walt Disney Company	Capodagli, B., & Jackson, L. (1999). *The Disney way: Harnessing the management secrets of Disney in your company*. New York, NY: McGraw-Hill.
Larry Ellison	Oracle	Symonds, M. (2013). *Softwar: An intimate portrait of Larry Ellison and Oracle*. New York, NY: Simon & Schuster.
Bill Gates	Microsoft	Lowe, J. (1998). *Bill Gates speaks: Insight from the world's greatest entrepreneur*. Hoboken, NJ: Wiley.
		Wallace, J., & Erickson, J. (1992). *Hard drive: Bill Gates and the making of the Microsoft empire*. New York, NY: Harper Business.
Hugh Hefner	Playboy Enterprises	Watts, S. (2009). *Mr.Playboy: Hugh Hefner and the American dream*. Hoboken, NJ: Wiley.
Lee Iacocca	Ford Motor Company, Crysler	Iacocca, L., & Novak, W. (1986). *Iacocca: An autobiography*. New York, NY: Random House.
Jeff Immelt	General Electric	Magee, D. (2009). *Jeff Immelt and the new GE way: Innovation, transformation and winning in the 21st century*. New York, NY: McGraw-Hill Professional.
Neville Isdell	Coca-Cola Company	Isdell, N., & Beasley, D. (2011). *Inside Coca-Cola: A CEO's life story of building the world's most popular brand*. New York, NY: Macmillan.

(*Continued*)

Table B.1 (Continued)

Steve Jobs	Apple	Isaacson, W. (2011). *Steve Jobs*. New York, NY: Simon & Schuster.
Charles Koch	Koch Industries, Inc.	Koch, C. G. (2007). *The science of success: How market-based management built the world's largest private company*. Hoboken, NJ: Wiley.
Gus Levy	Goldman Sachs	Cohan, W. D. (2012). *Money and power: How Goldman Sachs came to rule the world*. New York, NY: Random House.
Andrew Liveris	The Dow Chemical Company	Liveris, A. (2011). *Make it in America, updated edition: The case for re-inventing the economy*. Hoboken, NJ: Wiley.
Ralph Lauren	Ralph Lauren Corporation	Trachtenberg, J. A. (1988). *Ralph Lauren: The man behind the mystique*. New York, NY: Little, Brown.
Bill McDermott	Xerox, SAP	McDermott, B. (2014). *Winners dream: A journey from corner store to corner office*. New York, NY: Simon & Schuster.
Alan Mulally	Ford Motor Company	Hoffman, B. G. (2012). *American icon: Alan Mulally and the fight to save Ford Motor Company*. New York, NY: Random House.
Bob Munchin	Goldman Sachs	Cohan, W. D. (2012). *Money and power: How Goldman Sachs came to rule the world*. New York, NY: Random House.
Alan Murray	The Wall Street Journal	Murray, A. (2010). *The Wall Street Journal essential guide to management: Lasting lessons from the best leadership minds of our time*. New York, NY: HarperCollins.
David Novak	Yum! Brands, PepsiCo	Novak, D. (2012). *Taking people with you: The only way to make big things happen*. London, England: Penguin.
Barack Obama	The United States of America	Obama, B. (2007). *Dreams from my father: A story of race and inheritance*. New York, NY: Random House.

(*Continued*)

Larry Page	Google	Lowe, J. (2009). *Google speaks: Secrets of the world's greatest billionaire entrepreneurs, Sergey Brin and Larry Page.* Hoboken, NJ: Wiley.
Andrew Rosen	Kaplan, Inc.	Rosen, A. S. (2011). *Change.edu: Rebooting for the new talent economy.* New York, NY: Kaplan.
Bob Rubin	Goldman Sachs	Cohan, W. D. (2012). *Money and power: How Goldman Sachs came to rule the world.* New York, NY: Random House.
Howard Schultz	Starbucks	Schultz, H., & Yang, D. J. (1997). *Pour your heart into it: How Starbucks built a company one cup at a time.* New York, NY: Hyperion.
John Sculley	Apple	Sculley, J., & Byrne, J. A. (1987). *Odyssey: Pepsi to Apple: A journey of adventure, ideas, and the future.* New York, NY: Harper & Row Publishers.
L. Jay Tenenbaum,	Goldman Sachs	Cohan, W. D. (2012). *Money and power: How Goldman Sachs came to rule the world.* New York, NY: Random House.
Donald Trump	The Trump Organization	Trump, D. J., & Schwartz, T. (2009). *Trump: The art of the deal.* New York, NY: Random House.
Jack Welch	General Electric	Murray, A. (2010). *The Wall Street Journal essential guide to management: Lasting lessons from the best leadership minds of our time.* New York, NY: HarperCollins.
John Whitehead	Goldman Sachs	Cohan, W. D. (2012). *Money and power: How Goldman Sachs came to rule the world.* New York, NY: Random House.
Steve Wozniak	Apple	Wozniak, S., & Smith, G. (2006). *iWoz: Computer geek to cult icon.* New York: W. W. Norton.
Mark Zuckerberg	Facebook	Beahm, G. (Ed.). (2012). *The boy billionaire: Mark Zuckerberg in his own words.* Evanston, IL: Agate Publishing.

I read and analyzed these texts, pulling data from certain texts as themes emerged that indicated relevant occupational discourses. In particular, I included and later coded any mention of leaves of absence or other non-work pursuits as relevant data. Books that made no mention of leaves of absence or other work–life constructs were also coded as such.

The textual analysis portion of this study provided a discourse for how high-ranking men both supported and resisted leaves of absence and work–life balance as part of their personal organizational experience. These texts also provided data about occupational and entrepreneurial discourses, which were confirmed, contradicted, and modified by male workers in the interviews. As such, and as is further explained in the next section, interview data worked in conjunction with the popular text analyses to reveal a bigger picture of how discourses were promoted and manifested in individual identities and actions.

INTERVIEWS

Interviews are the most popular approach to answer questions about identity (Alvesson et al., 2008). Lindlof and Taylor (2002) described the research interview as "particularly well suited to *understand the social actor's experience and perspective*" (p. 173, italics in original). They pointed out that, interviews are complicated because people sometimes interpret their experiences in different ways, forget details, lie, and make mistakes in reporting but are nonetheless a fascinating and insightful way to study discourse. Moreover, Lindlof and Taylor identified one primary purpose of interviewing as drawing out "individual, interpersonal, or cultural logics that people employ in their communicative performances" (2002, p. 174). Indeed, in this study, I used interviews to gain insight into men's leave-taking choices, and through interviewees' stories and accounts, I learned something about the broad cultural logics (both produced and reproduced in discourse) that guided their choices. In particular, I was interested in the men's accounts of their own experiences and their perceptions of others' experiences.

I constructed an interview protocol (see the following discussion) based on published research and from insights from another interview project about men's experiences with gender equity (Ashcraft et al., 2013). My interviews were roughly scheduled into four sections. I first asked a series of background questions, including "How do you describe your occupation to others?" and "What are important characteristics of people in your line of work?" Second, I asked interviewees about their experiences with leave and leave policies, including questions such as "What is your company's policy for leaves of absence?" and "Was there ever a time that you thought about taking a leave, or would have qualified for a leave of absence but did not take it?" Next, I asked interviewees about their perceptions of leaves of absence, such as "Why don't men take leaves of absence as often as women?" Finally, I asked the men about their perceptions of work–life balance and asked questions such as "What does balance mean to you?" Although I used the interview protocol, I followed up on relevant stories that were important to interviewees and allowed the interviews to expand or decrease on some areas based on the interviewee's experience. I tried to minimize the "demand effect" (Nichols & Maner, 2008) when participants tended to respond to questions in ways that confirmed my research project by leaving questions open-ended and by not alluding to a specific definition of ambiguous terms such as *occupation* or *balance*.

Throughout the study, I paid close attention for declarations. As Jorgenson (2002) described, declarations are "direct claims made by speakers on attributes and identities (e.g., 'I was always good in math') or statements that give a report on how things appear from speakers' points of view (e.g., 'Engineering is a gender-neutral field')" (p. 361). When I heard an utterance that was a declaration, I followed up with probing questions so that I understood what discursive resources the interviewees drew upon to describe their work and leave choices.

People's identities and experiences are not independent of the interview context. Thus, the interviewees' perception of me as an interviewer inevitably shaped the way their experiences were presented in the interview. In particular, because I am a woman interviewing men, I paid special attention to gendered dynamics at play during interviews. For a similar example from scholarly research, Arendell (1997) described the way that the divorced fathers she interviewed consistently confirmed their identities *as men* and how the male interviewees frequently took the interview situation as a means to reproduce stereotypical gender roles by taking charge, questioning the interviewer, acting chivalrous, overstepping personal boundaries, and asserting superiority. Like Arendell, I assumed that my male participants would be "gender enlightened" (e.g., giving answers that seemed politically correct), which was sometimes not the case. This left me to work through a significant tension of playing into stereotypical gender role performances: on one hand, the desire to build rapport during interviews and, on the other hand, the desire to maintain my commitment to feminist premises, which necessitated a break from such performances.

In a few instances, my political commitments were directly questioned. I was at first taken aback by these questions. It did not occur to me that the men I was interviewing would feel threatened by my feminist commitments, because I attempted to remain neutral so that I could capture the interviewee's words rather than shades of my own. I also did not anticipate that some would vehemently resist the idea that they might want time away from work. However, this occurrence reinforced the precariousness of the interview setting and reminded me that my role in this research project is influential at every step of the project. When I was directly questioned about my commitments, I spoke about my personal desire to see more equitable workplaces and an increase in the opportunity for men to participate at home. While most of the interviewees who asked about my own views were satisfied with my honest responses, three interviewees explicitly disagreed that equality was desirable. Another became agitated that my feminist lens would skew his words, and he asked that I take care not to "cherry-pick" his words. This request gave me considerable pause, and ultimately resulted in a disciplining of my own voice as I started to write the findings. A tension started here, from within my feminist commitments. On one hand, feminist research is guided by the tenet that interviewees are collaborators. Thus, I did not want to "cherry-pick" words or slant what my interviewees intended in the interview. On the other hand, I wanted to critically evaluate his position that gender equality was not desirable. In the interview, I politely deferred to the interviewee and ultimately smoothed over the tension with an assurance that I was presenting the findings as I understood them, thus necessarily under my influence but with the intention to be true to my interviewees' experiences. It was only after the interview that I wondered how I could have handled the discussion differently so that I did not fall into the traditional deferent role.

Another relevant aspect of my role as the interviewer is my relative lack of experience with many of the occupations of the men I interviewed. I have worked as a consultant in many industries. However, there were numerous occasions that I did not possess knowledge of the ways that the men performed their work. This situation sometimes worked to my advantage in the interviews, because the men were able to "teach" me about their occupation. Other times, however, some men felt exasperated when I asked for clarification of acronyms or asked questions that might have seemed obvious to an insider.

In addition, my parental status was a regular point of conversation in the interviews. In many cases, the men asked me directly if I had children. In a couple of interviews, my children walked into my home office and were detected through the phone. Revealing my children worked both as an advantage in the interviews and as a disadvantage. In many cases, it seemed to help build rapport with the interviewee, particularly with fathers about my age. However, revealing that I am an employed mother also created some awkwardness when interviewees gave opinions (frequently negative) about moms working outside the home. Most would apologize or otherwise save face about comments that they thought might have been offensive to me, but one explicitly disciplined me with aggressive comments about the "irresponsibility of mothers who work." My response to this was much like my responses outlined earlier. I politely deferred during the interview and later questioned what the "right" feminist move would have been. In the end, I handled objections, questions, and concerns honestly, selecting transparency over rapport when forced to choose.

All interviews were conducted by phone, which allowed for participants from a wide range of geographic locations to be represented in the data. Despite the elimination of nonverbal communication, research shows that data from face-to-face and telephone interviews is often highly consistent (see, e.g., Aziz & Kenford, 2004; Sturges & Hanrahan, 2004). Moreover, Sturges and Hanrahan (2004) concluded that telephone interviews can be used productively in qualitative research and are preferable in some situations (e.g., when the study is about sensitive topics, when interviewees are hard to reach, and when researcher safety or cost are concerns). Sturges and Hanrahan further pointed out that technological advances should change the way we do research, and that with technology, research can fit better into the lives of interviewees. This project fit these parameters, as conducting phone interviews certainly made scheduling interviews with people dispersed around the country much easier and more financially practical.

Interviewees consented to the interview and the audio taping of the interview verbally during the digitally recorded interview. I conducted 68 interviews, with individual interviews varying in length from 22 to 95 minutes. Interviews were recorded through a phone service and were digitally downloaded from the site with a secure password known only by me, and were then transcribed. All individual names, companies, and locations were changed to pseudonyms or were deleted entirely to protect the privacy of participants.

Interviews are socially constructed sites that are political and involve impression management. Put simply, most people like to think about themselves as balanced, well-rounded individuals. However, private interviews allowed the participants to speak in-depth, and to think about how they prioritize their lives. Across the interviews, the examples and experiences provided allowed me to draw connections between occupational discourses and identities, entrepreneurialism, and leave-taking practices, and in doing so, illuminated a complex interplay of discourse and everyday lived experience.

Participants

The 68 men in this study volunteered to be interviewed. They were recruited through personal networks and referrals. The participating men ranged in age from 22 to 76. The majority of interviewees (48 men) identified as white, seven identified as Asian, four identified as African American, four identified as Latino, three identified as European, and two identified as biracial. These interviewees had a wide array of experiences and perceptions of leaves of absence. Thirty-four of the interviewees were fathers, and 19 were not. The men came from a variety of occupations, and a few men reported multiple occupations. In some instances, they held multiple jobs during the time of the interview. In one or two instances, the participant spent his entire career in one occupation but then retired and took a different job. In addition, some men noted special contexts for their occupations that they believed made their occupation different from others. For example, one accountant worked for a nonprofit company, which he believed made his life as an accountant different from other accountants in for-profit firms.

For these reasons, there are more occupations and occupational contexts reported than interviewees. Following is an alphabetical list of the participants' occupations:

- Accountant (3)
- Architect (2)
- Baseball consultant
- Casino dealer
- CEO, manufacturing
- Coast Guard employee
- Computer engineer (2)
- Computer programmer (5)
- Computer science (6)
- Contractor/construction (5)
- Courier
- Debate coach (2)
- Disc jockey
- Ditch digger
- Driver (2)
- Electrician
- Energy worker
- Engineer (6)
- Environmental tester
- Government worker (2)
- Graduate student/college instructor (3)
- Graphic designer
- Independent contractor (6)
- Information Technology technician (6)
- Insurance business intelligence
- Insurance manager
- Lifestyle coach
- Marketing associate (4)
- Mechanical engineer (3)
- Movie reviewer
- Music producer
- Network service provider
- Nightclub security
- Nonprofit employee (4)
- Physician
- Police officer
- Professor
- Property manager (2)
- Real estate agent (2)
- Researcher (2)
- Rock-climbing instructor

- Sales associate
- Small-business owner (4)
- Soccer coach
- Solar energy control/window tinting technician
- Start-up team member (3)
- Swim team coach
- Telemarketer
- Writer (3)

Interview Protocol

Background Information

1. How do you describe your occupation to others?
2. How did you come to be a xxx?
3. What is it like to work in xxx?
4. What is your biggest occupational challenge?
5. What makes you successful in your work?
6. What makes people unsuccessful in your type of work?
7. What are important characteristics of people in your line of work?

Leave Policies

1. What is your company's policy for leaves of absence?

   a. How do you know?

2. Who handles the logistics of taking leave?
3. Did anyone talk to you about the option to take a leave?
4. Is your company covered under FMLA?
5. How long can/do leaves of absence last?

Leave Experiences

1. Do you know a male coworker take a leave of absence?

   a. Why did he take leave?
   b. How long did he take leave?
   c. What was your feeling about his leave?
   d. How did coworkers talk about his leave?
   e. How do you think management felt about his leave?

      i. Why?

2. Have you ever taken a leave of absence from work?

   a. How long was your leave of absence?
   b. Why did you take a leave?

    c. Did you feel supported in your decision to take a leave?

      i. Why or why not?

    d. Would you take a leave of absence again?

    e. Would you recommend taking a leave of absence to a friend in the same company?

3. Was there ever a time that you thought about taking a leave, or would have qualified for a leave of absence but did not take it?

Perceptions of Leave

4. Why don't men take leaves of absence as often as women?
5. Are there reasons that are more acceptable than others for men to take leave?

Data Analysis

For all researchers, data analysis is about interpretation. For qualitative and feminist researchers, in particular, interpretation is laden with any number of influencers, including values, discourses, power, relationships, and contexts. Qualitative and feminist researchers believe that because qualitative data are produced in relational contexts, they should be recorded and interpreted in the same way. Viewed in this way, interviews are performances that should not be stripped of context during analysis. Qualitative and feminist researchers make choices at each step of the research process, including data management, data reduction, and conceptual development. As Borland (1991) explained,

> for feminists, the issue of interpretive authority is particularly problematic, for our work often involves a contradiction. On the one hand, we seek to empower the women we work with by revaluing their perspectives, their lives, and their art in a world that has systematically ignored or trivialized women's culture. On the other, we hold an explicitly political vision of the structural conditions that lead to particular social behaviors, a vision that our field collaborators, many of whom do not consider themselves feminists, may not recognize as valid. (p. 64)

Borland (1991) described interviewing her grandmother, who shared a narrative with Borland and then felt that Borland's interpretation of that narrative was completely incorrect. This example demonstrates classic tensions for feminist qualitative scholars, including how we represent our participants' words, who has the "textual authority" once the words are on paper, and how to accommodate both feminist commitments and our research collaborators. In light of these tensions, successfully handling data analysis in a feminist qualitative study requires reflexivity and an attempt to view narratives, interviews, and accounts from the participants' points of view.

To this end, I tried to balance my own agenda of emancipation with the actual words and feelings of my interviewees. I worked hard to hear what the interviewees were saying, even when it conflicted with what I hoped to hear or thought I would hear. As such, I have attempted to make sure that the voices of my interviewees are represented in this study and that I captured the nuanced and sometimes conflicting accounts of the interviewees' experiences. Dealing with these experiences during a research project was quite challenging, particularly in light of some data suggesting that men do not want or need leaves of absence. However, some techniques helped alleviate the bias in my own interpretation. First, my interview schedule was designed so that it did not frame leave policy in a negative light. Second, I interviewed both men who have taken leave as well as those who have not taken leave, which provided a variety of perspectives. Finally, I continually embraced and thought about the importance of reflexivity throughout the project, so that the ways in which I interpreted the data reflected what was actually said in interviews. To this end, I attempted to verify with interviewees the meaning of their stories during the interview so that I did not unduly apply my own lens to their words. Also, I include in my findings both quotes that support what I thought I might find and those that contradict my own views. Hence, these strategies help demonstrate the importance of engaging the tension between my own feelings about leave and honoring the feelings of my interviewees.

To begin analyzing the data for this project, I listened carefully for emerging themes as I collected data. These themes became the rough categorizations for the study. In this way, my technique is much like the "wave technique" described by Lindlof and Taylor (2002, p. 214), an inductive approach that allows categories to emerge from the data. Additionally, Strauss and Corbin's (1998) grounded theory was employed but with careful deliberation and consideration. Grounded theory was used here to contend with new experiences late in the study that continued to shape the project. The inductive analysis of grounded theory occurred throughout the data collection and analysis process and, hence, certainly shaped the research and interview questions throughout. For example, questions that were particularly illuminating were asked in most interviews, while questions that did not connect well with interviewees were dropped.

After the interviews were transcribed, I created a rough first list of coding categories. This initial effort produced 63 codes. As I finished coding the interviews, I eliminated codes that had minimal data and combined some codes that seemed similar. I went through this process four additional times. Coding in iterations allowed me to switch between broad, preliminary codes to more detailed codes that were evident across and through the interviews. Additionally, because I was interested in uncovering latent meanings, absent or missing discourses, gendered tensions, and discursive resources, the use of grounded theory afforded me the opportunity to recode multiple times until the coding scheme represented the data.

REFERENCES

Alvesson, M., Ashcraft, K., & Thomas, R. (2008). Identity matters: Reflections on the construction of identity scholarship in organization studies. *Organization, 15*, 5–28. doi:10.1177/1350508407084426

Arendell, T. (1997). Reflections on the researcher-researched relationship: A woman interviewing men. *Qualitative Sociology, 20*, 341–368. doi:10.1023/A:102472 7316052

Ashcraft, K. L., & Flores, L. (2000). "Slaves with white collars": Persistent performances of masculinity in crisis. *Text and Performance Quarterly, 23*, 1–29. doi: 10.1080/10462930310001602020

Ashcraft, C., DuBow, W., Eger, E., Blithe, S., & Sevier, B. (2013). *Male advocates and allies: Promoting gender diversity in technology workplaces.* Boulder, CO: National Center for Women & Information Technology.

Ashcraft, K. L., & Mumby, D. K. (2004). *Reworking gender: A feminist communicology of organization.* Thousand Oaks, CA: Sage.

Aziz, M., & Kenford, S. (2004). Comparability of telephone and face-to-face interviews in assessing patients with posttraumatic stress disorder. *Journal of Psychiatric Practice, 10*, 307–313.

Borland, K. (1991). "That's not what I said": Interpretive conflict in oral narrative research. In S. B. Gluck & D. Patai (Eds.), *Women's words: The feminist practice of oral history* (pp. 63–75). New York, NY: Routledge.

Carl, W. (2005). The communicational basis of the organizational text as macroactor: A case study of multilevel marketing discourse. *Research Reports in Communication, 6*, 21–29. doi:10.1080/1745943050026211

Jackson, B. (2001). Art for management's sake? The new literary genre of business books. *Management Communication Quarterly, 14*, 484–490. doi:10.1177/08 93318901143006

Jorgenson, J. (2002). Engineering selves: Negotiating gender and identity in technical work. *Management Communication Quarterly, 15*, 350–380. doi:10.1177/08 93318902153002

Lewis, L. K., Schmisseur, A. M., Stephens, K. K., & Weir, K. E. (2006). Advice on communicating during organizational change: The content of popular press books. *Journal of Business Communication, 43*(2), 113–137. doi:10.1177/0021943605 285355

Lindlof, T. R., & Taylor, B. C. (2002). *Qualitative communication research methods* (2nd ed.). Thousand Oaks, CA: Sage.

May, S. K., & Zorn, T. (2001). Forum introduction. Gurus' views and business news: Popular management discourse and its relationship to management and organizational communication. *Management Communication Quarterly, 14*, 471–475. doi:10.1177/0893318901143004

Nadesan, M. H. (2001). Fortune on globalization and the new economy: Manifest destiny in a technological age. *Management Communication Quarterly, 14*(3), 498–506. doi:10/CAX0240040001023

Nichols, A., & Maner, J. (2008). The good-subject effect: Investigating participant demand characteristics. *The Journal of General Psychology, 135*, 151–166. doi:10.3200/GENP.135.2.151–166

Strauss, A., & Corbin, J. (1998). Grounded theory methodology: An overview. In N. K. Denzin & Y. S. Lincoln (Eds.), *Strategies of qualitative inquiry* (pp. 158–183). Thousand Oaks, CA: Sage.

Sturges, J., & Hanrahan, K. (2004). Comparing telephone and face-to-face qualitative interviewing: A research note. *Qualitative Research, 4*, 107–108. doi:10.11 77/1468794104041110

Index

For Product Safety Concerns and Information please contact our EU
representative GPSR@taylorandfrancis.com
Taylor & Francis Verlag GmbH, Kaufingerstraße 24, 80331 München, Germany

www.ingramcontent.com/pod-product-compliance
Ingram Content Group UK Ltd.
Pitfield, Milton Keynes, MK11 3LW, UK
UKHW021608240425
457818UK00018B/436